# The Network Self

The concept of a relational self has been prominent in feminism, communitarianism, narrative self theories, and social network theories, and has been important to theorizing about practical dimensions of selfhood. However, it has been largely ignored in traditional philosophical theories of personal identity, which have been dominated by psychological and animal theories of the self. This book offers a systematic treatment of the notion of the self as constituted by social, cultural, political, and biological relations. The author's account incorporates practical concerns and addresses how a relational self has agency, autonomy, responsibility, and continuity through time in the face of change and impairments. This cumulative network model (CNM) of the self incorporates concepts from work in the American pragmatist and naturalist tradition. The ultimate aim of the book is to bridge traditions that are often disconnected from one another—feminism, personal identity theory, and pragmatism—to develop a unified theory of the self.

**Kathleen Wallace** is Professor of Philosophy at Hofstra University, USA. She has worked in American Philosophy, and is an expert on the work of Justus Buchler. She has also worked in the areas of Metaphysics of Personal Identity, Hume Studies, and Feminism. Some representative articles include "Personal Identity of an Intersectional Self," "On-line Anonymity," "Educating for Autonomy: Identity and Intersectional Selves," and "Autonomous 'I' of an Intersectional Self."

# Routledge Studies in American Philosophy

Edited by Willem deVries
*University of New Hampshire, USA*

Henry Jackman
*York University, Canada*

For more information about this series, please visit: www.routledge.com/
Routledge-Studies-in-American-Philosophy/book-series/RSAP

# The Network Self

Relation, Process, and Personal Identity

Kathleen Wallace

Routledge
Taylor & Francis Group

NEW YORK AND LONDON

First published 2019
by Routledge
52 Vanderbilt Avenue, New York, NY 10017

and by Routledge
2 Park Square, Milton Park, Abingdon, Oxon OX14 4RN

*Routledge is an imprint of the Taylor & Francis Group, an informa business*

First issued in paperback 2021

*Library of Congress Cataloging-in-Publication Data*
A catalog record for this title has been requested

ISBN: 978-0-367-07748-8 (hbk)
ISBN: 978-1-03-209355-0 (pbk)
ISBN: 978-0-429-02254-8 (ebk)

Typeset in Sabon
by Apex CoVantage, LLC

MIX
Paper from
responsible sources
FSC
www.fsc.org   FSC™ C013985

Printed in the United Kingdom
by Henry Ling Limited

# Contents

# Preface

I started on this book by way of several paths: working on the notion of anonymity, reading, and thinking about the philosophical literature on personal identity and about feminist theories of intersectionality and relational autonomy, but also by way of feeling a disjuncture between how persons identify themselves qua persons and how philosophers have approached the notion of persons.

When people introduce themselves to one another, they often identify themselves with a social characteristic relevant in some way to the context of meeting. "I'm a philosopher," or "I'm a professor at Hofstra University," or "I'm Jane's sister," or "I'm Isabel's mother," or "I'm from New York," or "I'm a bicyclist, but not much of a skier," or "I'm an opera lover," or "I'm Irish," and so on. Sometimes people will identify themselves in comparative terms (e.g., "I'm the tallest person in the room") or in terms of their beliefs or preferences (sexual, religious, political, ethical, aesthetic, and so on). Sometimes people identify themselves in terms of their past ("I am the person who lived down the hall from you in college") or take some feature of their projected future as a particularly salient feature about who they are ("I'm going to be awarded the Ph.D. at commencement in two weeks," or "I'm getting married next year"). People also experience memory and other psychological experiences as important to who they are. "I remember that like it was yesterday," or "I am very angry about that," or "I feel melancholy today."

Of course, most people feel that a present state or social locations do not exhaust who they are. Some people may feel that socially defined traits do not reflect who they "really" are, especially when they feel that in some or many contexts they can't express, or have to hide, their true feelings, preferences, beliefs, and so on. The desire to not be reduced to a social (or other) role, the experience of having to dissimulate in social contexts, and the experience of unexpressed personal thoughts and feelings are important to acknowledge. At the same time, it seems to me that social traits do pick out important features of selves as selves. Even if they don't exhaust what selves are, a philosophical theory of the self ought to encompass them. But, what is striking to me is the extent to which philosophical characterizations of persons have rarely included social traits.

Philosophical theories of persons in the Anglo-analytic tradition emphasize what are taken to be essential to, or necessary and sufficient conditions for, being a person, such as being some continuous concatenation of psychological experiences or being an animal or body of a particular natural kind; or essential to being that *particular* psychological stream or being that *particular* body. According to such theories, the ordinary ways in which people identify themselves mentioned earlier are simply social or other roles that are accidental. This has always bothered me. It seems to me that social and other relations and locations are fundamental to who and what a self is, not just causally, but constitutively. Had the infant that began my self been put up for adoption and grown up in a completely different kinship, educational, and social class environment, that self would be a different self, not me, even if that self started out as the same biological organism as the one that developed into me. Philosophical theories also address questions about persistence, change, and identity through time, but without, in my view, adequately acknowledging the extent to which a self is constituted by its history. This has always struck me as an under-recognized feature of what it means to be a self. For these intuitions to make sense, there must be more to the self than psychological or animalist theories suggest.

I propose a model of the self that I hope captures the ways in which a self is embodied and socially (although not exclusively socially) constituted, that recognizes the ways in which people ordinarily recognize themselves and conduct themselves as agents, and that allows us to think about how selves are constituted in both local and wide social contexts. At the same time the model addresses how such a self has an integrity as a whole, persists, and is continuous with itself as an ongoing process. The model incorporates social constitution in a more comprehensive view of the self as relational, or as I shall say, as a network, and recognizes the self as constituted by its history by also conceptualizing the self as a process. I call this model the cumulative network model (CNM) of the self. It addresses both "metaphysical" issues such as identity and persistence and "practical" issues such as autonomy and responsibility. In saying that social relations and embodiment are constitutive of the self, I am not suggesting that they are the sole constituents of a self, for selves are physically, genetically, culturally, semantically, and psychologically constituted as well. What I argue for is a comprehensive view of the self as plurally constituted and that such plural constitutedness is fundamental to understanding the multiple capacities and agential possibilities of selves.

# Acknowledgments

I am grateful to many for their comments, encouragement, and support. In particular, I would like to thank Dartmouth College for supporting me as a Visiting Scholar, and to members of the Dartmouth College Philosophy Department for stimulating conversations and comments. I also very much appreciate the Faculty Research and Development Grants and research leaves granted to me by Hofstra University. I am also grateful for feedback I received from participants in the following venues where I presented portions of this work: the Society for the Advancement of American Philosophy, the New York Society for Women in Philosophy workshop, the Central European Pragmatist Forum, the Nordic Pragmatist Network Conference on Pragmatism and Communication, the Philosophy Department Colloquium at Université Luxembourg, and the Philosophy Department Colloquium at Hofstra University.

A number of people have given professional and philosophical support in a variety of ways: Amy Allen, Susan Brison, Stephanie Cobb, Anthony Dardis, Terry Godlove, Eva Feder Kittay, Graham Priest, Ira Singer, Eric Steinhart, Christine J. Thomas, and Charlotte Witt. I would like to thank Amy Allen in particular, and two anonymous reviewers, for much constructive feedback and encouragement. Many thanks also to Bez Ocko for her patience and perseverance in making the figures. For different kinds of support, I am grateful to Eileen Bannon, Jacalyn Carley, Sharryn Kasmir, Gail Schwab, and Lisa Wager for friendship and pacts, to my siblings and best friends—Jeanne Ruttle, Laura Wallace, Mary Tilley, Barbara Wallace, and John Wallace—for their unstinting love, interest, and good humor, to my niece, Emma Wolfe, for her interest and curiosity, and to Jed and Perry Williamson for their generosity in providing such a congenial retreat in which to work. To my mother, Eileen McCormick Wallace, and to my mentor and friend, Sidney Gelber, I owe inspirational debts numerous and deep. And finally, this book would never have been completed without my spouse, Eric Steinhart, whose clarity of purpose and enduring love and commitment encouraged me to persevere.

## Permissions

Some of the material in Chapter 5 is drawn from my article "Autonomous 'I' of an Intersectional Self," *Journal of Speculative Philosophy*, 17, no. 3, pp. 176–191, Kathleen Wallace. Copyright ©2003. The Pennsylvania State University Press. The material from this article is used by permission of The Pennsylvania State University Press.

Quotations from Marya Schechtman in Chapter 2 and Chapter 3 from *Staying Alive: Personal Identity, Practical Concerns and the Unity of a Life*, Copyright ©Marya Schechtman (2014), are used by permission of Oxford University Press.

Kathleen Wallace
November 2018

# 1  Introduction to *The Network Self*

I am large, I contain multitudes.

(Walt Whitman)[1]

I am myself plus my circumstance.

(Ortega y Gasset)[2]

[A] man has as many social selves as there are individuals who recognize him . . . and as there are distinct groups of persons about whose opinion he cares.

(William James)[3]

## 1. Basic Thesis

*The Network Self: Relation, Process, and Personal Identity* develops an account of a relational process self that addresses both metaphysical interests in the nature and identity of the self and practical concerns about autonomy and responsibility.

First, the metaphysical thesis. The self is "relational" and a process; it is what I call a *cumulative network*. I argue that social features and relations, for example, familial, ethnic, or other cultural and social relations, are as central to conceptualizing the self as are physical, biological, and psychological traits. The claim is that the self is a *network* of interrelated traits, physical, biological, psychological, social, and so on. Second, the claim is that the self is a temporal, changeable network of accumulating traits and is, therefore, a *process*. This is a naturalistic, but not merely physicalistic, theory of the self.

The thesis as I develop it launches from the insights of two contemporary relational approaches to the self in philosophy, relational self theories and mereological theories. In feminist (and communitarian) theories a "relational" self has meant a "social" self, or a self that is in relationship(s) with others, causally determined by "outside" social factors, or that has its motivations and values shaped by social influences. My approach seeks to show how social relations are among the many kinds of relations constitutive of selves by giving an account of the self as a network. The self is plurally constituted, but is a unified, structured whole, a network with synchronic unity.

In contemporary analytic metaphysics, four-dimensionalist theories of objects conceptualize persons as spatio-temporal regions and understand relations mereologically. But, four-dimensionalist accounts entail that selves are multiple person-stages or person-parts, and hence, weaken the notion that the self is one "thing" re-identifiable as such through change. My approach seeks to remedy that problem by giving an account of the diachronic unity of the self as a process (which may not be the same as narrative unity). My positive account develops this account, borrowing some ideas from the American pragmatic and naturalist tradition. I comment in Section 7 on some of the ways in which that tradition is a rich resource for addressing contemporary philosophical issues, but my account does not require prior familiarity with it.

Second, the practical concerns about autonomy and responsibility. By "practical" I mean related to practice, action, and agency. I argue that a metaphysical theory of the self helps to interpret the extent to which responsibility is an identity-presupposing concept, and the nature and possibility of autonomy. Conceptualizing the self as a network also gives reasons for why we should think of the self as continuing *as a self* (and as possibly deserving of care) even when it is severely psychologically impaired or compromised. I'm suggesting not that the theory establishes how and when care ought to be provided; rather, it gives an account of why it would make sense to think of a compromised self as a self deserving of care. Perhaps tangentially related are the approaches of Haslanger (2012) and Thomasson (2015). Haslanger argues that concepts of race and gender ought to be shaped by normative concerns about social justice. Thomasson suggests more generally that metaphysics can be understood as a "project of 'conceptual engineering,'" that is, as "working out . . . what concepts would be most useful for a given purpose and in a given context."[4] I am not, however, suggesting that the concept of the self should be shaped by specific normative goals (e.g., social justice, care, etc.). But, my approach is normative in so far as I am recommending that we ought to conceive of the self in a particular way (as a cumulative network) at least in part *because* doing so allows us to account for an array of practical dimensions of selves, such as autonomy, responsibility, continuity as a self in the face of impairments. My approach then is not just "descriptive metaphysics" in Strawson's (1959) sense, not only because I do not limit myself to "common sense" categories, but because it is also a recommendation for how we ought to think of the self. In proposing the cumulative network model of the self, I am also suggesting a revision, if not in common sense, at least in philosophical approaches to the self. The latter are not just abstractions from or more articulate statements of common sense. They need to do different interpretive work from that done by common sense.

Prevailing philosophical conceptualizations of the self—e.g., as a psychological or biological entity or as a physical object or as narratively constructed—don't do all the interpretive work, descriptive and normative, that I think a theory of the self ought to do. I think we want a theory that recognizes that a self is both socially constituted and autonomous, is responsible even if it has changed over time, continues as a self in the face of change, even in the face of impairment, and so on. There is practical work that metaphysical concepts can and ought to do. Thus, my approach is (1) that a theory of the self can and ought to be evaluated by its implications for practical questions (one respect in which my work is "pragmatic"), and (2) that treatments of practical issues can and ought to be evaluated by the merits of their metaphysical assumptions. This is contrary to what some personal identity theorists have recently argued, and I side with those who are on the other side of that debate.

## 2. The Practical and the Metaphysical

Shoemaker (2007) suggests that contemporary philosophers' analyses of persons and personal identity develop out of two distinct areas of interest, (1) an interest in practical concerns on the one hand, and (2) an interest in the nature and identity of objects on the other. Velleman (2002) argues that answers to metaphysical questions about the nature and persistence of the self do not coincide with answers to practical questions about self-regard and self-governance (autonomy).[5] Olson (1997) argues that the two areas should be kept separate: practical concerns should be dealt with by ethicists, issues about persistence and identity should be dealt with by metaphysicians, conflating the two just leads to confusion (69). Korsgaard (2003) argues that the unity of the self is a pragmatic, not a metaphysical matter. By "pragmatic" she means what is necessary for the possibility of agency. She argues that the unity of a self as an agent has practical grounds in the "raw necessity of eliminating conflict among your various motives" and because of "the unity implicit in taking a standpoint when one deliberates and chooses" (169). On one hand, Korsgaard accepts the idea of a division of labor between metaphysics and ethics; on the other hand, in arguing that a problem that arises from metaphysical treatments of the self (Parfit's in particular, Parfit [1986]) can and should be solved "pragmatically" she is also reflecting the idea that both "practical" and metaphysical perspectives are necessary to a full understanding of the self.[6] Schechtman puts this point more explicitly, arguing that metaphysical concerns about identity and persistence are important to practical concerns *and* that issues of practical significance should have some place in a philosophical account of personal identity:

> facts about personal identity are incredibly important in our day-to-day lives. This does not mean that this is all there is to our lives, or that everything about our identities can be learned by looking at judgments of practice and value. But it is a strong indication that we should not simply ignore the practical in understanding what we are and how we continue.
>
> (Schechtman, 2008, 52)[7]

West (2008) argues that metaphysical questions about identity over time are inextricably tied to practical questions and that those practical considerations may justify the conclusion that "there is no single correct answer as to whether a bodily criterion or a psychological criterion is correct" (73). Gallagher and Marcel (1999) criticize purely introspective methods and theorists who approach an analysis of self in "a manner that is abstract or detached from behavior and action normally embedded in pragmatically or socially contextualized situations" (274). They suggest that "problems and paradoxes concerning the notion of the self are the result of searching for the self within these abstract perspectives" (274), and that a different approach is needed:

> [F]or this more comprehensive model [of the self], considerations about agency and ethical action are most pertinent. We are led to a perspective that takes ethics (in the most general sense of "having to do with how one lives one's life") as a suitable starting point for working out an understanding of the notion of self.[8]

Metaphysical and practical issues are not always the same. However, theories that address practical concerns—such as a theory of autonomy or of reflexive self-regard—can't help but make some metaphysical assumptions, even if unarticulated. And, a theory of the self that ignored practical issues would be incomplete in virtue of ignoring important aspects of what it is to be a self. As Schechtman argues, if we want to understand the self as it actually is we have to consider the social and cultural infrastructure that contributes to defining what a self is (Schechtman, 2014). Additionally, the merits of a theory might be weakened if it had problematic implications for practical concerns. Baker (2009), for example, criticizes four-dimensionalism for having "an anemic conception of material objects" (1). By treating objects as merely occupied space-time regions, four-dimensionalism, she argues, fails to recognize the ontological distinctiveness and significance of different kinds of objects, and specifically, of persons. Ordinary objects are merely a matter of convention, of our picking out particular space-time regions for our purposes. Baker also argues that four-dimensionalism clashes with presuppositions of morality and makes it difficult to understand ourselves as human agents with responsibility for our actions (12–13). It might be argued that such a criticism is motivated by practical and value concerns and thus represents exactly the confusion that ought to be avoided. However, my approach is that some metaphysical and practical concerns should be commensurate with one another and therefore, that it *can* be legitimate to raise a practical concern as a relevant consideration for a general theory about the self. This might mean that practical concerns about agency or autonomy should be revised in light of metaphysics, but it might also mean that a general theory of the self should be reconsidered in light of practical concerns.

Thus, I attempt to walk a fine line between being sensitive to the distinction between practical and metaphysical concerns, while at the same time addressing some of the ways in which the practical may be important to understanding who and what we are. I develop an account of practical capabilities, such as autonomy, as a (norm governed) way in which a self as a particular kind of relational process functions. And, I also discuss responsibility as an identity-presupposing concept and how this bears on the attribution and distribution of responsibility. I show how practical concerns about identity and agency may be relevant to deciding fusion and fission thought experimental cases in philosophy, which were originally introduced as a way to test metaphysical intuitions and theses about identity.

## 3. Origins: Relational and Temporal Self Theories

As noted earlier, the view advanced in this book takes off from the work of two areas of philosophical work:

1. The idea of a relational self, proposed by feminists and communitarians, whereby relations are conceptualized in terms of relationships, social and interpersonal. The idea I take from this work is that a self has multiple dimensions or traits and is in important ways socially constituted, although in my view a relational self is more than a social self.
2. The four-dimensionalist (temporal parts or stage theory) idea of a person, developed by metaphysicians concerned with problems in the constitution and identity of material objects, according to which an object (a person) is a spatio-temporal region composed of relations between spatio-temporal parts, stages, or (sub-)regions. I take the idea that a self has temporal features in a different direction and argue that the self is in an important sense its history, and thus, a process.

While they have different provenances, both approaches aim to demystify or to naturalize (not necessarily in a reductive sense) the self and both are "relational" views of the self, albeit in different senses. A "social" relational view of the self arises from objections by feminists, communitarians, and others to an atomistic view of the self that ignores the extent to which the self is a product of its social relations and cultural or community locations.[9] Four-dimensionalism concerns part/whole and temporal relations and problems in the metaphysics of identity of physical objects that change over and persist through time. Four-dimensionalism argues that objects perdure[10] as four-dimensional spatio-temporal regions; time and space are dimensions of objects. Four-dimensionalism contrasts with three-dimensionalism, according to which an object has spatial dimensions and is something that endures, persists, through time.

### 3.1. Temporal Self Theories

Four-dimensionalist theories in contemporary metaphysics come in two varieties, the temporal parts theory and stage theory. On a temporal parts theory, a person or a self consists of temporal parts (e.g., the Monday-part, the five-year-old part; the "size" of the spatio-temporal region can vary). The person as a whole is a space-time worm. This entails that at a time a self is never wholly present, but only a part of a self (e.g., the "today" part) is present. On stage theory, there are multiple, three-dimensional person-stages that are united in some appropriate way to form a person-career. Thus, I the person today writing this sentence am a different person (person-stage) from (albeit a "counterpart" to)[11] the person yesterday who wrote a different sentence, but those two persons are stages in my person-career.

Both varieties have odd results for conceptualizing aspects of selves, such as agency and responsibility, that are important for practical concerns. That only a part of a person is present or that a person (person-career) is multiple persons (person-stages) has weird implications for understanding who acts (a part of a person? of a stage? is that a person?) and who is responsible for actions (a different part or stage?). While I find four-dimensionalism unappealing in this regard, I take the stance that it is worth exploring further how to retain the important and compelling insights about the nature of the self as a temporal spread. I will propose that the self be modeled as a process as well as a network, what I call the cumulative network model of the self. I see myself as working in the spirit of four-dimensionalism, moving away from thinking in terms of static spatio-temporal regions. I will introduce a way to think more dynamically about the self as *cumulatively* related to its past.[12]

### 3.2. Relational Self Views

Feminists and communitarians object to atomistic views of the self that ignore the extent to which the self is a product of and constituted by its social relations and cultural or community locations. Feminists such as Meyers, Alcoff, and others have advocated for a notion of a "relational self." They appeal to the idea of multiple locatedness, by which is meant *social* locations and positions.[13] Meyers (2000b) and others use the phrase "intersectional self."[14] Alcoff (1988) proposed the notion of "positionality" for conceptualizing a self as constituted by plural cultural, gender, and ethnic "positions." Communitarians, such as MacIntyre, Sandel, Taylor, Walzer, and others, reacting to so-called "liberal" views of the self as atomistic, overly individualistic and autonomous, also argue for a conception of a social self. Selves are embodied in social contexts, that is, in social and communal practices, habits, and roles that shape conative and cognitive structures and form an essential part of the well-being of selves. The very identity of the self is wrapped up in at least some of these social roles, that is, in membership in a family, society, culture, and political structure.[15]

I agree, with feminists and communitarians, that the self is socially constituted. But, I seek to show how the relations constitutive of a self include, but are not exclusively, social relations.[16] Feminist theorists have been more important in my own thinking and more forward-looking than communitarians in exploring alternative ways of conceptualizing the self as social and relational, and in recognizing the importance of autonomy as well as the nature of interdependent selves. My interest in a relational self, though, is not situated in the context of political theory. Rather, my aim is to give a broad account of a self that is relational throughout, and without commitment to specific political norms. At the same time, I am interested in practical dimensions to selfhood, such as the capacity for autonomy and responsibility. Feminists have grappled with the question of autonomy, and offered some ways of preserving autonomy for a relational self. I build on such accounts of the ways in which a plurally constituted relational self is capable of autonomy, or self-governance (what I call self-directing norm-generation). I suggest that autonomy for a relational self is rooted in reflexive relations between the multiple constituents of such a self, and that relationality is not in conflict with, but provides a basis for autonomy.

## 4. The Basic Thesis: The Self as Network and Process

In modeling the self as relational, the issue is not simply to consider ways in which the self may be socially determined or causally determined by factors "outside" of itself. Nor is it simply a matter of considering the extent to which a self borrows motivations and values from or is shaped in the formation of such by social influences. Rather, it is a matter of considering the self as relationally constituted throughout. The self is a relational, plurally constituted complex, that is, a *network* of interrelated biological, genetic, physical, social, psychosocial, linguistic, semantic, and so on traits. I have an expansive view of relations constitutive of a self as a network, and therefore, "relational" does not mean only "social."

In philosophy, the concept of a network has been most conspicuous in computational theories of mind with such concepts as neural nets, connectionist models of mind and brain, and to some extent in philosophy of biology (biological networks) and philosophy of ecology, wherein ecosystems may be conceptualized as types of networks.[17] But, I am suggesting that the self, the individual person, be conceived as a network. As a network it would exhibit a structure or typology (Barabási, 2002), and thus, is not a mere bundle of properties. While there is contingency among the actual, multiple constituents of a self, the self is a structured unity with characteristic functionalities.[18] I also propose that the self is a process. I call this the cumulative network model of the self (CNM). According to CNM, the self is a complex of plural constituent relations, that is, a *network* of traits, with synchronic unity and a *process*, that is, a temporal spread with diachronic unity.

As a process, a self is a *cumulative* changeable totality that takes up, includes in some sense, its own past. At any time, a self is a diachronic unity because it is a cumulative upshot of what it has been and the leading edge of the process. Imagine a physical process, like an avalanche. It is spread out in space and time. Any phase of an avalanche is what it is in virtue of the intersection of forces, energy, and matter that have been accumulating and those that are present at that phase. So, too, the self. The self is not merely a succession of distinct selves or self-parts or -stages, but like an avalanche, is one process spread out in space and time, a structured and active unity of multiple constituents that include biological, social, cultural, and semantic, as well as physical relations. The self is constituted of "stuff" (e.g., bio-physical stuff), just as the avalanche is constituted of "stuff" (e.g., snow). There are other physical forces and factors (e.g., the steepness of the slope) functioning and interacting such as to constitute the avalanche as a structured activity, qua an avalanche process. Similarly, there are social, psychological, cultural, semantic relations, and factors functioning and interacting to constitute the self qua process self. The avalanche is a process constituted of multiple traits, and so, too, is a self. I show how this model of the self avoids the problems associated with standard four-dimensionalist temporal parts and stage theories, viz., either that only a part of the self is present at a time or that there are multiple persons making up a "person-career." I suggest that since the self at any time is the process as it is up to that time, there is a sense in which it is a whole self as it is up to that time that is present.

The cumulative network model (CNM) of the self has implications for practical dimensions of the self, such as reflexivity, autonomy, and responsibility. These are not only psychological dimensions of a self. I use the term "self" more broadly. It does not refer only to subjective experience, an "I," consciousness, or self-consciousness. Rather, it refers to the self as a whole, the person. I am aiming to model the self as it generally is, a "macro-level" conceptualization of the self as functional whole. I will, however, also aim to provide some conceptual tools for discussing subjective experiences, such as reflexivity, autonomy, and responsibility that I think of as practical dimensions of selves.

## 5. Practical Implications

The first part of the book, Chapters 2, 3, and 4, addresses the general theoretical issues. In Chapter 2, I march out the view, elaborating the notions of network and process just described. In Chapter 3, I address the specific issue of identity over time or persistence. I show how the structured unity of a relational process self satisfies conditions for persistence as that one self. In Chapter 4, I analyze some recurrent thought experiments about fusion and fission of selves from the metaphysical literature on persons and personal identity, and show how the model I am proposing differs from (and improves on) current treatments of whether and how the self would continue in such cases.

Chapters 5, 6, and 7 address "practical" issues of autonomy and responsibility with which many theorists about persons are concerned. For these we need to grapple with how it is that a self engages in reflexive processes of self-identification and self-interpretation. If a self is relationally constituted, then in what sense is there an "I" and a first-person perspective? Isn't an "I" in some sense, by definition, non-relational, a perspective that remains constant at least in conscious experience and that is the executive decision-maker of the self, however much the self may be relationally constituted in other respects? Moreover, isn't some single chief executive capacity necessary for autonomy, for self-direction as an ongoing agent?

Some have proposed that because a self is a multiple, an intersectional self (typically, of race, class, gender, occupation, ethnicity, language, and so on), it has no unitary identity.[19] There have also been strong and important critiques of the notion of a substantial "I" or of an inner "self" that is an independent subject, among them those offered by Wittgenstein, Anscombe, Dennett, and Baker.[20] I largely agree with the latter critiques and with a rejection of the "I" as some sort of Cartesian mental substance, or of any substantivizing conception of it as a continuant across imaginative or counterfactual transformations of a first-person perspective. However, if we can't fully understand agency, our own and others without *some* notion of a first-person perspective, then some account of the capacity for self-representation, identification, and re-identification as indexical or reflexive functions is needed.[21]

In Chapter 5, I show how such capacities can be conceptualized as relationally constituted.[22] The cumulative network of traits is conceived as a *community* of first-personal perspectives. A reflexive "I" perspective is not an observer or evaluator perspective *apart* from the locations of the self. Rather, "I" is a reflexive function, by which the self as a network of traits evaluates or mediates from some location(s) or other. For example, suppose a self who is a feminist and a spouse. The self can reflexively identify itself as and reflect on itself qua feminist (I-as-feminist), or qua spouse (I-as-spouse), or mediate between the two (I-as-feminist/ spouse). This reflexive activity, I suggest, should be thought of as "self-" or "reflexive communication." It is reflexivity in a perspective, that is, always from or within some location or other. (The perspective could also be the self as a whole.) Imagine a network of lamps wired to one another. One or more can be turned on at a time. Each lamp illuminates the room in a different way. Take this as a metaphor for the self as a network of traits. The wire(s) are the relations between locations or perspectives and the light(s) when on the "I" reflecting on itself in that perspective(s). Even if it feels as if there is one lamp (one "I") that moves from one location in the room (in the network) to another, it is rather that different lamps are turned on or off (different perspectives of the self are functioning reflexively).

This approach gives up the notion of a single executive "I," and reconceives reflexivity as multi-faceted.[23] I suggest that modeling the self as plurally constituted is essential to understanding the self's capacity for multiple ways of acting and being. Relational constitution does not undermine but rather makes self-mediation possible. Through reflexive communication the self actively contributes to its own self-constitution and practical identity, and is also capable of directing itself through higher level reason-giving and reason-responsive activity. When the self does so in norm-generating and norm directed ways, it is self-governing, or autonomous.

In Chapter 6, I analyze the notion of autonomy as consisting in what I call norm-generation, execution, and assessment. (For simplicity, I will sometimes refer to it as simply norm-generation.) I do not consider autonomy in the context of free will/determinism debates. Rather, I take the issue to be more helpfully thought of in terms of autonomy versus heteronomy, by which I mean thinking about autonomy as self-governance or self-rule.

According to proceduralist accounts personal autonomy consists in the possession or exercise of certain abilities, irrespective of the substantive content of the choices. Thus, on a proceduralist account, personal autonomy would consist in the right kind, or in properly developed exercise, of reflexive capacities. But, a substantivist theorist would worry that an apparently autonomous choice might merely express inculcated values or beliefs over which one has exercised no control or ones which, even though endorsed, are repressive or stultifying. (An example expressing feminist worries would be that of a wife who unreflectively endorses submissiveness to her husband's wishes; another would be that of a husband who unreflectively expects and endorses such submission.) A substantivist approach argues that only certain kinds of choices constitute autonomy, that choices ought to conform to objectively autonomy-conducing standards. A proceduralist worries that *self*-determination would be compromised by objective standards being imposed on, rather than shaped by, the self.

If autonomy means the capacity for self-governance, then the substantivist is right that autonomy involves norms. But, a substantivist approach is limited if it doesn't account for norms themselves as being in some sense self-produced. Norms are not only universal standards of rationality or consensus (even if there may be some contexts in which universal norms are appropriate) or social standards defining the appropriate behavior in a given social role (e.g., caregiving standards of good parenting). Norms can also be seen as produced in at least some sense by selves; and they may be diverse, revisable and generated by human selves in specific contexts or for specific purposes. My suggestion is that an autonomous self mediates among, and sometimes transforms, its own locations. Autonomy need not entail transcending social locations, although it could entail transcending, in some sense, some of them. An autonomous self is one in which reflexive capacities are engaged in the process of generating norms. That might mean endorsing existing, internalized norms, but it can also mean revising and inventing the norms by which a self governs or rules itself.[24] Thus, returning to the example of a woman who is a feminist and a spouse, suppose she aims to articulate guidelines (norms) for herself for how to be both. Each of these is a constitutive trait of her. Each self-perspective (self-as-feminist and self-as-spouse) communicates to itself and to the other, to generate a norm (or norms) with respect to, for instance, marriage-in-light-of-feminist-concerns. This process of establishing a norm for self-governance may involve assimilation, as well as modification or rejection, of social norms, as well as communication with others. The "I" is both "I"-as-feminist and "I"-as-spouse. These constitutive locations of the self communicate with one another to normatively direct and to shape perhaps a new constitutive location for the self (the network), "I"-as-feminist/spouse.

In Chapter 7, I take up the notion of responsibility. Many discussions of responsibility are tied up with discussions of whether selves are really free. Again, as with autonomy, the free will/determinism debate is not the focus of my interest in responsibility. I am concerned with three different aspects of the notion of responsibility.

(1)  The extent to which responsibility is an identity-presupposing concept, particularly in so far as the self is a target of forensic concerns. What is often taken to be of primary concern in matters of ascription of responsibility is that the self that performed an action is one and

the same self as the self that is held responsible, that the self that at time $t_1$ performed an action *is* the self that at time $t_2$ is held responsible. This issue reconnects with some of the discussion of identity in Chapter 3, where I suggest that the relevant concept is not identity, but what I call numerical unity. Other responsibility affecting considerations, such as whether a change in character or ability is relevant to legal competence, are distinct from this core issue of (re)identification. I explore how the issue of identification bears on distribution of responsibility by reconsidering some of the fusion and fission thought experiments considered in Chapter 4.

(2) Responsibility as a forward- and backward-looking concept. In so far as responsibility is a backward-looking concept, it is concerned with whether a self has the appropriate causal and counterfactual dependency and continuity relations with some action at a previous time. Insofar as a self is cumulative, it includes its past as a trait. Therefore, the basis for backward responsibility, for a self's relation to and responsibility for its own prior actions, is built into the very model of the self.

But, there are forward-looking considerations—for instance, living a life going forward with or without impunity—that bear on the issue of responsibility ascription. The nature of a relational *process* self that is both autonomous (or, at least has the capacity of autonomy or self-governance) and incomplete supports the notion that responsibility is also a forward-looking concept. Even though a self is "determinate" with respect to its past, it also is incomplete. It contributes to the shaping of its future, and therefore, takes responsibility in a forward-looking sense. I mean "taking responsibility" in two senses. First, in something like what Fischer and Ravizza (1998) suggest—that a person recognizes the conditions that helped to create who she is and takes on responsibility for being that person or agent going forward. Putting this in an admittedly awkward way, this is a kind of forward-looking perspective on the backward-looking aspect of responsibility whereby a self takes up her or his past incorporating it into who and what the self is going forward. Thus, second, the self takes responsibility for how it moves forward, for how it projects itself into the future with its cumulative past.

(3) How the scope of responsibility is affected by the plural character of a relational self: I argue that in so far as a relational self is constituted by—not just causally influenced by—its social relations (as well as biological, cultural, linguistic, political, etc. relations) the self may share responsibility for the character of the communities by which it is constituted and for the impact of communities with which the self identifies and is identified. By this I do not necessarily mean that a self is responsible for the sins of the ancestors of its social constituents.

Nor am I endorsing Jaspers' notion of metaphysical guilt whereby one may be morally tainted merely in virtue of who one is or by association with those who engage in wrongful action (e.g., according to Jaspers, the German who would be metaphysically guilty for the Holocaust simply by virtue of being German). Rather, I am suggesting that a relational model of the self provides a better explanation than an atomistic model for why in at least some contexts one is or ought to be responsible or share in the responsibility for behavior or the consequences of behavior that are attributable to groups, collectives or institutions to which one belongs and in which one participates. Recognition of oneself as at least partially socially constituted by these locations gives some basis for calling it a failure when one does not recognize oneself as, for example, contributing to a harm in virtue of one's participation in a group, society or institution that is, collectively causing harm or engaging in wrongful behavior. Whether recognition of one's participation calls for specific action, let alone what such action would be, is a complicated ethical and political issue and not one that I will attempt to resolve. My suggestion is that the cumulative network model of the self can at least offer an answer to the question, why should an individual regard collective harm or wrongdoing as posing any obligation for or any ascription of responsibility to the individual? If participation in a society, institution or collective is at least partly constitutive of who one is, then that may provide some basis for individual responsibility for collective actions and harms.

To summarize, *The Network Self: Relation, Process, and Personal Identity* offers a theory of the self as a relational process, that is, as a cumulative network. The self is modeled as a network where the constituents are biological, social, cultural, semantic, and so on, as well as "purely" physical. In order to address practical issues, such as the capacity for first-personal activity, autonomy, and responsibility, I conceive the self as a community of first-personal perspectives that reflexively communicate with one another. When the self does so in norm-generating and norm directed ways, it is self-governing, or autonomous. Finally, I explore how the cumulative network model (CNM) of the self meets a cluster of concerns about responsibility, about re-identification, about responsibility in collective contexts, and about backward- and forward-looking aspects of responsibility.

## 6. Other Relational Self Theories

The idea of a relational self has been in circulation for quite some time and in many different areas of thought—psychology, sociology, religion, neuroscience—as well as philosophy. I have already mentioned feminism as one of the originating touchstones of my thinking. While I can't review all the different theories, I will briefly situate my approach in comparison to some other views that have explicitly thematized relationality as a basic feature of the self.

The most recent and well-worked out philosophical view—a narrative constitution view—is Schechtman's (2014) person life view of persons. A person is a being who has a person life. Schechtman's view explicitly incorporates social determinants of a person. It does not however conceptualize the self as a network. As a narrative constitution view, it relies on social and cultural practices to define what a self is. I argue that while social and cultural experiences and practices may be constitutive elements of selves, the model of the self is not based on, or at least is not intended to be based on, social and cultural practices. Schechtman's view acknowledges that a person life develops. It does not however explicitly conceptualize the self as a process. Schechtman incorporates "practical" concerns into a conceptualization of persons as they actually are and as they are the "target of forensic concerns." She does not, however, address how to conceptualize autonomy for such a socially constituted self and does not consider some of the aspects of responsibility (such as an individual having a share in collective responsibility) that I do.

Another relational, but not social, view is Ismael's (2007) dynamical system view of the self. This view is developed in the context of philosophy of mind and of addressing the problem of mental self-representation in light of the "apparent unanalyzability of the notion of a self" (3). By the latter is meant the apparent absence of any interior identifiable subject or "I" whenever the mind turns to examine its own inward contents. The dynamical system view of the self as embedded in the natural world is meant to replace and resolve the problems of a mind/body dualism while introducing a naturalistic account of how it is possible to form thoughts about and refer to oneself without having a conception of the self (200).[25] Some of Ismael's treatment of first-person (reflexive or indexical) reference and identification resonates with my own discussion in Chapter 5 of a first-person perspective and reflexivity. Here the point is that to view the self as a dynamical system is a kind of relational model of the self.

Ismael's analysis was anticipated by previous philosophers including the prescient John Dewey, who argued for a transactional self for which experience is a relational process of engagement between an organic self and world.[26] Related to, but also predating Ismael's theory, some externalist theories of mind may also be suggestive of the kind of view I am proposing. For example, Clark and Chalmers (1998) in the extended mind thesis suggest that the self should be viewed as "an extended system, a coupling of biological organism and external resources," and that rather than viewing the self as a "mere bundle of occurrent states" or as "bounded by the skin," it is "far better to take the broader view, and see agents themselves as spread into the world" (18). A theory of the self as relational is not developed, nor is the social constitution of a self explicitly thematized, except in so far as a social relationship may be a component of a self's cognitive processing, as for example, when one self relies on memories of another self for its cognitive processing.

Another relational (but not exclusively social) view is advanced by Lysaker and Lysaker (2008). In their analysis of the first-person perspective experience of schizophrenia, they, like Alcoff, use the term "position" to develop their notion of a "dialogical self." Drawing on work[27] inspired by Nietzsche and Bakhtin, Lysaker and Lysaker characterize a self as "a multiplicity of souls" or as consisting of "multiple self-positions," e.g., self-as-brother, self-as-anxious, self-as-teacher, and so on, positions which "converse with one another, and without ever collapsing into one, overarching position" (45). They also distinguish between three types of self-positions, what they call "organism-positions," "character-positions," and "meta-positions" (54). (Examples of each of these: self-as-male would be an "organism-position," self-as-teacher would be a "character-position," self-as-angry would be a "meta-position.")

Lysaker and Lysaker's view of the self provides an intriguing framework for understanding mental illness, and in particular schizophrenia, and in that regard the focus of their concern is very different from mine. They do not characterize the self in temporal terms as I will, nor do they deal directly with the issues I will address in this book (i.e., identity and persistence, autonomy, responsibility). But, their analysis resonates with mine in three respects: (1) it does not limit constitutive relations to the social (but includes biological, psychological, emotive, reflexive and so on); (2) it advances the idea that the multiplicity or complexity of the self is irreducible; and (3) it introduces the dimension of reflexivity, via the category of "meta-positions." (I discuss reflexivity in Chapter 5.)

The psychologist Kenneth Gergen (2009) argues that "the bounded self" of individualism should be jettisoned and replaced with a recognition of relational process as prior to the individual. The self should be understood as a manifestation of relationships. Gergen proposes four theses about the relational self, namely, that mental discourse (1) originates in human relationships, (2) functions in the service of relationship, (3) is action within relationships, and (4) that discursive action is embedded in traditions of co-action (70–74). Gergen attempts to show the implications of his relationship self for practices, such as therapy, education, and for moral and sacral experiences. He eschews the term "self" for "being" because of individualist associations of "self."

Gergen's treatment focuses on human relationships and is thus a social self view. Gergen's work draws some of its inspiration from feminism and acknowledges "philosophical inheritances" in the works of Mead, Merleau-Ponty, Heidegger, Buber, Levinas, and the Wittgenstein of the *Philosophical Investigations*. But, it is not a philosophical treatment of the concept of social self or "relational being" and does not address issues such as identity and persistence. It does resonate with my theory in at least two respects: (1) it recognizes the self as a relational process, even though its view of "relational" is social and hence, more restricted than mine; and (2) it attempts to reconceive practical dimensions of human experience, such as moral responsibility, in relational terms, although it doesn't address the same issues about responsibility that I do (for instance, the extent to which responsibility is an identity-presupposing concept).

Actor-network theory in sociology (Latour, 2005) rejects substantialist, essentialist, and natural kind theories of the self. It presents a self as an object or "actant" that, like any other object, is what it is and is able to act only through relations (conceived largely in terms of forces and power) with other objects (actants), both human and non-human. While there may be some resonances between my view and actor-network theory, my view aims to articulate within a relational model what is distinctive about selves, and not collapse the difference between selves and other constituents of social systems. Thus, I aim to give an account of reflexivity and autonomy and to address the notion of responsibility, which I take to be distinctive practical dimensions of selves.

## 7. Pragmatism

My work is "pragmatic" in several senses. It is pragmatic in the sense expressed by Korsgaard, noted earlier, when she argues that aspects of the self should be understood with respect to what is necessary for agency. In addition, my thinking reflects the influence of classical American philosophy and such figures as William James, Josiah Royce, Charles Sanders Peirce, George Herbert Mead, John Dewey, and Justus Buchler. While the work of these philosophers predates the maturation of and progress made by analytic metaphysics and feminist philosophy, their work informed the development of my thinking about a relational self in a number of ways. While classical pragmatism is typically associated with the slogan about truth as "what works," and thus, with a kind of anti-realist stance, that is a superficial and somewhat distorted reading of the positions of the pragmatist philosophers. The pragmatist commitment to fallibilism does not entail anti-realism, but the view that beliefs are revisable because better approximations to reality are achieved and achievable. Peirce thought that an ideal community of inquirers would approach truth. The facts of the world would demand that ideas that led to habits of thought and action that defied the brute given-ness of the world would eventually have to be abandoned, because the irritation of doubt (sometimes experienced in direct practical terms, not only in rational terms involving inconsistency or cognitive dissonance) would force their reconsideration. Most pragmatists were realists and developed substantive views about human nature, nature, science, religion, views which were not merely about "what works" for a believer or believers. Kitcher (2007) suggests, in his discussion of whether "race" is a natural kind,[28] that the core insight of the pragmatists is pluralism, "an insistence on the indefinitely multiple possibilities of classification" (300).

Many of the pragmatist philosophers were naturalists, broadly understood. A naturalistic approach entailed the breakdown of a sharp distinction between subjective and objective, and a recognition of the centrality of relation in ontology. James argued for an ontology of relations. Dewey conceived experience as "transactional," a process of doing and undergoing that takes place between an organism and nature qua its environment. For Dewey, the individual is a process. The Deweyan "situation" of organism-environment is also social, not only physical. Mead developed a social ontology of the self and argued that a system of social roles and relations is constitutive of the self.[29] Royce argued that interpretation is a distinct cognitive function of a self and is fundamentally social in nature. For Buchler, a self is a process and a "natural complex" as much as any other being is (whatever it is, physical object or process, social institution, abstract object, possible entity).[30] Complexity is analyzed in terms of relationality (and what Buchler calls "ordinality") and relation is analyzed in terms of relevance. I draw on some specific ideas from Mead's, Royce's, and Buchler's work,[31] but I do not presuppose familiarity with their work on the part of the reader. Where some specific background is needed, I will provide it at the relevant juncture.

Contemporary work in pragmatism and feminism is a background to and is resonant with my work. Seigfried (1991a, 1991b, 1996, 2002) presents a strong case for the affinities between feminism and pragmatism, in particular with pragmatism's emphasis on experience, and on context and situated knowledge, and its idea that philosophy ought to be responsive to its social and political world. She also argues that pragmatism historically was influenced by feminist thinkers such as Jane Addams and Charlotte Perkins Gilman, and that pragmatism should be recovered for the rich resources it offered for feminist thinking. Sullivan (2001) aims to show the affinities between pragmatism and continental thought for developing feminist themes, particularly around the notion of embodiment. McKenna (2002) suggests that a pragmatist feminist notion of the self could be found in Dewey, one that would transcend "abstracted notions of the self found in the social contract/justice models and the organicist/care models" (149). This notion, McKenna says, would be

> a new concept of the individual, an integrated individual, a social self. Dewey calls this the "unified individual." Such an individual is

attentive to his/her context; s/he acts more than s/he is acted upon; s/he is involved in and responsible for his/her own creation. S/he is not thrown around by natural or social forces, but uses such forces with intelligence, purpose, and foresight. Without this new concept of the self we will find ourselves being moved by external forces; we will experience a loss of agency.

(148–149)

I do not pursue a historical or comparative project here. And my work is not offering a specifically feminist or pragmatist theory of the self. I am interested not so much in developing a notion of the self that addresses particular problems identified by feminism or pragmatism, although as discussed previously, I do think that a philosophical theory of the self should be able to address, if not practical questions of a specific time and place, general functional or practical features of a self, whatever its context. I offer a general theory of the self that has been inspired by insights from feminism and pragmatism about the social constitutedness of the self, as well as by issues raised in the Anglo-analytic literature on personal identity.

Methodologically, I have also been influenced by pragmatism. I am interested in exploring the connections of an idea to practices and agency *and* in exploring how an idea "works." By that I mean that I am interested in exploring the implications of an idea in the world, and specifically, in how an idea of the self makes sense of the nature of the self. This involves both "agreeing" with reality, but also interpreting it. Ideas may refer to or correspond to something, but they also interpret and give meaning to what it is we aim to understand. The pragmatists were also committed to the notion of improvement in belief and understanding, and understood that in terms of making better approximations to the nature of reality (allowing for the possibility that at least in some contexts or respects there could be a plurality of approximations). Of course, they, Dewey in particular, were interested as well in ideas leading to improvement in human life, but such improvement, Dewey believed, was not independent of improvement in understanding the world. I am not as optimistic as Dewey about progress, but am pointing out that a commitment to progress entails a commitment to a reality that is at least partly independent of us. This is more the realist or objectivist crux of the pragmatist slogan about truth being what works (rather than meaning just whether an idea "works for me," by, for instance, improving my own or a subject's outlook on, or prospects in, life). In the pragmatist spirit I am less concerned with offering decisive rebuttal of other theories (although I do note what I take to be weaknesses or unsatisfactory aspects of some theories) than I am with developing a model of a relational process self and seeing how that model interprets and makes sense of the self.

# Notes

1. Walt Whitman, Song of Myself [Section 51], in the 1891–92 edition of *Leaves of Grass*.
2. Ortega y Gasset (2000, 45).
3. James (1890, 294).
4. Thomasson (2015), no page number in text file available at https://www.amiethomasson.org/publications
5. For Velleman, practical questions are psychological questions. See also Schechtman (1996), who distinguishes between what she calls the re-identification question and the characterization question in discussions of personal identity.
6. Korsgaard's approach is not pragmatic in the sense meant by the classical American pragmatists (see Section 7), but one can see the resonance with some strands of pragmatism, and in particular the notion that metaphysics is not necessarily divorced from practice and the requirements of living in a social and natural world.
7. Schechtman (2014) argues that to understand the person as s/he actually is, we need to conceptualize it as the target of practical concerns.
8. Gallagher and Marcel (1999, 275). By self they mean consciousness, or the capacity for conscious access to itself. This is a much more restricted meaning of "self" than what I intend, but the methodological point is still relevant.
9. Similar concerns may motivate the development in psychology of explicitly relational or social theories of the self. For example, see Andersen and Chen (2002) and Gergen (2009).
10. Or "exdure." The difference between these two is not important for my purposes. For a succinct and clear introduction to the difference between these two, see Kurtz (2006).
11. For counterpart theory see my discussions of four-dimensionalism in Chapters Two and Three.
12. While I incline toward some version of four-dimensionalism (I do think that objects are spread out in space and time), I agree with Seibt (2009, 2015) that four-dimensionalism doesn't do justice to the ontology of processes. (I don't however pursue questions about the ontology of processes generally.) I also think that if general ontology aims to delineate categories for whatever is, then there are many aspects of reality (such as mathematical realities, possibilities, laws, fictional characters, social practices) that are not helpfully conceptualized as spatio-temporal regions. But, that is not the subject of this book; I mention these points only to clarify why, although I am sympathetic to four-dimensionalism in some respects, I don't fully sign on to the theory.
13. "Relational" and "social" are often simply interchangeable. For example, Christman (2004) in an article on relational autonomy says, "I will use the term 'relational' and 'social' more or less interchangeably" (159). However, elsewhere in the same article, he says,

> '[R]elational' views seem to express more thoroughly the need to underscore interpersonal dynamics as components of autonomy, dynamics such as caring relations, interpersonal dependence, and intimacy. 'Social' accounts imply, I think, a broader view, where various other kinds of social factors—institutional settings, cultural patterns, political factors—might all come into play.

> (161)

In my taxonomy, both interpersonal and "broader social factors" would be characterized as social self views. I do distinguish familial and other social

clusters of traits for purposes of illustrating the idea that there is organization and structure (of sub-clusters of traits) to the network self. See Chapter
2. But, my point is that while there are many different kinds of social traits
(interpersonal, familial and kinship, cultural and political) as a broad kind
category, all are social.

14. Meyers (2000b) builds on the work of Crenshaw (1993), Lugones (1992),
and Mouffe (1992). See also Crenshaw (1991), Collins (1990), Lugones and
Spelman (1999), Anzaldua (2001). In a later article, Meyers distinguishes
between what she calls the social self and the relational self. By the former,
the "social" self, she means a "socialized or enculturated self" that has assimilated social norms, values, attitudes, and interpretive frameworks (Meyers,
2005, 29). By the latter, the "relational" self, Meyers means an "interperson-
ally bonded self" (2005, 30). On my view, both of these are social interpretations of "relationality." See previous Note 13. Witt (2011), too, identifies
relationality with what she calls the "social individual," one of three ontologically distinct entities—the human organism, the person, and the social
individual—that constitute a self. In an earlier piece I used the term "intersectional self" (Wallace, 2003). However, I note that "intersectionality" has
a distinct history as a concept for identifying the ways in which multiple
cultural and social locations, and specifically, race and gender, interact in
the production and experience of discrimination and injustice. Since I do
not engage with this literature or these issues in this book, I do not here use
"intersectionality" to characterize my view.

15. For representative works see, MacIntyre (1984), Sandel (1998), Taylor (1989),
Walzer (1983). See also Kymlicka (1989).

16. However, with communitarians' emphasis on social and cultural traditions
as positively valued determinants of selves, and feminists' critiques of the
limiting roles allowed to women in such traditions, the two approaches are
not necessarily philosophically allied. Communitarian theories tend to be
more concerned with the issue of selves being located in and defined by
the traditions in which they find themselves and with challenging political liberalism's stance that the State ought to protect liberty and individual
autonomy. On the communitarian view, political liberalism overlooks the
importance of duties to the community and the role the State should play in
preserving the community and the public good. The merits or faults of the
communitarian critique of political liberalism as far as the public good goes
is not my concern here, other than to note that a communitarian emphasis
on preserving existing social and cultural traditions puts it at odds with
feminist critiques of the effects of many such traditions on women. For a
good discussion of tensions between communitarianism and feminism see
Barclay (2000).

17. There are many, too many, different views that could be cited here. One
theory that resonates with the view I develop is the dynamical system view
developed by Ismael (2007). Ismael's focus is the development of a non-
representational theory of mind. By "self" she means the mind's capacity to
develop a self-centered portrait of the world in which it, as an aspect of a
dynamical, coordinating system, is located.

18. While I do not have the mathematical or theoretical background to pursue
formal network theory, it may be a fruitful line of connection for exploring how networks are organized and capable of retaining their functional
capabilities in spite of change, even extensive change, in a wide range of
constituents.

19. Post-modern and "diversity" critiques of the "unitary self" argue for this
view of the self. See Mackenzie and Stoljar (2000b). Young (1986) cites

Kristeva as characterizing the self as an "intersection of influences" with no center (4). On a post-modern view of a thoroughly decentered self see also Lyotard (1988).

20. Anscombe (1975), Baker (2013), Dennett (1992, 2001), Wittgenstein (1972, 66–67).

21. In a different, but perhaps related vein, Strawson argues against no self views by suggesting that our capacity to self-ascribe entails the ability to other ascribe (to other *persons*) and that therefore persons must have both physical and mental aspects; they must be more than a mere consciousness. Thus, when we refer to ourselves, we are referring to *something*, just as when we refer to others. "Person," he says, is a primitive concept (Strawson, 1959, Chapter 3).

22. Other recent reconceptualizations of the first-person perspective include Baker's (2013) naturalistic but irreducible "personal" account and Ismael's (2007) more thoroughly naturalized account of such capacities. However, neither account specifically addresses how social and interpersonal relations are constituents of such capacities.

23. Some research from psychology and neuroscience seems to be similarly suggestive of a plural first-person perspective. See, for instance, Andersen and Chen (2002), Bloom (2008, 2010). For earlier work, see Minsky (1988). Thus, my account of the self as a relational process may be consistent with neuroscience, but doesn't provide explanations of brain functions and processes that may explain how memory and other conscious (and unconscious) behaviors work.

24. My point here is only with regard to autonomy, not about the general extent to which selves may be subject to normative considerations. Of course, a self need not be aware of or endorse a norm to, nonetheless, be subject to or evaluable according to it. For example, a parent who does not take care of his child does not have as a morally legitimate excuse that he doesn't endorse the norm of parents caring for their children.

25. In Ismael's work (2007), sometimes "self" means the organism, the whole dynamical system that is capable of mental experiences, reflexive identification and so on, and sometimes it means mind, that is, just that subset of capacities of the whole dynamical system. In this context, when I use the term "self" I mean the former (the dynamical system) unless I specifically note otherwise.

26. Dewey's views can be found in many of his voluminous writings. But, see for example, his *Experience and Nature* (Dewey, 2008a) and *Art as Experience* (Dewey, 2008b).

27. Such as the work of Hermans (1996a, 1996b) and Hermans et al. (1993).

28. He argues that it is not (Kitcher, 2007). See also Kitcher (2012).

29. In cognitive science, some proponents of 4E cognition—cognition that is embodied, embedded, extended, and enactive—suggest that pragmatists such as James, Dewey, and Mead anticipated such development in cognitive science and that their work still has much to offer, for example, in integrating the 4Es (Gallagher, 2014; Johnson, 2005).

30. Buchler argues for the irreducibility of complexity and against ontological simples (Buchler, 1990, 17–30).

31. I make some use of Mead (1934) in Chapter 5 on the first-person perspective. I make some use of Buchler (1979, 1990) in developing the notion of the relational process self in Chapter 2 and the notion of reflexive communication in Chapter 5. I think of Buchler as a transitional figure between early 20th century pragmatists and naturalists, and contemporary metaphysicians. Buchler himself was not a pragmatist, but a metaphysician who

worked prior to the maturation of contemporary analytic metaphysics. Buchler's insights are surprisingly prescient, and offer some pathways for pushing conceptual boundaries about complexity, the nature of objects, modality. I draw rather freely from the Buchlerian framework as it suits my purposes. I am interested in problems posed by the nature and identity of the self, not in providing exposition or defense of Buchler's theory. The theory is of interest in so far as it helps in conceptualizing the nature of the self as both relational and as a process. I will indicate when I am using specific Buchlerian categories.

# 2 The Relational Process Self: The Cumulative Network Model

By nature, I am a sort of meeting place of countless streams of ancestral tendency.

(Josiah Royce)[1]

I think the next century will be the century of complexity.

(Stephen Hawking)[2]

I cannot compare the soul more properly to any thing than to a republic or commonwealth, in which the several members are united by the reciprocal ties of government and subordination, and give rise to other persons, who propagate the same republic in the incessant changes of its parts. And as the same individual republic may not only change its members, but also its laws and constitutions; in like manner the same person may vary his character and disposition, as well as his impressions and ideas, without losing his identity.

(David Hume)[3]

[T]hings, however absolute and entire they seem in themselves, are but retainers to other parts of nature, for that which they are most taken notice of by us. Their observable qualities, actions, and powers are owing to something without them; and there is not so complete and perfect a part that we know of nature, which does not owe the being it has, and the excellences of it, to its neighbours; and we must not confine our thoughts within the surface of any body, but look a great deal further, to comprehend perfectly those qualities that are in it.

(John Locke)[4]

## 1. Preliminaries

The approach I take to the self is located at the intersection of metaphysical and practical interests. It is distinguished from other contemporary work at this crossroads by its aim to offer an explicitly relational theory of the self. This chapter focuses on the metaphysical interest in developing a relational or network model of the self.

By self, I do not mean something merely psychological or mental, as in having a sense or concept of self or as in self-consciousness. By self I mean the whole being, human, biological, psychological, social, and semantic. I prefer the term "self" to the term "person" because it seems to me to be the more neutral term. The concept "person" is often distinguished from the concept "human being." Philosophical theories of "person" include the animalist view, the constitution view, the brain view, the temporal parts view, the bundle view, the soul view, the special composition view, and most recently, the person life view.[5] I do not examine the extensive literature on these in detail, but refer to them and draw contrasts between them and my view where appropriate. The term "person" also often has honorific connotations, such that "person" may connote an object of respect or of some other proper moral attitude.

My view was stimulated by (1) in contemporary analytic metaphysics, the approach known as four-dimensionalism, which views objects and persons as spatio-temporal regions (Sider, 2001) and (2) feminist theories of a relational (or "social") self. The former, by conceiving of the self as temporally constituted, inspires the notion that the self is temporally constituted and thus is a process. From the latter, feminism, I borrow the insight that the social and the practical are also constitutive of a self. However, I aim to move beyond these. I have an expansive view of relations and don't equate "relational person" solely with "social person." Rather, the cumulative network model (CNM) of the self includes social, but many other relations (biological, physical, psychological, and so on) as constitutive of selves.[6] In addition, my view of the self as a *process* avoids worries about a relational self being too fixed by particularities. Here is Christman (2004) expressing such a worry:

> Just as conceiving of persons as denuded of social relations denies the importance of such relations to the self-understandings of many of us at various times in our lives, to define persons as necessarily related in particular ways similarly denies the reality of change over time, variability in self-conception, and multiplicities of identity characteristic of modern populations.
>
> (145)

Rather, as a relational process, the cumulative network model (CNM) aims to capture the changeableness, variability, and multiplicity of a self, while also accounting for its persistence as a and as that self.

My view is also "naturalistic." This might raise the question, whether it is reductivist or non-reductivist. I am not proposing that a self is an *entity* separate from its elements and relations (a non-reductivist view). But, I am also not proposing a crude reductivist view by which the self reduces to "lower level" constituents, such the occurrence of impersonal events and relations, or a conventional selection of spatio-temporal regions, or of some present arrangement of psychophysical elements. Rather, a self is a structured unity as a macro-level "thing." A self is like a nation, but a self, like a nation, is an interrelated network of its constituents and as such has a distinct integrity in virtue of those relations. As such it has its own distinctive way of functioning. A self is a network, and networks have their own distinctive features and principles qua networks and thus cannot be reduced to being a mere sum of their parts (Barabási, 2002). For the network self, molecular, psychophysical, cellular, neurophysiological events and components are indispensable—for example, blood flow in areas of the brain and the firing of neurons are constituents of a functioning self—but so are "macro-level," biological, social, semantic, linguistic, and interpersonal ones. "Macro-level" traits are really the traits of that macro-level thing, even if a causal explanation for them could be derived, at least in principle, from "micro-level" or atomic events and particles.[7] This is nothing special about persons or socially constituted complexes. The same is true of purely physical things. The traits of water qua water (e.g., its density, viscosity, that it freezes at 32 degrees Farenheit/0 degrees Celsius, and so on) are the traits of water as the molecular network that it is, not the traits of the constituents of water—hydrogen and oxygen—even though water is constituted by their appropriate combination. Hydrogen, for example, doesn't freeze at 32 degrees F. Likewise, when my body freezes, the atoms in my body do not freeze, nor do electrons in atoms freeze. The freezing point of water depends on intermolecular forces of the water molecule. If one wants to understand water, *its* characteristic features, behavior and functions, one has to consider the complex water, and not only its "lower level" components, oxygen and hydrogen, even if it is also true that it wouldn't be water without those atomic components.

Similarly with selves. Molecular biology and neuroscience may tell us a great deal about how selves work, but we still want to understand selves qua selves, that is, qua macro-level complexes, and to conceptualize their characteristic features and functions. For instance, suppose a self that is an alienated cousin. The psychological and social relations of alienation constitute the self differently from the way in which neurochemical features of the self do, but all these aspects are intertwined to constitute the self qua alienated. The concept of relational constitution as I develop it is meant to recognize the reality of these different aspects of the self. I am taking as the "object" of analysis selves as we ordinarily understand them to be: human beings with a range of distinctive capacities (biological, cognitive, semantic, linguistic, normative, active, artistic, and so on), social relations and locations, and a temporal trajectory. The "object," the self is a relational process that I conceptualize as a cumulative network of traits.

The self "as it really generally is" is an adaptation of a phrase from Gendler (2002):

> Recent philosophical discussion of the nature and value of personal identity, however, have tended to treat these "facts of life" as *provincial* truths—as facts about persons-as-they-happen-to-be, not facts about persons-as-they-really-generally-are.
>
> (34–35)

The "facts of life" that Gendler refers to are that "persons are produced by well-known sequences of biological and social processes" (34), not the thought experimental processes of fission, fusion, and teletransportation that dominate much discussion in the personal identity literature. Extending this thought, I suggest that the "facts of life" include not only organismic and biological constitution, but that a self is a relational network and process, a particular history, character, biological, social, semantic (that is, meaning-laden) trajectory, a particular personality with habituated (but changeable) ways of acting, communicating, and judging.[8]

Schechtman, too, is concerned with how selves (persons, she would say) actually are, and she and I come to similar views about what the concept of self (or person) should include. According to Schechtman, a person is constituted by a person life, "a unified locus of the sorts of practical concerns and interactions that typify the lives of those who generate and maintain the social/cultural infrastructure within which these lives take place" (Schechtman, 2014, 118).[9] On Schechtman's view to be a person is dependent on being recognized as such, and therefore appears to be dependent on social, narrative construction by others. This construction is not arbitrary, but reflects how things actually are. While I agree that social relations are constitutive of others, I argue that social relations constitute traits of a self; they are not just ways in which others treat or construct a self. I also allow for the possibility that even socially isolated selves can under some circumstances count as selves (see discussion in Chapter 3, Section 4.2.1). I also explicitly conceptualize the self as a process, which Schechtman does not. My account of identity, or what I call numerical unity, is different from Schechtman's. I do, though, agree with Schechtman's critique of Baker's view on constitution and identity for presupposing a strong *de re* essentialism and for assuming that there is a single defining feature of persistence conditions for distinct substances (Schechtman, 2014, Chapter 7). In contrast, Schechtman argues that a locus or cluster of properties can be sufficient for distinguishing persons, a position with which I agree.

Philosophically, one might be tempted to classify my cumulative network model (CNM) as a kind of bundle theory. However, at least some of the traits constitutive of a self may involve relations to particulars and therefore, are not necessarily universals or properties in the usual sense of that term (even though there may be universal, that is, common traits of selves, such as species, bodily, psychological and developmental structure and capacities). Second, "bundle" tends to suggest a collection without necessarily implying structure or constitutive relations among members of a bundle. In contrast, I will argue that the self qua network of traits has a unifying structure or integrity. On the practical side, the self also has an ability to engage in reflexive activity that contributes to that integrity, to the direction of the self and to its awareness of itself as a self. This is a system theory of self rather than a bundle theory. Thus, the terms "complex" or "network" should not be equated with "bundle."

My approach might be associated with Wittgenstein's notion of family resemblance.[10] However, in my case the idea of a network self arose from my reading of pragmatist philosophers and in particular, Buchler. More importantly and in contrast to the Wittgensteinian notion, the notion of a network is not a mere convention. It is not just a matter of use that we decide to group together some set of traits and designate an entity of some kind. Even if there are conventional (e.g., social) elements the claim is that the self qua network, is constituted by interrelated traits that form a whole independently of our naming and classificatory practices.

## 2. The Relational Self: The Cumulative Network Model (CNM)

In the remainder of this chapter, I will delineate the model of the self as a cumulative network (a relational process). The goal here is less to argue for the model than it is to build it, to march it out. In a sense, the argument for the model will be the work that it does as explored in subsequent chapters.

On the relational model that I am proposing, the self is a network of traits and relations. What do I mean by that? Consider the following hypothetical example: Lindsey is mother, novelist, English speaker, Irish-Catholic, feminist, professor of philosophy, automobile driver, psycho-biological organism, introverted, prone to a cheerful disposition, fearful of heights, brown-haired, myopic, left-handed, and so on. (This is not an exhaustive set, just a selection of some traits in order to convey the general idea.) These traits are related to one another to form the network of traits that is Lindsey. The self as a whole, *Lindsey*, is an inclusive network, a plurality of locations related to one another such as to constitute *a* whole self. The overall character of a self is constituted by the unique interrelatedness of its particular relational traits (psycho-biological, social, political, cultural, linguistic, physical, and so on). See Figures 2.1.

Another way of representing the idea is to use a web structure, modeled after one way of representing ecological networks (Figure 2.2).

Representing the idea in yet another way, by using a matrix to represent the interrelatedness of traits, we can see that they may form clusters of traits within the overall network. In the matrix, Figure 2.3, I have omitted some of the traits that were included in Figure 2.2 in order for

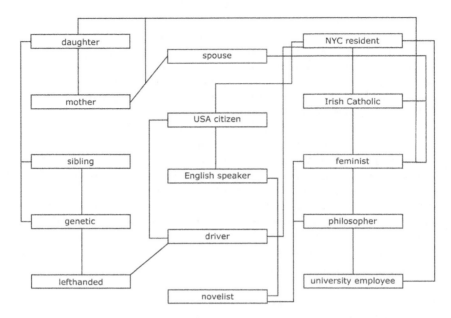

*Figure 2.1* A partial, simplified representation of Lindsey as a network of
traits, at some non-specified time as an adult and without reference
to particular contexts. This figure is suggesting that as constituting
Lindsey, the trait being an English speaker is relevant to the trait being
a novelist, being a novelist is relevant to being a feminist and to being
a philosopher, being a resident of New York City is relevant to being a
driver, being a spouse, a daughter, a mother, a philosopher are relevant
to being a feminist. (These are not necessary relations; it might be that
for someone else being a philosopher and being a feminist are only
weakly relevant, or not relevant at all to one another.) This figure also
does not represent Lindsey as a process; here, the idea is to represent
only the idea that the self is a network of multiple, interrelated traits.

the matrix to be readable. The simplification doesn't matter for the purpose of representing the idea of clustering of traits.

A graphic and even further simplified representation of the clustering
idea might be represented by gathering the clustered traits into "hubs"
(Figure 2.4). For example, the body itself is a network of traits (genetic,
molecular, cellular, organismic, and so on), a "hub" or "sub-network" of
the more comprehensive network that is the self.[11]

However, and as the next figure, Figure 2.5, is meant to illustrate, we
shouldn't think of clusters or sub-networks as isolated, or self-enclosed
"hubs." Any trait may be related to any other trait, such that a particular
"bodily trait" and a particular "social" trait are relevant to one another,
and so on. Traits may be related in a variety of ways, crossing over these

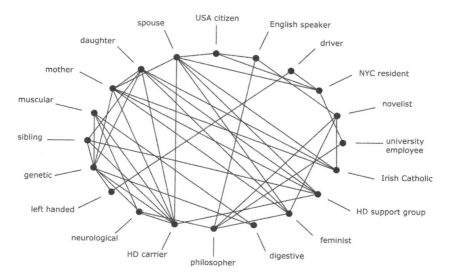

*Figure 2.2* Network as a Web. Each node is a trait and the lines between the nodes represent traits that are related to one another.

general categorizations. Thus, the trait "Huntington's Disease Carrier"—which we might think of as a primarily "biological" trait constituted by genetic, molecular, and biochemical relations—is also related to family and social traits. If the carrier status is known, psychological relations and social relations to other carriers and familial and medical communities are related to the genetic traits and to how together they are constituents of the self qua Huntington's Disease Carrier. Or, a "social" trait may be related to familial traits. In addition, some traits may be more dominant or organizing than others; for instance, in the examples illustrated, being a feminist may be strongly relevant to the overall character of that self whereas being an aunt may be weakly relevant. Relations between traits and sub-networks of traits are more complex than can be represented in such simple figures.

Every trait is itself relational: being a language speaker entails neuro-physiological relations and brain structures, as well as relations to other speakers, to vocal possibilities, to semantic and grammatical structures, and so on; being a (biological) son or daughter entails genetic relations and kinship relations in a network of such relations; and so on.[12] Some of its traits and relations just happen to a self, e.g., being the daughter of someone, being a national of a particular country by virtue of birth, the speaker of a particular language, being left-handed, or being the carrier of a genetic disease; others may be chosen or "self-determined," e.g., redefining one's status or character as a daughter, being the spouse of

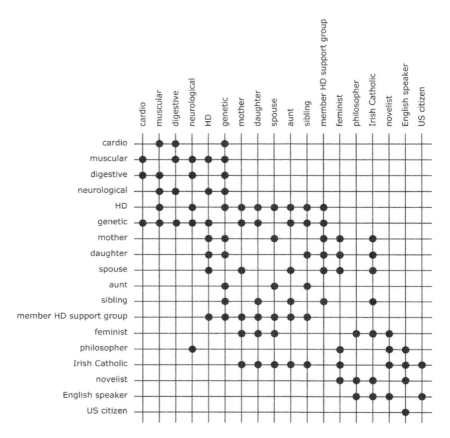

*Figure 2.3* A grid showing traits forming clusters of relations within the overall network.

someone, becoming nationalized in a country other than the land of one's birth, learning a new language, being tested as a genetic carrier of a disease, being a feminist, and so on.

Each network self is individuated and identifiable as distinct from other network selves in virtue of it being a unique configuration of interdependent relations. What makes for the network being *that* network is that there is commensurateness or mediatability of traits. In the comprehensive network that is the self not every trait is related to every other; but every trait is related to some other. Between traits there are routes of access to other traits (mediatability of traits), and every trait is related not just to other traits, but to the whole. The unique combination and interrelation of traits constitute the person's overall integrity or the overall characteristic determinateness of the person.

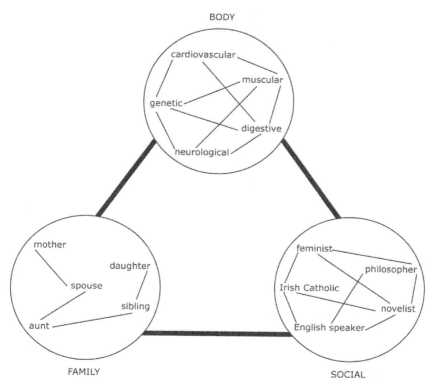

*Figure 2.4* An illustration of the structural organization of a self whereby traits are clustered as different "hubs" or sub-networks of traits.

I do not mean "integrity" in a moral or value sense, as in the phrase "a person of integrity." While "integrity" has value or moral associations, it also connotes the idea of definiteness or determinate nature.[13] Of course, "integrity" may include psychological and moral character. A person's integrity is both a unity and a plurality; it is the unity that is the unique interrelation of the plurality of her traits. Traits identify a self in so far as they are continuous with the unique interrelation of traits that is that self.

That traits are related to one another, does not mean that they are necessarily harmoniously related, or "integrated" in a psychologically or narratively coherent way. It just means that they are relevant to, conditions of one another and of the comprehensive configuration that is the self. If a self is psychologically "conflicted," or "disintegrated" or "dissociated" in ways characteristic of some types of mental illness, it is still that self (that network) experiencing conflict and constituted as conflicted. Its traits are still relevant to one another qua being in conflict or tension, or being

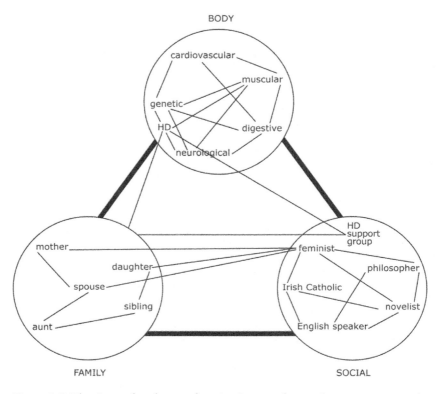

*Figure 2.5* The interrelatedness of traits is complex and crosses over sub-
networks. Being a Huntington Disease Carrier (HD) is related not
only to other bodily traits, but to familial traits and to a social trait,
such as being a member of a Huntington Disease support group (HD
support group).

disintegrated rather than harmonious. Imagine a dissonant musical composition as analogous to the idea of a conflicted or disintegrated self. The
notes or chords that are disharmonious are still related to one another in
such a way as to produce the characteristic determinateness of the overall
piece. Similarly, the unity I am talking about is a feature of any self being *a*
self (that network), not the narrative unity that might be thought to be necessary for agency and self-reflection, and that is a high level, sophisticated
achievement of a self.[14] There might be conditions of such extreme psychological and social disintegration that the network of traits is too fragmented for the realization of communicative and judicative capacities that
we normally think of as distinctive of fully functioning selves. But, whatever its psychic distress, the self is still constituted as a psycho-biological,
social, temporal network, even though a psychically fragmented self may
be unable to function in many of the normally valued ways.

A self is also temporally constituted. Lindsey was not always a mother or a novelist, or a professor of philosophy or a licensed driver; nor was she always of the organismic size and functionality that she is now. When she was five years old she was a kindergartener, a budding English speaker, 42 inches tall, had latent reproductive potential and so on. But, before discussing the temporal nature of the self as a process, the *cumulative* part of the cumulative network self, I want to flesh out more what relatedness means, and in particular the distinction between relations that are constitutive (or really determinative) versus those that are simply incidental (or trivially determinative). While waiting for a subway train one is standing on a platform and is therefore related, in virtue of the standing-on relation, to the platform. Yet, that relation, standing on the platform, seems to be pretty trivial and not constitutive of who or what the self is.

## 3. Network Relationality

### 3.1. Some Standard Distinctions

Among philosophers, the distinction between constitutive and incidental traits has often been made in terms of essential or necessary and accidental or contingent properties or qualities. One might say that her genetic constitution is necessary (essential) to Lindsey being the self that she is, whereas she could have been born somewhere else and spoken a different native language (accidental). However, on CNM, being a native English speaker is constitutive of Lindsey being the self that she, in fact, is. Even if it is "accidental," being a native English speaker is a trait that shapes what a self actually is and contributes to the integrity of the self. For example, Lindsey's signature authorial style as a novelist may be shaped by her linguistic affinities and capabilities as native English speaker. If both essential and accidental traits are really constitutive, then an essential/accidental distinction would not make the one I am looking for.

Another way of framing the distinction is in terms of intrinsic and extrinsic properties, or between pure and impure properties. An intrinsic property is "a property that a thing has (or lacks) regardless of what may be going on outside of itself" (Yablo, 1999, 479). "If an object has a property intrinsically, then it has it independently of the way the rest of the world is. The rest of the world could disappear, and the object might still have that property" (Weatherson, 2008). The intrinsic/extrinsic distinction as defined would not exclude relational properties (for example, that my one foot is bigger than my other is relational but not dependent on anything outside of my bodily constitution). But, it is not a very helpful distinction for CNM according to which traits include relations to particular things "outside" of the self that would, according to this distinction, be classified as extrinsic. For example, being an English speaker and a philosopher are constitutive traits of Lindsey, even though on the intrinsic/extrinsic distinction, both would be classified as extrinsic (dependent on what goes on outside her, such as, the existence of the language English, the culture she was born into and educated in, how philosophy as a discipline is defined, and so on).

A distinction between pure and impure properties also does not make the distinction I am looking for. One way of thinking about "pure" properties is to think of them as differentiating individuals only by means of abstract, structural arrangements of their features and relations.

> I have some of my properties purely in virtue of the way I am. (My mass is an example.) I have other properties in virtue of the way I interact with the world. (My weight is an example.) The former are the intrinsic properties, the latter are the extrinsic properties.
>
> (Weatherson, 2008)

Another way of thinking about the pure/impure distinction is to think of properties as abstract universals that therefore, as such, can't contain or be related to concrete particulars. A pure property doesn't involve relation to any other *particular* (such as parents, other people, or things in the world). Thus, "being a mother of someone" and "being a speaker of some language" would be pure properties, while "being the mother *of Lindsey*" and "being a speaker *of English*" would be impure properties. Or, consider the fictional character Clark Kent/Superman. "Being vulnerable to some element" is a structural feature of Clark Kent/Superman (setting aside issues about the being of dispositions) and in that sense is a pure property, whereas "being vulnerable to the element *kryptonite*," or "being the adopted son *of the Kents of Kansas*" would be an impure property. "Impure" properties contain constants (kryptonite) or named particulars, such as particular persons (Lindsey, the Kents), and therefore, are not pure properties.[15]

I am not disagreeing with the distinction between pure and impure properties. It's just that it doesn't make the one that I'm looking for between a constitutive and a trivial relation. On CNM weight may be really constitutive of a self, that is, it may be a distinguishing and determinative feature of a self in a variety of contexts, e.g., medical and social. Being the parent or the child of a particular person or persons may be really constitutive of a self.

### 3.2. Relation: Strong and Weak Relevance

I turn to a distinction made by Buchler between strongly relevant and weakly relevant traits (1990, 104–128). This distinction does not map directly onto an essential/accidental, intrinsic/extrinsic, or pure/impure distinction. Nor does "trait"—whether strongly relevant or weakly relevant—map directly on to "property." One might think of traits as ways complexes are rather than as properties that things (individuals) have.[16]

Minimally, a relation is a condition or determinant of scope or reach of the relata, or more strongly a condition or determinant of the integrity of one or both (or more) of the relata (Buchler, 1990, 104). When two or more complexes are related, the character of the relation is a trait of each of the relata (Buchler, 1990, 111). A strongly relevant trait is one that conditions (reinforces, sustains, modifies) the integrity or overall character of the being, while a weakly relevant trait conditions only the scope (the "reach" of the complex). A relation may also be strongly relevant to one relata and weakly relevant to the other, and thus in one respect constitute a strongly relevant trait, and in another a weakly relevant trait. There are many different kinds of relations, physical, social, legal, normative, mereological, causal, etc., and this definition of relation does not distinguish between them. It is meant as a wide definition of relation in general, any kind of relation.

To illustrate the distinction between strong and weak relevance consider another example, of something other than a self. Suppose that the population of New York City, several million people, were 100 people more or less than it currently is. Unless among those 100 individuals is someone who for reasons other than mere addition to the population makes a significant contribution to the overall character of New York City, such a change in population is, in all probability, weakly relevant to the overall integrity of New York City. The loss or addition of 100 people contributes to a trait (the population of New York City) that is strongly relevant to New York City, but this alteration in population per se would not alter the integrity of New York City. *Population* is strongly relevant, but this *difference* in population would be weakly relevant, to New York City. That's not to say that in some respect the difference of 100 people might be strongly relevant to New York City, say, in a census count which aims to determine the size of cities and rank them according to their population size. In such a case, that difference could be strongly relevant to New York City in a specific context, even if not with respect to its integrity overall. That's also not to say that repeatedly many reductions or additions in population couldn't alter the overall integrity of New York City, but there may not be a precise algorithm for assessing that or a precise boundary between an alteration in integrity and an alteration in scope (Buchler, 1990, 106).

A trait is the character of some relation[s], geographical, political, legal, cultural, architectural, and so on qua constitutive of New York City. As such some of those traits are strongly relevant to one another and to the overall whole that is New York City, while some are weakly relevant. Population and geographical structure[17] may be strongly relevant to one another in constituting the population density of New York City, which may be a strongly relevant trait of New York City.

The nature of relevance might be different for different relata. For instance, being a resident of New York City might be a strongly relevant trait of an individual self, S, and moving away from New York City might alter the overall integrity of that individual, S, while S being a resident of New York City is weakly relevant to New York City. Hence, the "same" fact, that S is a resident of New York City, is a relation between and thus a trait of two complexes (New York City and S), and in respect to one it may be weakly and in the other strongly relevant. Relation is reciprocal, but not necessarily symmetrical.

Now a self is not the same kind of thing as a city—it is not a geographical, political, economic, cultural, architectural complex but a psychological, biological, social kind of complex. The purpose of the analogy is only to introduce the idea of strongly and weakly relevant traits as constitutive of something as a network. A self is an interrelated network of traits, some of which are strongly relevant, some of which are weakly relevant to one another and to the whole that is the self. I will continue with the New York City analogy for another step, introduce the analogy to a property cluster in philosophy of biology, and then return to a discussion of the self.

### 3.2.1  Integrity

The overall character—the integrity—of New York City is the unique interrelatedness of its strongly relevant traits. The extent to which it can lose or modify one or more strongly relevant traits and remain New York City depends on the traits. New York City might tolerate a considerable alteration in its population size such that its integrity evolves, but is still the integrity of New York City. But, if the five boroughs of New York City were to disaggregate into five distinct cities, New York City would be a different city with a different integrity. The persistence of sub-complexes or parts (the boroughs) does not entail the persistence of a whole. Yet, it may be difficult to be precise; New York City could persist even with the loss of some neighborhoods (sub-complexes), and maybe even the loss of a borough. On the other hand, if New York City had consisted only of what is known as Manhattan Island, it would be different city with a different overall character, that is, a different network of traits in population size, landmass, legal, economic, political and cultural traits, tax base, and history.

The integrity is an evolving unique structure or configuration of interrelated traits or conditions that are commensurable with one another and that form a whole. In the case of the self, each self is an evolving and unique configuration of interrelated traits, psychological, biological, physical, social, cultural. The ways in which such traits are interrelated may be quite similar—biologically, for example, most human organisms have similar bodily configurations. But, even so the particularities of each are unique and hence the integrity is unique and characteristic of the self.

However, a self changes and develops, and whether and to what extent particular features have to be present is not precisely determinate. Rather there may be a cluster of traits constituting a self, some commensurable subset of which has to persist from one phase to the next in order for the integrity, and hence the self, to persist. But, the integrity may tolerate a wide range of changes and types of loss or deprivation and addition. A self may require a body, such that a brain in a vat or the preservation of information alone in a digital format is not sufficient for being a self. But, it is difficult to specify precisely exactly the extent to which a self may tolerate bodily enhancement, diminishment, alteration or replacement, or to prescribe in general what is necessary or sufficient in any particular case. This may entail the discomfiting conclusion that there are borderline cases when we can't be certain whether the integrity has been preserved.[18]

It might be argued that selves are "natural kinds" or at least are rooted in natural, i.e., biological, facts. But, biological kinds themselves have been conceptualized philosophically as "clusters." Cluster kind realism has been proposed for biological species by Boyd (1991, 1999), Millikan (1999), and Slater (2015). Boyd proposes that a biological natural kind be defined in terms of a homeostatic property cluster (HPC). While HPC is introduced initially to define a natural kind (or species), the idea can be extended to individuals (Boyd, 1999). Natural kind members share contingently clustered family of properties that may alter over time and none of which is necessary for kind membership. These are objective similarity, causal, spatio-temporal relations that are not merely a matter of convention.[19] Similarly, an individual is a contingent network of properties that may alter over time, no one of which may be necessary, but some subset of which may be sufficient, for persistence of the individual or for its inclusion in the kind.[20] Preserving the clustering concept, but loosening the causal requirements of HPC, Slater (2015) has proposed SPC, or stable property cluster view. SPC allows for domain and context-relativity and can meet some of the problems that HPC's causal requirements might pose for defining membership in a kind. But, SPC affirms the basic cluster idea, namely, that not all properties have to be present for kind membership to obtain. While I am neutral on HPC and SPC, I find the idea of a cluster-concept germane to the view I am developing. If the idea of a cluster concept makes sense for understanding biological individuals, then the notion of a self as a biological *and* social and psychological network could be seen as a continuation of that concept (as long as cluster and properties are not understood in static terms).

### 3.2.2 Relation: Constituting a Network Self

I am not going to characterize particular kinds of relations and how they constitute a self. Rather, I am interested only in advancing the idea (1) that self be conceptualized as a network of traits, where traits are understood as constituents (nodes) that are the expression of relations (to other traits or to "things" that are not themselves traits of the network), and (2) that relation be understood in terms of relevance. Thus, Lindsey is constituted as "mother" in virtue of relations to her spouse and to her daughter. Her spouse and daughter are relevant to her qua mother. Lindsey's spouse and daughter are not themselves traits of her network, but each one's relation to her and perhaps their relation to one another are (just as those relations are relevant to, traits of their networks, albeit in different respects).

Consider now a particular individual, Mozart. Being a musical composer was a strongly relevant trait of Mozart. A strongly relevant trait is one that conditions (reinforces, sustains, modifies) the overall character (integrity) of the network, the self. Being a musical composer is itself a complex trait, the expression of genetic and neurological relations ("native ability") as well as of training, and cultural exposure and opportunity. The determinate nature, the integrity of Mozart—his definiteness and identifiability as the self that he was—is inextricably bound up with (is constituted by) his being a musical composer, setting aside, for the moment, that as an infant he was not a composer. Wolfgang Amadeus Mozart was also constituted by other traits—for example, son of Leopold and Anna Maria Mozart, sibling of Maria Anna (Nannerl) Mozart, German speaker, collaborator of Lorenzo Da Ponte, born in Salzburg, with genetic composition, bodily structure and functionality, psychosocial dispositions and habits, and so on. Some of the relations expressed in these traits were strongly relevant, some weakly relevant to his being the self that he was. His relationship to his father appears to have been strongly relevant to the development of his musical talent as both a performer and a composer through his teenage years and until he left Salzburg for Vienna, where he married Constanze. His relationship with his sister was strongly relevant in his early musical performance career, but became only weakly relevant, if relevant at all, in his later career as musical composer and musician. His relationship with Lorenzo Da Ponte was strongly relevant to at least one aspect of his being a musical composer, viz., with respect to being a composer of opera. See Figure 2.6. A biographer with more intimate knowledge of Mozart could provide a much more detailed and accurate account of Mozart. Here I am just illustrating the idea that some traits are strongly relevant to the overall character of a self, whereas some are only weakly relevant. Some trait may be so dominant that it is an organizing trait of all or most of a self's other traits, and is the major identifying feature of a self, such as Mozart being a musician and musical composer.

Mozart *is* the unique intersection, the network of all these traits, biological, familial, cultural, social, psychological. There is no one subset of traits that by itself is constitutive of Mozart. Even if it is necessary that a self, that Mozart, be a living organized human body, by itself that is not sufficient to constitute a self. A self is understood as typically having a distinctive range of functional capacities, psychological and

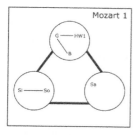

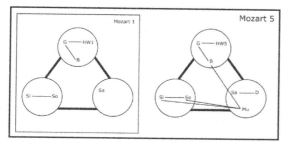

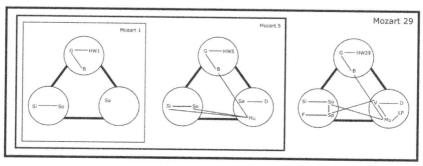

*Figure 2.6* Mozart's sibling relation (Si) as different at different temporal cross-sections of Mozart.

Abbreviations: B = brain; D = German speaker; G = genetic traits; HW = height/weight (at a time); LP = collaborator of Lorenzo da Ponte; Mu = musician; Sa = Salzburg resident; Si = sibling; So = son; Sp = spouse; V = Vienna resident

This figure anticipates the subsequent discussion of a self being a cumulative process such that at a temporal cross-section, a self includes its own past as a trait (represented by the nested boxes).

developmental capacities, communicative, agential, intentional, semantic, judicative capacities, although these admit of considerable variation in individual expression and achievement.

I have been arguing that rather than thinking in terms of a particular set of necessary and sufficient conditions, the integrity of a self—like with the previous example of New York City and recalling the cluster concept argument—should be thought of in terms of a network of interrelated conditions or traits. Some subset may be sufficient for preservation of a self, for preservation of the integrity of the network and it is contingent exactly what would be sufficient in any particular case. Normally, that is for selves as they really, generally are, living bodily continuation is a necessary (although not necessarily sufficient) condition of being and persisting as a self. On CNM what matters is that the *network* continues and the network is more than a body.

How much or what kind of alteration could a self undergo and still be a self? Does a self *have* to be socially related? Normally, yes. But, a self may lose all its social relations and still be a self, if there are other constituents of the self, e.g., capacities to speak and communicate, to process information, capacities of motor coordination (all of which are both biologically and socially constituted), and memory and expressive capacities that sustain the integrity of the self. A network can lose traits, or even "hubs" (a strongly relevant cluster of traits) and still persist provided there are sufficient other hubs and traits to sustain the network, even if in a diminished state.

For example, a person stranded on a remote, otherwise deserted island, may have been severed from her constitutive social relations (a cluster or "hub"), but may retain memory and capacities (e.g., linguistic and symbolic expression), such that she is still a self, albeit diminished.[21] One might characterize this as disablement (something like when someone loses their limbs) or even as the beginning of a process of dying, whereby an irreversible loss of social relations might be social death, preceding biological death. It could also go the other way. A self could lose memory, consciousness, and many if not most capacities (for example, a seriously diminished Alzheimer's patient), but be sustained as a (diminished) self by the ongoing social relations that constitute it. At some point we might characterize such a self as undergoing a process of dying.

Could a human organism be a self if it *never* had social relations with other selves? Practically, that is difficult to imagine since a human infant cannot survive without extensive care for at least the first few years of life. Almost all accounts of feral children are hoaxes or cases of mental illness or of abuse and in some cases, of escape from human abuse to living in the wild after some initial period of human contact and socialization (however dysfunctional). If social relations and other distinctively human capacities, relations, and modes of functioning are constitutive of a self, then genuine feral cases may not be selves at all, even though they are genetically human.[22] Or, they may be severely damaged or diminished selves. Perhaps, in some cases, they might be able to become selves if social relations could be established and other capacities develop. What feral cases may demonstrate is that the border between being a self and not being a self is vague and not precisely determinable.

A *particular* self is located in particular social relations and roles, causal and dependence relations, and has a particular origin and social, genetic, biological, and personal past. The integrity of a particular self, of a network of traits *may* be preserved in the face of a wide range of changes (in biological characteristics, in capabilities and dispositions, in social, legal, cultural, political roles) and types of loss and deprivation (amnesia, dementia, replacement of, loss of or severe alteration in physical parts or social roles, trauma, physical disability). Selves change in multiple ways; they grow, develop, age, learn, have psychological conversions, and so on. Many of these are normal and unremarkable aspects of a process self. Some discussions of whether someone is still a, or that particular, self or a person often focus on unfortunate developments in psychological features such as cognitive disability or loss of cognitive and memory functions, for example, with dementia or amnesia. On CNM, comprehensive amnesia and Alzheimer's disease happen to, are constituents of a self. They are damage to bodily and psychological (sub-) networks (trait clusters) of the self. That damage may have profound effects on other, e.g., social, intentional, communicative, (sub-) networks of the self. With cognitive damage, there may be shedding, so to speak, of many constituting social roles, as in the case of Clive Wearing, who suffers severe anterograde and retrograde amnesia,[23] or as in an Alzheimer's patient, but other social roles may still persist. Participation in communicative, social, and meaning relations, may still be possible and ongoing, however rudimentarily, as with selves cognitively disabled from birth. Or, as in Alzheimer's, there may be a threshold after which the process is better understood as one of dying.

The idea of a self as consisting of a network of interrelated conditions or traits, *some* subset of which may be sufficient for preserving the integrity of the network of traits, allows for the possibility that a self may still be preserved in the face of a wide range of types of change, addition, loss, and deprivation. It is *that* self that is developing and growing or dying or that has become damaged or disabled. This does entail that there may be borderline cases when we can't be certain that it is (or isn't) a or that particular self and that at the margins, membership in the category may be vague.[24]

## 3.3. Contingency

For any particular self what is strongly relevant to it being the self that it is largely a contingent matter. There may be necessities, of course. If one is the first-born offspring of one's genetic parents, then one is necessarily older than a subsequent born offspring of the same genetic parents. Or, if one has a certain genetic structure, then one will necessarily have brown eyes. Or, if one is six feet tall, then one is necessarily taller than someone who is five feet five inches tall. Or, if one is a mammal, one necessarily breathes oxygen. Contingency means that traits may become or cease to be relevant and traits that are strongly relevant to the self at a time, may become weakly relevant to the self at a subsequent time and to the overall integrity of the self.

Contingency is most naturally explored by thinking counterfactually about alternative scenarios.[25] Returning to Mozart, at five perhaps his sibling relation to his sister was strongly relevant to Mozart being the self that he was at five. However, at 27, his sibling relation to his sister was weakly relevant to Mozart qua musical composer. Suppose he had not had a sister and had not performed with her during his early years. In so far as other traits would have obtained—his genetic disposition and talent, his father's training, and so on—enough conditions would (probably) have obtained that he would still have been a musical composer, he would still have been very much the self that he in fact was. An aspect of his process would have been different, but his overall integrity would not have been markedly different.

But, now suppose Mozart's father had died when Mozart was two years old, his family ended up destitute and in a poor house where Mozart had no access to musical instruments and training, and where he had to beg just to avoid starving to death. The self, the *network* of traits that was Mozart, might not have existed. There would have been a biological organism with the same genetic lineage and same name, but it would have been a different self, a different network of traits. Even its physical characteristics, due to the effects of poverty, environmental and possibly epigenetic mechanisms, could have been different and that self would probably not have been a musical composer at all. If the self is, as I have been arguing, a network of traits, and if the network of traits were sufficiently different such that it had a different integrity, then such a network named Mozart would be a different self from the self (the network) who actually was Mozart.

Returning to the earlier example of Lindsey. Suppose that instead of being one of five siblings, Lindsey had been an only child. Would she have been the same self? The answer, on CNM, would have to be, "It depends." If sibling relations were strongly relevant to Lindsey's overall integrity, then the absence of siblings might have resulted in a different integrity. Perhaps she would have had a different personality, or different dispositions and habits of interaction with others. If a self is a network of traits and relations constituted not only by its organismic features, but by a much fuller range of particular relations (social, political, psychological, semantic, etc.), then depending on the differences, whether they are strongly or weakly relevant and how they are interrelated with other traits and the whole, the self might have been a different self, a different network of relations with a different integrity. If her sibling relations were weakly relevant to her being the self that she is, then the integrity of her network might not have been significantly altered. It's conceivable that as single offspring she still would have become a philosopher. In principle, it is not ruled out, for there is no contradiction between not being a sister and being a philosopher. But, conceivability alone isn't determinative of what is in fact relevant. Whether the kinship relations are strongly relevant to—that is, a condition for (a determinant of)—that talent and career path being realized is not a logical or principled but a contingent matter. Perhaps Lindsey would have had the same talents, but with no other children in the family, she might have had different nurturing experiences, different educational experiences and opportunities, and thus possibly have realized a different talent or pursued a different career path. Maybe philosopher would have been a strong contender, but maybe other relational conditions would have worked in favor of another direction. While for some self, talent may be strongly determined (genetically or however) regardless of many social relations and conditions, for another self it may not be. We explored previously the example of Mozart where the actualization of his musical talent would (probably) have obtained absent a sibling relation. Sibling relations don't have to be strongly relevant to the realization of a talent, but in a given case, they might be.

Imagine another scenario. Suppose the biological organism (BO), a sub-network of Lindsey, had been one of five genetic offspring of the same parents, but each of the five was raised as a single child by adoptive parents. BO would have been a constituent of a different network of social and legal kinship relations, upbringing and educational relations, nutritional and medical care relations, and so on. Hence, the interrelated network of relations that constitute that self would have been different from the network, the self, Lindsey, that has actually obtained; let's call this counterfactual self Linda. Perhaps Linda with BO as a constituent would still have been very similar in some ways to Lindsey, for instance, by becoming a philosopher and a novelist, but perhaps not. It depends on what is strongly relevant to what, and that is contingent. The genetic sibling relation still obtains, but might not be strongly relevant. On the other hand, suppose Linda marries and reproduces with someone who, unbeknownst to her, is genetically her brother. Genetic possibilities and actualities obtain in virtue of that sibling relation whether Linda knows it or not, and they are very different from the sibling relations of Lindsey. Alternatively, suppose there were a genetic bank (perhaps like the Icelandic DNA database), where DNA records of all citizens were stored such that anyone could trace their genetic lineage and locate genetic siblings. (In Iceland, the database is used to determine permissible marriage partners based on genetic distance.) In that case, genetic sibling relations might be strongly relevant even if the siblings were not raised together.

The distinction between a strongly relevant and a weakly relevant trait is neither *a priori* nor fixed. Trivial relations could become strongly relevant in some context. In most contexts, being a stander on the subway platform at any particular time is a fleeting, trivial trait. However, there could be a context in which that trait becomes strongly relevant. For instance, suppose that while standing on the subway platform one is seriously maimed by a bomb. In that (unfortunate) case, the normally trivial relation, standing-on-the-subway-platform-at-time-t is strongly relevant; it is a determinant of one's overall integrity (which now includes being maimed).[26]

This approach may seem very counterintuitive. Each of us tends to have the strong intuition about oneself that it still would have been "me," that there is something essential that is me and that would be present in a counterfactual situation. But, when I wonder counterfactually, when I hypothesize or imagine what "I" would have been like, or what my life would have been like had I had different parents or sibling relations, had I missed the train and been standing on the platform when the bomb went off, or any other counterfactual, I carry over into that hypothetical case myself as I am. In imagining the alternative scenario, I cannot help but do so from my already formed first-person perspective. I imaginatively project myself as I already am into another, imagined, scenario. But, the self that I am, including my first-person perspective, is constituted by the relations and locations that I do have, and which constitute the overall integrity of who I am. In the imagined alternative life, if the strongly relevant traits are different, then the overall integrity and first-person perspective would be different from what they actually are, and it is ambiguous what is meant by saying that it still would have been "me."

At any time, the perspective from which a self views itself is a cumulative expression of what the self is up to that time. When I hypothesize a different self-scenario, I am imagining a different process self. If the hypothesized self is sufficiently different in strongly relevant traits, then there would have been a different self than who I am with a differently constituted first-person perspective. For CNM, if the process that is the self were to have taken a different path or course such that the network of relations constitutive of the self were different, then the resultant network would be a different self.

## 4. Relational Self in Process: A Cumulative Whole

I have suggested that the relational self is a network of traits. The network of interrelated traits is distinct from other networks in virtue of how the traits, the locations, are uniquely related to one another to form a self. But, the self is different at different times. Lindsey-at-5-years-old is a kindergartner and is 42 inches tall, Lindsey-at-48 is a philosophy professor and 68 inches tall. Lindsey-at-5 is not qualitatively the same as Lindsey-at-48. But, these stages are not distinct selves; rather they are stages *of* one self, and that self is a process.[27] At any time, the network as it is at that time is the way the process self is at that time. The configuration of the network at a time is the cumulative upshot and leading edge of the process. The self is a network and a process that is spread out in space and time.

## 4.1. Four-Dimensionalism

Our ordinary view of objects, including selves, is to think of them as three-dimensional things—substances, entities, organisms—that move through time. Philosophically, development, difference, and change are then conceptualized in terms of some thing having different properties at different times or as having time-indexed properties. An object—a table, a tree, a self—endures through time as that one thing with its different properties.

In contrast to three-dimensionalism, the philosophical approach known as four-dimensionalism says that objects are perduring spatio-temporal regions. For example, Mozart is a space-time region (physical stuff arranged in a particular way in the 1756–1791 space-time region).

> Perduring things are processes that have stages . . . persons [are] processes, that is, [are] time-ordered sets of person stages. For convenience, . . . suppose every person contains only finitely many person-stages, each of which persists for some very short finite period of time. Every person X is some series of person-stages $\{x_0, x_1, \ldots x_n\}$. Any series of person-stages is one person if and only if it is made continuous in the right way by some unity relation that connects its earlier to its later person-stages. Perhaps the *personal connection relation* is psychological; perhaps it is biological.
>
> (Steinhart, 2002, 306)

However, each of the two main contemporary four-dimensionalist theories, the temporal parts theory and the stage theory, has a static view of the object in so far as each temporal part or stage is a distinct three-dimensional object with just the properties that it has. (Instead of the term "self" the term "person" is used in this literature.) On the temporal parts theory, the person is conceptualized as a succession of spatio-temporal parts. The "five-year old part" and the "thirty-year old part" are parts of a larger space-time worm, the entire filled region constituting the self as a whole. Thus, the person is never wholly present in each of its parts or segments, or alternatively put, the person is never wholly present at a time.

Four-dimensionalist stage theory (Sider, 2001) addresses the odd result just noted, viz., that only a part of a person is present at a time. According to stage theory, at any time there is, wholly present, a person ("person-stage"), a three-dimensional object that is a stage of a four-dimensional person-career. Each person-stage is a counterpart of other person-stages to which it has some appropriate unity relations (e.g., psychological, biological, causal) such that all the person-stages add up to a "person-career." On this version of four-dimensionalism, each stage is a discrete three-dimensional object (a person). Since three-dimensional objects do not endure but only exist at a time, the thirty-year-old person(-stage) is a different (three-dimensional) object from the five-year-old person(-stage), another object. There are many persons (i.e., person-stages), although there is just one person-career.

Whether it is person-parts (of a person as space-time worm) or many persons (person-stages of a person-career), four-dimensionalism presents practical issues for conceptualizing agency, responsibility, and the nature of a sustained first-person perspective. With person-parts, one might ask whether responsibility for an act transfers from one part to another part, particularly if the parts are separated by many other temporal parts. Similarly with stage theory, is a person-stage responsible for an act of another person-stage? Do person-stages perform acts at all? Lewis pointed out that the abrupt existence of person-stages means that person-stages can't *do* what a person can do. Most acts and activities of persons take time and would involve the coordination of many person-stages (or person-parts) (Lewis, 1983a, 76). Lewis distinguished between a stage, which can have a temporal duration, but only very brief, and a segment so perhaps segments would be of sufficient duration to carry out an extended act. But, even so, it seems to me to lead to an oddly stilted, episodic, and static view of agency. One of the philosophical motivations for developing CNM is wanting a theory that more aptly captures the self as something that acts and functions as a whole, rather than *its* agency being jury-rigged out of multiple person-parts, stages, or segments. While it might make sense to talk about the operations of a computational device as time slices or segments, I don't think that accounts very well for human functioning and action. For example, an action can have a time disrupted nature—driving to Vermont from New York occurs in a segment of time, let's say, but it could take place in disrupted segments, say over two days with a stopover in Massachusetts. Is it then two or more acts?[28] How many persons (parts or stages) are involved? Buying a house is an extended act, constituted by many smaller acts, but aptly characterized as a cumulative act with numerous other unrelated things happening in between the constituents of the act of buying a house. I think we want a theory that can conceptualize acts as those of one self, not aggregated acts of many different selves.[29]

In the part and stage analyses of four-dimensionalism temporal parts or person-stages are discrete, isolated units in a temporally ordered series (something like successive film frames in a film, without the film strip, and with the frames causally related in a particular way). Temporal seriality with appropriate unity relations and connections is a necessary condition for a succession to be *a process*. Processes have spatio-temporal locations to be sure. But, I want a thicker way of conceptualizing a process self, and in turn the practical dimensions of selves that are involved with agency and responsibility.[30]

In philosophy of biology there has been interesting work done on developing a thicker notion of process for conceptualizing biological individuals as processes.[31] Some of the features proposed for individuating biological individuals have included reproductive capacity; spatio-temporal restrictedness; cohesiveness; homology and collocation; that, as distinct from aggregates, an individual interacts as a whole with an environment and that the interaction has unitary effects on the constituents of the individual; that an individual produces outcomes due to causal interactions among its parts in contrast to an aggregate where, if it produces outcomes, they are due to aggregated causal contributions of the constituents of the aggregate.[32]

Such biological relations and structures are among those that constitute a process self, although I am suggesting that a process self be understood more comprehensively as social, psychological, cultural as well as biological relations and structures. Among all of these constituents there is an evolving commensurability that individuates the self and constitutes the self's integrity. The integrity of the process self evolves; it continues between stages, and stages themselves are the cumulative upshot of the process as it is up to that time. Alternatively put, between stages the evolving integrity of the network overlaps or maps from one to the other stage.[33]

### 4.2. Overlapping Integrity

To get at the idea of overlap and mapping of integrity, consider another, non-self, process, a chess game, which is clearly not an individual or a self. I use the analogy to make only one point about processes.

A chess game is a structured process, one that has as its constituents configurations of the chessboard, moves that are ordered temporally, governed by rules, where the moves are responsive to one another (defensively or offensively) constituting a series of strategic and tactical maneuvers oriented to a particular goal (checkmate), and where the totality of moves constituting a game has a clear beginning and end. Each move is both discrete and determinate, and responsive to or anticipatory of another move(s). Each move is located in, belongs with, and alters a configuration. Each configuration is the leading edge of the game. The rearrangement of the board produced by a move is the cumulative state of the game at that stage. (A particular configuration might be producible by a different preceding pathway in a different game. I am considering it only as a constituent of a particular game with its history or sequence of chess relations.) Possibilities of movement for a piece or pieces may be foreclosed or opened up by a particular move, such that a move produces change and forward momentum in the game. But, no move rearranges every piece on the board. Rather, some (most of the) configuration of pieces continues from one move to the next. The configuration, the integrity, evolves, but is continuous with itself. It is expressed by each stage. Each stage represents the cumulative upshot of the game at that stage. Another way of describing it from the point of view of each stage is to say that the configuration overlaps stages, or the configuration of one stage maps onto another. The evolving configuration of the chessboard at a time overlaps with the configuration of the chessboard at both a previous and a subsequent time. Chess games are often described as sequences of discrete moves. But, such descriptions are elliptical representations, for each move presupposes a continuous, evolving configuration.

Taking the chess game as analogous to the self, the self is a network of traits (genetic, biological, social, linguistic, political, psychological, and so on). At each time or stage, traits are related to one another to form an integrity, a distinctive character with structure, and functional, communicative, and causal relations. The integrity is analogous to the chess configuration, the arrangement of the chessboard at a time. Just as some arrangement of the chessboard at one stage maps on to the arrangement of the chessboard at the next stage, so, too with the self. The integrity of the self evolves, but is continuous with itself. Interrelated traits of the self at one stage—its integrity—map on to the next stage of the self. Just as the arrangement of the chessboard does not remain exactly the same from one stage to the next, the integrity of the self does not remain exactly the same from one stage to the next. What overlaps is not just individual traits but a related network of traits, as the chessboard configuration is meant to suggest.

Of course, that the integrity overlaps or maps onto the next stage means that traits overlap or map as well. So, for example, recall Lindsey. Suppose she is now 48 and became a professor of philosophy at 35 years old. The trait, "being-a-professor-of-philosophy" characterizes, overlaps with, stages of Lindsey from Lindsey at 35 through Lindsey at 48. DNA configurations that constitute Lindsey genetically characterize, overlap with, every stage of Lindsey. Lindsey as sibling characterizes, overlaps with, every stage of the process that is Lindsey from sibling's birth to at least the sibling's death (if that precedes Lindsey's); and so on. See Figures 2.7 and 2.8. But, the important point is that those traits are related to one another to form an evolving integrity and that that overlaps or maps onto the next stage. This is meant to capture the idea that a stage of a self is not an isolated three-dimensional object, but is the cumulative upshot of the evolving process.[34]

One limitation of Figure 2.7 is that it does not represent the *interrelatedness* of overlapping traits with one another, the traits as constituting a network. Nor does it represent the idea of stages of the self as cumulative. To capture the latter idea, we might modify the figure as in Figure 2.8.

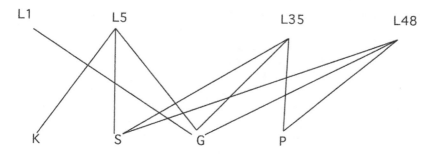

*Figure 2.7* As represented here, genetic traits (G) overlap every temporal cross-section, sibling relation (S) overlaps from L5 (birth of sibling) through L48, being a kindergartner (K) is a trait of the network only at L5, and being a philosophy professor (P) is a trait that overlaps temporal cross-sections L35 through L48.

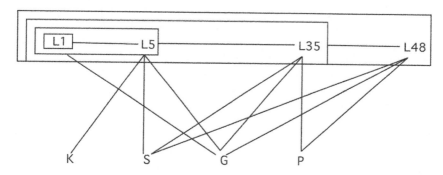

*Figure 2.8* An illustration of a prior stage as a trait of a subsequent stage. Each stage includes its prior stage as a trait such that the self is its own past (the nested boxes). The self is cumulative because it is a process, where each stage is the process as it is up to that time.

"Overlapping" and "mapping on to" are two different ways of conceptualizing the same phenomenon. Consider a stage of a self, say the 14th month stage of Lindsey, and suppose that it is a 30-day spatio-temporal region or stage. That same region (stage) could be further broken down, say into sub-regions (also stages) e.g., 30 days (or 1,020 hours, and so on). The description of the 14th month spatio-temporal region (stage) will be of a network, an arrangement of traits of that region. That arrangement spans the sub-regions (stages), the 30 days. I am simplifying, of course, because even within the 14th month stage the integrity evolves. But, if the *region* (stage) has a distinctive integrity, then the integrity must overlap or spread over the stages (days) of the region. On the other hand, if one takes a region (stage) as a discrete unit and asks what is its relation to a previous or subsequent region (stage) such that the regions (stages) constitute *a* process, the integrity of the arrangement of one region (stage) maps on to the other. Its unity as a comprehensive region is conceptualized in terms of an evolving integrity. How the integrity got to be the evolving structure that it is depends on and is explained by the particular causal relations (both within the network and external to it), counterfactual dependency, the interdependency of processes, psychological and social relations, biological relations (as noted earlier), the actions of the self and their effects on the evolving integrity, and so on.[35] These relations underpin the process self as an evolving ordered sequence of discrete stages such that between stages there is a mapping of the integrity from one stage to the next.[36] The integrity that maps from one stage to the next is a structural feature of the self, not a merely epistemic tool. The evolving configuration in chess *is* the chess game; the evolving integrity *is* the self.

How much change or difference does a process tolerate while persisting as *that* process (how exact does the mapping have to be)? It will depend on the kind of process and there may be variation in what would count as sufficient. Consider again the chess game. Suppose midway through the game all the pieces on the board were knocked over, leaving intact the arrangement of only a few pieces in one corner of the chessboard and none of those pieces is the king of either side. Suppose further that there is no record of the moves, and that no one can remember the arrangement of the pieces that have been knocked over (this would probably be a chess game involving inexperienced players!). A subset of relations (the pieces in the corner) overlaps the time prior to the pieces being knocked over and the time after the pieces have been knocked over. But, that subset is not a sufficient set of the arrangements that constituted the game for that subset to now be a stage *of the game*. The game—the cumulative network of configurations produced by play—may have been destroyed such that the corner arrangement is not a stage *of it*, of the process that was the game.[37] A chess game is a particular, ordered succession of moves embodying particular strategies and tactics, and not merely an agreement between players to play. For the latter, "play" might resume by setting up the board again in some agreed upon configuration. The players may be continuing to *play chess* in some sense, but it's not clear to me how they could be said to be continuing the previous game.[38]

Similarly with a self. Suppose Lindsey were in a plane crash and her body were almost completely incinerated, except for a finger. DNA analysis might be able to identify the finger as having been a constituent of Lindsey, but at the time in question, it is no longer a constituent *of* Lindsey because the network of relations, Lindsey, has been destroyed. In contrast, if a maimed living body survived the crash a sufficient set of strongly relevant traits of the self—the self's integrity—prior to the crash would map onto the self after the crash (depending on the scope of the maiming). While a living body is a necessary condition of a self, the body is itself a network of relations, molecular, genetic, physiological, structural, and so on the integrity of which admits of alteration in the bodily network. Therefore, a maimed body, depending on the scope of the maiming, may be such that the integrity of the prior network of which it is a sub-network maps on to the subsequent network of which the body, now maimed, is a sub-network.

As a structured network ("configuration") of traits, a self has structural features some set of which is preserved, some set of which maps from one stage of the process self to the next. The configuration includes not just bodily relations, but social, communicative, semantic, psychological, intentional, and agential relations.[39] The configuration of the self can map onto the maimed body, but not onto the finger; the finger is not a sufficient set of related traits and functionality. In saying that the integrity of the network (configuration) has to overlap with or, has to map onto the successive stage, some set of causal, counterfactual dependencies, biological, social, communicative, judicative and meaning relations has to be preserved, although there may not be a single, necessary condition or set of conditions that has to be preserved.[40] The configuration is changeable, but change has to be commensurate with the structural features of the configuration. Just as a physical process has an integrity as that physical process—for example, an avalanche cannot become, cannot go from being at one time an accumulating pack of snow to at a subsequent time being a chess game—so, too, with a self. A self (an interrelated network of traits) cannot just become, cannot map on to just any other network that succeeds the self. Rather, the self is a unified and structured process with interrelated and overlapping traits.

### 4.3. Cumulative Stages

The notion of an evolving integrity captures another aspect of how each stage is a stage of a process. Each stage is the state of the process up to that stage. Each stage is cumulative, and in so far as the process continues, is the leading edge of the process. To get at this idea, return to the chess analogy. Consider what appear to be two qualitatively identical chessboard configurations, where each corresponding piece is on the corresponding square of each board. Suppose each configuration consists of 28 pieces arranged in the formally or qualitatively same pattern; call that 28a ('a' designating one of the many 28 piece configurations possible in chess). One configuration is a stage of a game (28a qua Configuration$_n$ or Cn of Game$_n$ or Gn, or 28a-Cn-Gn) and the other is how someone happened to arrange some pieces on a board independently of any game (28a qua in a chess practice, or 28a-p).

So the distinctions are between:

- a formal configuration (a type), e.g., 28a;
- a game, Gn, qua a formal sequence of moves (a type since games formally defined can be replayed as multiple instantiations);
- a playing of the game, e.g., Gn.1, Gn.2, and so on (each a token of the type Gn);
- an occurrence or instantiation (a token) of the type, e.g., 28a-p, 28a-Cn-Gn, 28a-Cn-Gn.1.

As a stage *of the game*, 28a-Cn-Gn has the prior sequence of moves, that is, the sequence of play, as a trait, a relevant condition of what it is, whereas 28a-p does not (even though it could substitute for 28a-Cn-Gn going forward; see Chapter 3). The stage, 28a-Cn-Gn, is not qualitatively identical with 28a-p because they have different traits, different relevance conditions in spite of formal similarity of the 28a arrangement. The stage is the result of play, of a series of moves the cumulative upshot of which is 28a-Cn-Gn; 28a-Cn-Gn is counterfactually dependent on previous play. Once the game has commenced, each stage, configuration, of the game is the cumulative result or upshot of the game as it has been played up to that stage and the leading edge of the game as play continues. The final stage (checkmate or stalemate) is the cumulative state of the game qua end of the process as determined by the rules of chess.

A stage of a game represents the game as it has been played up to that stage. This cumulative relation of each stage to previous stages is relevant to the stage being what it is, what configuration it is, and to it being the leading edge of the game, that is, to its relation to successor stages. A relevance relation is not necessarily a whole/part relation. A previous stage (the past) is not *a part* of a current stage (the present); it is relevant to the previous stage being what it is. A relevance relation may not be strictly causal either; what moves the rules of chess allowed at a previous stage are relevant to what move occurs at that stage and thus, to how the board is reconfigured at a subsequent stage. But, the rules and what they allow are not causally but normatively relevant to each stage.

In a game, a prior stage is a condition for a successor stage being what it is. Each successor stage has the prior stage as a trait. Therefore, each successor stage has the game's past as a trait, that is, as relevant to it being what it is. And that is included in what maps onto each successor stage. Each stage is both the cumulative state of the game up to that stage and the leading edge of the game in so far as it continues. Chess games, represented as a series of discrete moves, are elliptical representations of what is going on. At each stage the configuration of the board represents the sequence of moves (the game as it is) up to that stage. The chess *game* as a whole process is not just a succession of discrete moves, but is a cumulative sequence of overlapping chess configurations. The game at any stage is a changeable directional network of chess relations (forces, positions, tactics and strategy, rule governed possibilities, and so on).

The point in using the chess analogy is to illustrate the idea of stages being cumulatively related to one another such as to constitute a process. There are of course many differences between chess and selves. Chess is a rule-governed process; the process self is not (although there may be biological and developmental "rules" or patterns). Moreover, as we noted, chess games can be both types and tokens. Selves are individuals that do not admit of multiple instantiation (unless entire worlds are reinstantiable).

Just as each stage of a chess game is the cumulative state of the game up to that stage, each stage of the self is a cumulative state of the self up to that stage and the leading edge of the self in so far as it continues. Lindsey at 14 months is the first-born child of her parents, has a genetic structure, is embedded in kinship relations, wears diapers, crawls, has other rudimentary motor, communicative and social skills. At 15 months, Lindsey becomes the sibling of a second child. Each stage is the cumulative network, is the process as it is up to that stage. What this means is that the 15 month stage has the 14 month stage as a trait, not a part, but as relevant to it being what it is. Each stage—the 14 month stage, the 15 month stage—is the cumulative state and leading edge of the process, Lindsey, at its respective time. What is strongly relevant at one stage may not be strongly relevant at another stage; recall the Mozart example at Figure 2.6 and the discussion in Section 3.3.

### 4.4. Cumulative Whole

At any time the self is identified and identifiable as having a particular constitution and determinate overall character, which I have called the *integrity* of the self. Because each stage is the cumulative self up to that stage, there is a sense in which each stage is the whole self, Lindsey up to that stage. The five-year old Lindsey—who is daughter, sibling, kindergartner, budding English speaker—is the cumulative totality of her experiences and locations as of that time. The 48-year old Lindsey—who is daughter, sibling, mother, philosopher, English speaker, novelist, citizen, and so on—is the cumulative totality of her experience and locations as of that time; she is the upshot of the cumulative process which includes five-year old Lindsey. Each stage includes the previous stages, not as literal parts, but as relevance conditions (some of which are counterfactual dependency relations) of the cumulative whole at that time. See Figure 2.9 (and recall Figure 2.6).

"That was me at an earlier time, but I was a different person then." This can be interpreted as distinguishing between the cumulative self experienced each time as a present whole, while also affirming that there is an overall cumulative process of which each stage is a temporal

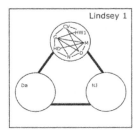

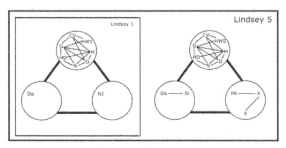

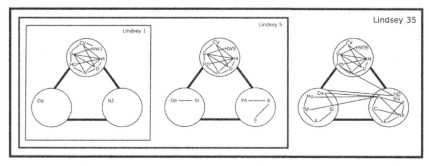

*Figure 2.9* This represents Lindsey as cumulative, structured sub-clusters of traits at a few different temporal cross-sections or stages, Lindsey one, Lindsey five, Lindsey thirty-five.

Abbreviations: A = aunt; CV = cardiovascular system; Da = daughter; D = digestive system; E = English speaker; F = feminist; G = genetic structure; HD = Huntington Disease Carrier; HDG = member Huntington Disease support group; HW = height/weight at a phase; IC = Irish-Catholic; K = kindergartner; Mo = Mother; M = musculoskeletal system; N = neurological system; NJ = resident of New Jersey; No = novelist; P = philosopher; PA = resident of Pennsylvania; Si = sibling; Sp = spouse

The first box is not nested because it is assuming that this is the starting point of the network of relations that is Lindsey and therefore, as such it doesn't yet have its own past qua network. A causal past that brings about the network may make it difficult to conceptualize exactly when the network comes into existence. For the sake of simplification this just stipulates that there is some initial time, birth, which is the beginning of Lindsey qua a distinctive self-network.

cross-section. Thus, Lindsey at 48 is different from Lindsey at 5, but the referent of "I" and of "me" is the process, Lindsey, that expresses itself differently at different times. The notion of a cumulative self allows for a way of characterizing the whole self as present at a time, while avoiding the consequence of many selves. Each stage is a way in which the process "expresses" itself at a time, a way in which a self is represented at a time, is characterized as, acts, remembers, is responsible for *its* prior self-expressions and actions, and so on at a time.

Reid (1895) and Butler (1736) criticized Locke's memory criterion for personal identity on the grounds that the stringing together of memories couldn't constitute personal identity, but rather presupposed something unified that had those memories *as its*. Similarly, a succession of spatio-temporal regions alone does not constitute a process. While I don't subscribe to a substance view of the self, I do endorse Reid's and Butler's points about presupposing a unity, a whole. The notion of a cumulative whole that carries its past with it is meant to provide a model of the structured unity of a process self. (On this view, a memory may be a contributing constituent to the whole, but it presupposes a whole to which it contributes and of which it is the memory.) The whole is not a substance but a uniquely interrelated changeable, complex cumulative network of traits constituted of molecular, biochemical, genetic, organ, function and limb relations, of neurochemical and neurophysiological relations, of psychological, mental, social, economic, political, linguistic, cultural, and so on relations.

A relational approach could be developed that would not in principle rule out that psychological relations or relations that produce psychological relations are the essential ones for a relational process to be a self. However, while psychological connection and continuity are typically strongly relevant to a relational process self, on CNM they may not be necessary for continuation of that self. I have been arguing for a broader approach to what is sufficient for being and persisting as a self. In profound cases of memory loss or amnesia, for instance in Alzheimer's disease or severe cases of retrograde amnesia, the self has and continues to be constituted by its past, *even though* it may have no conscious access to it. Loss of memory and cognitive ability have profound implications for such issues as agency and responsibility, for what we normally mean by a functioning first-person perspective, but this diminishment is still something happening to, a diminishment *of*, that self.

The CNM model captures the senses in which the self is constituted by its history and by plural relations, and is a cumulative whole self present at any time. To sum up the model's features:

(1) a self is a network of multiple relations and locations (in this respect, this view is in sympathy with feminist conceptualizations of the self as relational, but with "relational" understood more broadly than "social");

(2) a self is a process and therefore temporally constituted and spread out in space and time (in this respect, this view is in sympathy with four-dimensionalism);

(3) at any time, a self is a cumulative whole that sums up or "expresses" the process at that time. As a cumulative network, a self is the upshot of and counterfactually dependent on its own past relations. It also projects itself, it evolves, into a future. Therefore, at any time during its existence a self is incomplete as long as it has a future. Thus, four-dimensionalist part and stage theories are right that there is a sense in which at a time what is present is an incomplete self. At the same time, while incomplete or open (as long as it is alive), the self as it is at any time, is a cumulative whole of what it has been up to that time.[41]

What I would like to address next is the issue of identity over time or the persistence of the self. If a self is a process, and a process by definition is incomplete and changes over time, then in what sense does a self persist as itself? How is it possible to re-identify a self, that self, from one time to another? The next chapter considers these questions, and proposes that the issues raised are better understood in terms of the concept of "numerical unity" rather than identity in the strict sense of the term.

## 5. Affinities

I have mentioned in the text of the chapter possible associations to or affinities with or similarities to other theories or concepts where it seemed appropriate. Here I just want to give a nod to other possible associations. While I am not conversant enough with the literature in the Continental tradition to say definitively how my view might resonate, or not, with that tradition, there are a few affinities that occur to me.

According to CNM, the self is irreducibly complex. This may resonate with Levinas's notion of the infinity of each self, that no person can be reduced to a single role or aspect, and that no description can fully capture a person's identity.

I have also been very struck by Bourdieu's idea of *habitus*. It seems to exemplify something like the idea of a cumulative whole, except at a social level rather than at the level of an individual self. *Habitus* embodies the notion of cumulative shaping, in Bourdieu's case of social and cultural practices, enacted by and transmitted through both individuals and societies.

> The *habitus*, a product of history, produces individual and collective practices . . . [and] ensures the active presence of past experiences. . . . This system of dispositions—a present past that tends to perpetuate itself into the future by reactivation in similarly structured practices . . . is the principle of continuity and regularity which objectivism sees in social practices.
>
> (Bourdieu, 1990, 54)

There may be something here that also resonates with Merleau-Ponty's notion of sedimentation, by which Bourdieu may have been influenced (Merleau-Ponty, 1962).

The aspect of CNM that suggests that the self is a process that evolves or projects itself into the future might have affinities with a Heideggerian view of the self as, at any time during its existence, incomplete and living as a "pro-ject" towards its future. However, I am not concerned with Heideggerian themes such as how death functions as the horizon of that future and with other existential themes.[42]

I mention these—there may be others—in order to suggest avenues of connection between otherwise distinct traditions, even though these are avenues that I do not have the expertise, or the space, to follow.

## Notes

1. Royce (1969), *The Philosophy of Loyalty*, 865.
2. Stephen Hawking, January 23, 2000, *San Jose Mercury News*.
3. David Hume, *Treatise on Human Nature*, Bk. I, Pt. iv, sec. 6, "Of Personal Identity."
4. John Locke, *An Essay Concerning Human Understanding*, IV, vi, 11.
5. I borrow this list from Olson's (2007) helpful overview of the different approaches to the notion of person and personal identity. The animal view is that human selves are fundamentally human animals; the constitution view is Baker's, that the human self is a distinct (psychological) kind of being that coincides with a human body; the brain view, that a self is that which self-consciously identifies as "I" and thus the self goes with the brain; the temporal parts view, is the four-dimensionalist view, already mentioned, that the self is some occupied spatio-temporal region, such that at any one time, it is a part of the self that is present; the bundle view, that the self is just a collection (unstructured) of properties; the soul view, that a human self is fundamentally a soul distinct from the material conditions of existence; the special composition view, that there are special conditions under which material objects (microscopic parts or spatio-temporal regions) compose human organisms. I discuss the person life view (Schechtman, 2014) in the text, this chapter, Section 1, and elsewhere.
6. I have offered preliminary versions of my view in a number of places: Wallace (1999, 2003, 2007, 2008, 2009). The last is a very early version of this chapter and of part of the next, although my thinking has evolved since the article was written and departs from some of what I said there.
7. The reductivist assumption drives research programs in much of science. For example,

> Like any organ, the brain consists of large parts (such as the hippocampus and the cortex) that are made up of small parts (such as 'maps' in the visual cortex), which themselves are made up of smaller parts, until you get to neurons, billions of them, whose orchestrated firing is the stuff of thought. The neurons are made up of parts like axons and dendrites, which are made up of smaller parts like terminal buttons, and receptor sites, which are made up of molecules, and so on.
> This hierarchical structure (of the brain) makes possible the research programs of psychology and neuroscience. The idea is that interesting properties of the whole (intelligence, decision-making, emotions, moral sensibility) can be understood in terms of the interaction of components

> that themselves lack these properties. This is how computers work; there is every reason to believe that this is how we work, too."
>
> (Bloom, 2008, 2)

8. The extent to which selves can be cyborgian, incorporating non-biological traits and parts, would depend on many factors. Transhumanist beings that might "live" as information patterns in computer networks would be different kinds of beings than selves as they generally actually are, even if they "evolved" from selves. See Bostrom (2003), Haraway (1991), Moravec (1998, 1999), Steinhart (2014).

9. Schechtman does not draw out the implications of a network and process view and her treatment of personal identity is different from mine (although we agree about what should be inferred from some of the thought experiments employed in the philosophical literature). In the course of my discussions, I will refer to Schechtman's work and where we agree and disagree as pertinent.

10. Wittgenstein rejects the idea that necessary and sufficient conditions are required for definitions of terms. Rather the meaning of terms can be understood in terms of "family resemblances," following the use of terms through "a complicated network of similarities overlapping and criss-crossing" (Wittgenstein, 2009, 66).

11. This may bear some similarity to the dynamical system model developed by Ismael (2007), mentioned in the Introduction. In network theory, one might characterize the body as a "hub" in the typology of the self conceived as a complex network (Barabási, 2002).

12. Each location is itself a complex network. As mother, Lindsey is a network of social (kinship, interpersonal, legal) relations, such as, daughter, spouse, sister, aunt, niece, cousin, etc.; of emotional relations, and of (usually, but not always, for instance in cases of adoption) genetic relations; as introverted is a network of neurological, emotional, social dispositions and habits; as feminist is a network of social, cultural, and political beliefs and commitments. There are many sub-networks or configurations that overlap and work together to form a more comprehensive network.

13. I am borrowing from Buchler's use of the term "integrity" (1990, 22).

14. As proposed, for example, by Rovane (1998). We should note that even a narrative, or rational, unity need not be *harmonious*:

> [A]gents can manifest sensitivity to rational requirements without being successfully moved into complying with them. So perceiving one's online activity as conflicting with the other projects in one's life is as much a way of manifesting rational unity as perceiving it as in harmony with those projects.
>
> (Ward, 2011, 509)

15. It might be argued that if impure properties were included as real properties, then that would guarantee that indiscernibility *is* numerical identity and would trivialize the principle of the identity of indiscernibles (Forrest, 2006). I consider identity in Chapter 3.

16. That every trait is relational means that every trait is complex. Many of the general distinctions and overall conception here on offer are not metaphysically exceptional, that is, are not characteristic only of selves. I do not mean that everything is a process (although there are many more kinds of processes than just self processes) or human like, or that there are no distinctions between different kinds of complexes or networks. What I mean is that complexity and the distinctions being made about relational traits are more

general ontological categories. Every being is complex and the term "a complex" is a generic term of identification (Buchler, 1990). The pervasiveness and irreducibility of complexity means that it is complexity all the way down. That doesn't preclude dependencies, both symmetric and asymmetric, of all kinds. It just means that we wouldn't ever get to some ultimate foundation that was itself not related or supported in some way by other complexes. If that is right, then there is no ground of fundamental reality and it's "turtles all the way down" as Cameron (2008) so charmingly put it in a paper that argues for the opposite intuition.

One could, however, go along with the relational conception of self that is here on offer as long as one thought the claim being made about relational traits and the conception of self as so constituted were appropriate to (non-reductive) categorizing of "middle-size" existents (ordinary objects like tables, chairs, rocks, trees, buildings, animals, selves). One could avoid the broader metaphysical question about subscribing to a principle of ontological priority (and hence, a requirement of fundamentality of some sort) or to a principle of ontological parity, endorsed, for example, by Buchler (1990) and Priest (2009). Latour (1988), a proponent of actor-network theory, might also be characterized as exhibiting a commitment to a principle of ontological parity (all objects are actors or actants, there is nothing special about human agency). However, in my view, Latour's claim that everything is the same kind of thing (an object or an actant) throws out the baby with the bathwater. Ontological parity requires only a commitment to the equal reality of whatever is, not the eradication of all distinctions such that everything is one kind of thing. I note, though, that actor-network theory has interesting things to say about the interaction and interdependency of human and non-human actants in the "assemblage" of the social (Latour, 2005).

17. New York City comprises five boroughs spread over two main islands (Manhattan and Staten Island), part of Long Island (the boroughs of Queens and Brooklyn), part of the New York state landmass (the borough of the Bronx and a small portion of the borough of Manhattan), and numerous smaller islands, Roosevelt, Governor's, Ellis, Rikers, and others.

18. This aspect of the network model of the self bears some similarity to the argument advanced by Gallagher (2013), in the context of cognitive science, for a "pattern theory of self," although there "self" means "mind." Gallagher invokes the pattern theory again in Gallagher (2014):

> One can also ask whether intentionality, whether derived or non-derived, is necessarily the only mark of the mental. If one carefully considers such phenomena as emotions and the experience of self, one can argue that these phenomena, and more generally the mind itself, are really constituted by a pattern of factors, no one of which is necessary, but some number of which are sufficient for that constitution (Gallagher, 2013; Newen et al., 2015). . . . One could argue that more generally this same pattern theory applies to the mind itself. The mind (or the mental) is constituted by a pattern of aspects or elements not all of which are necessary in every case, but some of which are constitutionally sufficient.
>
> (Gallagher, 2014, 121–122)

19. I am not concerned with whether HPC satisfies criteria for natural kind classification. The theory does seem to satisfy quite a few (e.g., identify as having some [natural] properties in common; permit inductive inferences; participate in laws of nature) even though it allows for vagueness in the boundaries between natural kinds, rejecting the idea that natural kinds must be distinct. And it could be neutral or not on whether natural kinds form a hierarchy

(see Bird and Tobin, 2012). I am only interested in HPC as a theory that conceptualizes an individual self as a cluster of properties, or in my terms, a network of traits.

20. Schechtman (2014) makes a similar comparison to HPC in the development of her person life view of persons.

21. See Chapter 3, Section 4.2.1, for further discussion of abandonment or deprivation of all social roles.

22. In a related vein, Freeman (2011) suggests that, "A feral child, for example, would not *exist* qua human being on Heidegger's account, since she would lack the relational structures that constitute Dasein" (370).

23. Anterograde amnesia is the loss of ability to form new memories; retrograde amnesia is the loss of ability to recall past memories. Clive Wearing suffers a severe and chronic case (30 years) of both that began after he contracted herpes encephalitis. He knows he has a wife and children. He has some general or semantic knowledge and language, and thus can engage in some conversation. However, his episodic memory has been catastrophically affected. He has muscle memory and can still play the piano (he was a musicologist and keyboardist before the amnesia). Although he can't say what he remembers, he can sometimes enact it, such as playing a musical piece, or finding his way to the bathroom in his residence, or finding the equipment to make coffee. Every time he sees his wife (whom he does recognize), it is as if for the first time in years, even if she had been in the room only a few minutes before. Sacks (2007) gives a very interesting account of Wearing's case, accessible to the non-medical specialist.

24. For a different analysis of vagueness see Braddon-Mitchell and West's (2001) temporal phase pluralism, a theory according to which survival is defined relative to an individual or a society, and that rests on the psychological beliefs of a self or society.

25. I am not committing myself to any particular theory of counterfactuals or of possible worlds. Nor am I committing myself more generally to a possible worlds analysis of modality. I am only using counterfactuals to explore the sense in which what a self is a contingent matter.

26. Or, normally going for a walk in the French countryside would be a trivial (momentarily enjoyable) experience, but if one is assaulted, raped, beaten, and left for dead, a walk that becomes occasion for indelible trauma may be strongly relevant to the self who one is. (For an account of such an experience see Brison, 1993, 1997.)

27. The idea that the self is a process is not a widely held view, although there are some who appear to hold some such view (e.g., Gergen, 2009). Perry (1975) explicitly denies that persons are processes; "there is no one natural way to break up a person's life into discrete events" (10). According to Perry, while we can think of a person as *having* a life or personal history that is a process, the person is not a process. (See also Perry 1976 for other aspects of the self, for instance, the importance of unity, on which we may be more in some agreement.) In contrast, I am saying that the person, the self, is a process.

28. Four-dimensionalism allows for "gappy" objects; non-contiguous space-time regions may count as objects. I'm not sure what it would say about acts or events. But, in any case, my concern is about whether this approach is adequate to capturing the nature of agency and extended acts.

29. Thanks to an anonymous reviewer for suggesting clarification of this point.

30. Seibt has developed a general process ontology that is an extensional mereology, with a non-classical theory of whole-part relations. She argues for a distinction between being "a part of" and "part of," the latter meaning "belonging with," and for what she calls a leveled mereology. Her "general

process theory" is more general, and more technical, than what is needed here, but I note that she, too, conceptualizes individuals as processes. Seibt has developed her "general process theory" in numerous places; see for example, Seibt (2009, 2015).

31. See for example, Bapteste and Dupré (2013), Ereshefsky and Pedroso (2013), Hull (1976, 1978, 1980). Armstrong (1980) and Shoemaker (1979) argue that the identity of an individual depends on parts being properly causally connected.

32. For the latter, one might think of the outcome of an election as due to the aggregated causal contributions, the votes, of members of the electorate, an aggregate, not an individual.

33. Overlap means something different from the idea of overlapping spatio-temporal regions. For standard four-dimensionalism, in one sense, no part overlaps with another part, just as spatially, parts of the body do not overlap, but occupy distinct spatial regions. But, in another sense, temporal parts can share temporal parts and thus, have overlapping parts. Spatio-temporal regions can be divided into many different sub-regions, just as spatial regions can be. For example, my left hand can't overlap with—it cannot occupy the same spatial region as—my left arm from shoulder to wrist. However, parts of my left hand may also be parts of a larger object, the left limb from shoulder joint to fingertips. Therefore, my left hand and left limb share parts and thus overlap. Similarly, one could argue that the same is true of temporal parts. The yesterday part of me and the today part of me do not overlap, but the part of me that spans yesterday at noon to today at noon shares temporal parts with the yesterday and the today parts of me and thus yesterday/noon-yesterday-to-noon-today/today parts "overlap," that is, share parts. This overlap is just different ways of carving up the space-time continuum. By itself it doesn't have anything to do with how we might define ordinary objects or distinguish them from one another. In fact, on this view, my hand and the desk on which it is resting could be an object, that is, a spatio-temporal region that partly overlaps with the rest of my body and with the desk. Other features, such as causal relations between spatio-temporal parts, are required to distinguish what we take to be ordinary objects. Four-dimensionalists admit this. However, person-stages understood as spatio-temporal slices would be abstractions, a "thinner" view of stage than how CNM uses the term.

34. The view I am proposing may have some affinity to Peirce's discussion about the nature of a continuum. According to Peirce, there are infinite indenumerable relations between any two stages of a continuum such that stages are not discrete and there is no "gap" between them, *qua* stages *of* a process. The context of Peirce's argument is philosophy of mathematics where he advances the view that a continuum cannot be comprised of discrete points (infinitesimals), and thus he rejects atomism for what he called synechism. See Dauben (1977) and C.S. Peirce (1976, Vol. 3: 87–89). If a process self were a continuum, then that would further distinguish this view from stage theory, which conceptualizes the self as built up out of distinct space-time regions. I think this might be an intriguing line of argument to pursue, but I am not equipped with the requisite expertise in philosophy of math to do so.

35. Further specification of what would be relevant to and constitutive of a particular self would need to be made since the universe of causal relations and counterfactual dependencies is indefinitely wide. Even events upon which one might say a self is counterfactually dependent are not therefore constituents or traits of the self's *own* past. For example, suppose a bicyclist is "doored" by a driver who happened to be exiting their car just as the bicyclist rode by.

The bicyclist's experience and subsequent injury are constituents of the bicyclist. But, the driver having parked just when they did is not, even though the bicyclist having been doored is counterfactually dependent on that. So while the self has counterfactual dependency relations among its constitutive relevance conditions, counterfactual dependency by itself it is not sufficient for identifying particular traits *of* a self and its past. Perhaps another example, Christensen and Bickhard (2002), in discussing living systems as processes, distinguish between (sub-)processes that contribute to and depend on the system and those that contribute to it without depending on the system for their occurrence. They give the example of a plant depending on its leaves and the sun for photosynthesis: leaves are "part of" the plant, while the sun is not (10). The existence and processes of the sun are independent of the plant even though the plant is counterfactually dependent on sunlight. At the same time, sunlight is a constituent of the process of photosynthesis. (Therefore, photosynthesis is what I would call part of the scope of the sun. Recall the New York City analogy—an individual may be a constituent of the scope of New York City.) Photosynthesis is a strongly relevant constituent of the plant and is strongly relevant to, is interdependent with other constitutive processes of the plant, such as the plant's growth and reproduction. Thanks to an anonymous reviewer for pushing me to clarify this section.

36. Normally, for selves as they really are. As we will see in Chapter 4, there may be thought experimental cases, where the normal causal relations are loosened, and the integrity *may* still persist.

37. Or, recall the earlier city analogy. Suppose a city and all its inhabitants are destroyed save for a small neighborhood. It is conceivable that a particular neighborhood might be sufficiently important or central to the integrity of the city such that we might say that the city is present, albeit in a diminished sense. But, it is more likely that the presence of a small neighborhood alone would not preserve the integrity of or constitute the city.

38. Or, at least not in standard chess. Perhaps some variant version of chess would allow such types of game continuations. Or, perhaps play continues for the purposes of continuing a practice session.

39. In network theory more generally, some networks are robust, can lose traits and even a "hub" of traits, and still persist, if there are sufficient connections or hubs that remain, depending on the hubs, the amount of redundancy, and other assortative principles (Barabási, 2002). Similarly with a self.

40. See also discussion of identity over time and numerical unity, Chapter 3, Sections 4.1 and 4.2, where I also consider the issue of sudden and dramatic change in a self.

41. The cumulative whole self at a time would also include the possibilities of the self. Treatment of modality is beyond the scope of this discussion. I mention it only to indicate that notions such as dispositions and capability, as well as the notion that a process self is incomplete, at least until it is dead, would entail some notion of possibility.

42. For another resonance of Heidegger with a relational model of the self, and picking up on the feminist inspirations for this project, see Freeman's analysis of the Heideggerian notion of *Mitsein* and its implications for a relational conception of autonomy (Freeman, 2011).

# 3   Identity and the Network Self

At night, as Ruth lay in her old bed, she felt she had come back to her adolescence in the guise of an adult. She was the same person and yet she was not. Or perhaps she was two versions of herself, Ruth$_{1969}$ and Ruth$_{1997}$, one more innocent and the other more perceptive, one needier, the other more self-sufficient, both of them fearful. She was her mother's child, and mother to the child her mother had become. So many combinations, like Chinese names and characters, the same elements, seemingly simple, reconfigured in different ways.

(Amy Tan)[1]

## 1. Introduction

In the philosophical literature on the metaphysics of personal identity the term "identity" refers to a formal relation. This is different from its meaning in the literature on identity politics or in feminist treatments of, for example, women's sense of identity in comparison to men's, or in communitarian understandings of cultural identities. In the latter views "identity" refers to some positive content, for example, some specific gender, racial, sexual orientation, ethnic, religious, social, or cultural set of categories, in terms of which someone or some group of people understands who she is or who they are, or in terms of which they are so understood by others. According to CNM, cultural, gender, racial, or other social "identities" are specific locations or relationally constituted traits of the individuals and groups of individuals who are constituted in those ways. Schechtman (1996) calls this set of concerns, a characterization question.[2] I will come back to the "characterization question" (this chapter, Section 5) and its implications for understanding the formation of a first-person perspective (Chapter 5) and autonomy (Chapter 6).

In the metaphysics of personal identity, the issue is what Schechtman calls the "re-identification question." Logically, identity is a one-to-one, formal relation that any thing or person has to itself. But, re-identification is different from identity *tout court*. The question, "Is this the person now who committed a crime then?" isn't a formal identity question because the self at each time may have different traits. But, it's not a persistence, or not only a persistence, question, either because it's a "what" question— what is this self now such that it can be described as the self that then committed a crime? CNM suggests that the question is about "numerical unity." According to CNM, the self at any time includes its past as a trait, and therefore, is the numerically one self as it is up to that time. As a cumulative network the self is both a synchronic unity (a structured whole) and a diachronic unity (a unified process).

First, I will briefly comment on some other treatments of identity and identity over time or persistence, and then discuss the notion of numerical unity. In Chapter 4, I will discuss how CNM would treat some of the examples offered in fusion and fission thought experiments in the philosophical literature on personal identity.

Many discussions of personal identity understand the identity of a person in psychological terms, for instance as being a psychologically continuous or connected stream of conscious states (memories, intentions, propositional attitudes and so on). Others argue that bodily identity is a necessary condition for personal identity,[3] and among these, some reject the psychological criterion altogether.[4] CNM agrees that it is normally characteristic of selves that they have psychological characteristics, and that these are important in many re-identification contexts, such as when persons are the target of forensic understandings.[5] Persons have intentional and deliberative states; they enter into communicative, judicative, and meaning relations and processes; and they can be held morally and legally responsible for their choices and agential decisions. But, according to CNM, the forensic target is more broadly understood as a physically, socially, naturally, as well as psychologically constituted cumulative network. It is the self so understood that I mean by "person" in a phrase such as, "the person in the courtroom is the person who committed the crime two years ago." The term "person" is embedded in ordinary language and it is customary to use it rather than "self" in a phrase such as "*the person* in the courtroom." Where it is more natural to do so, I will use "person," which for this purpose is interchangeable with my usage of "self." (I will use scare quotes to mark other conceptions of the person, for example, when summarizing or referring to views that hold that a "person" is to be identified with the psychological stream.)

## 2. Identity and Indiscernibility

Identity is a formal one to one relation that any thing has to itself. It is an equivalence relation with the properties of symmetry, reflexivity, and transitivity. The logic of identity is based on the principle of the indiscernibility of identicals. If something is one and the same thing any complete enumeration of its traits or properties will be exactly the same (indiscernible from one another).[6] For example, the morning star is identical with the evening star, that is, the planet, Venus. For any trait or property that the morning star has, the evening star has it. Venus can be called or identified as the morning star or the evening star and in so far as it can be identified in two different ways (from two different perspectives) someone might not realize that ontologically there is only one thing, Venus, that is numerically (*one*) and qualitatively (the *same*) identical.[7] The morning star and the evening star could appear to be discernible from one another, in so far as each is only a partial, incomplete enumeration of the traits of Venus. But, a complete enumeration starting with the morning star and another complete enumeration starting with the evening star would be exactly similar, that is, indiscernible from the other.

Normally, when identifying particular things, we don't need to give, and in practice are unable to give, a complete enumeration of traits; typically, some subset of distinguishing, strongly relevant features is sufficient. For example, Lindsey is in one respect a biological organism, that is, a network of biochemical, physiological, psychological, etc. relational traits. In most contexts, I am able to securely assert that biological organism Lindsey is professor of philosophy Lindsey. However, neither I nor Lindsey may have complete or precise understanding of either aspect of Lindsey; for instance, neither of us may know her DNA profile. Moreover, many traits of a self involve relations to other selves, institutions, and objects in the world. Relatedness may entail that at any time the exact boundaries of the self are indeterminate (which may present a practical difficulty in some contexts) and that a complete enumeration of traits is impossible. The same thing is true of Venus. It's just that relative to us its constitutive relations (e.g., its material composition, its location, its orbit) may be less in flux and the traits that we can easily identify are sufficient for securing the identity claim.

Returning to the self, Lindsey is a unique network of traits: mother (aunt, daughter, sibling, niece, cousin, mother, etc.), novelist, fluent native English speaker, of Irish-Catholic heritage, professor of philosophy, licensed driver, social security contributor, psycho-biological organism, novelist, opera lover, optimist, and so on. To say that Lindsey the philosopher is identical with Lindsey the psycho-biological organism is to say that the network of traits that includes the trait philosopher and the network of traits that includes psycho-biological organism is one network.[8] The network is identical with itself. The traits of psycho-biological organism qua psycho-biological organism are distinct from the traits of philosopher qua philosopher. But, the self that is the psycho-biological organism Lindsey is the self that is the philosopher Lindsey. This is no different from Venus. The planet that is the morning star is the planet that is the evening star; or the planet that is the third planet from the sun is the planet that is the hottest of the sun's planets.

There could be some circumstance in which a more than normal detailed enumeration of traits or a focus on a not readily available or obscure set of traits (e.g., DNA analysis) would be required, but in most contexts, like with Venus, an enumeration of some subset of traits can be given that is sufficient to secure an identity claim. While a complete enumeration of traits may be impossible or difficult for us to provide, and an exact boundary difficult to circumscribe, that is not, most of the time, a barrier to making justified identity claims, even if it is, in principle, a limitation of a perhaps necessarily perspectival view of which we are capable.[9]

## 3. Identity Over Time

Re-identification is typically characterized as asking whether a person at one time is one and the same as a person at another time. The concern here is with issues such as whether the person in the courtroom today is the person who committed a crime two years ago; or, whether the person today who is obligated to fulfill a promise or contract is the person who, say, a year ago made the promise or contract; or, how to account for the fact that someone at 45 is radically different from that person at 5 and yet is in some sense *that* one person. The person as s/he is today has characteristics today that s/he didn't have two years or forty years ago and lacks other ones that s/he did have two or forty years ago. A complete description of the person as s/he was two or forty years ago is discernible from a complete description of the person today. Therefore, the person as s/he is today is not logically identical with the person as s/he is two or forty years ago.

One might deal with the problem of re-identification by conceptualizing the object as remaining the same in some sense, for instance, in virtue of time-indexed properties,[10] or by identifying a subset of properties that don't change and that are present at every time the entity exists. The idea would be that there is a subset of traits that remains qualitatively the same and it is on those that the identity of the person from one time to the next would depend. While on such an approach, the identity over time question would really be about identity, it would give up the idea that identity has to do with sameness as a whole. Identity would rest on the indiscernibility of just those core, invariant traits, however much the thing, in this case, the person, would otherwise change. DNA, in so far as it is presumed to be invariant and unique, might be thought to fill the bill.

Another strategy might be to argue that it's the unique origin that is the key. Origin, Kripke (1972) argued, is a necessary trait: a person, *this* person, came from the parents that she or he came from, that is, from the people "whose body tissues are sources of the biological sperm and egg" (112).[11] This wouldn't be distinctively or uniquely true of one monozygotic twin compared to the other, so "origin" might have to be moved to the time of the splitting of the zygote. Monozygotic twins develop as similar, but different processes of intra-uterine development, are typically different weights and sizes, have different times of birth, have different social experiences and exposure and so on, such that each twin is a unique process and intersection of traits. Therefore, even twins could be said to have unique origins. But, for CNM, more importantly each twin is unique and discernible from the other because they are distinct cumulative networks of traits (even if a second or third party has difficulty distinguishing them physically from one another). While DNA and splitting of the zygote may each be necessary for the distinct existence of monozygotic twins, it's the integrity of each process, of each cumulative network of traits that matters for the (re-)identifiability of each. Each twin as it is at one time (e.g., born second weighing 2,500 grams) would also be discernible from itself as it is at another time (e.g., at 5 it has not just been born, even though it is true that it was born second, and at 5 it weighs much more than 2,500 grams).[12]

Other strategies abandon a search for sameness of some kind and argue that it's about persistence or continuity. One might look to animal (bodily) continuity or psychological (consciousness) continuity to account for persistence. Four-dimensionalists have accounted for persistence in terms of succession of distinct objects, either parts or stages, with appropriate dependence and causal relations.[13] On the stage view a four-dimensional object, a person-career, consists of successive, numerically distinct and isolated three-dimensional objects (stages) that are counterparts of each other.[14] A stage just is a filled spatio-temporal region; so is a person-career, but it's a bigger region, a concatenation of three-dimensional objects (regions), none of which overlap. An object is numerically identical at different times to many distinct stages that bear the appropriate counterpart relation to one another. Relation between stages is not identity, but a counterpart relation. No stage *is* identical to another stage, but a stage *was* (or *will be*) identical to—viz., is a counterpart to—an earlier (or later) stage (another object) that has traits that the present stage does not.

As I have already noted counterpart theory entails that there are multiple persons (person-stages). This it seems to me is not what the identity over time or re-identification question is after, namely, the basis for being able to identify a single self, say Lindsey at 48 as the self who was Lindsey at 35. Counterpart theory says rather that there are similarity, causal and dependence relations between distinct person-stages. CNM agrees that between discrete stages there is not identity, but it does not have the multiple persons implication. Rather, there is one process, one cumulative network. There is overlap of strong relevance relations or mapping of the integrity of one stage onto the next; the self at a time includes its past as one of its traits. This is different from mere succession of distinct stages and from a counterpart relation between *distinct* entities. The cumulative self is changeable, but because the self's past is a trait of the self at any time, it is the *one* process as it is at that time. A cumulative stage may have (some) different traits from another cumulative stage, but each is the process self as it is up to each time. This is what I am calling numerical unity. Identity is a relation that the person has to itself. If identity means the indiscernibility of the whole from itself, then at any time the identity of the whole with itself is a different relation (the identity relation) from, even if it might depend on, the unity of the whole.

## 4. Numerical Unity and Network Preservation

CNM interprets the re-identification question as being about numerical unity. "Unity" here is not the kind of issue raised by Dennett (1992, 2001) and others as to whether there is a *unified* "I" or self-conscious self or first-person perspective. Nor is it the unity of rational agency posited by Rovane (1998) as defining of personhood. (See also Wallace 2000.) I will have more to say about a first-person perspective for a relational self (see Chapter 5), but that is not what is at issue here. I am also not referring to a problem in the Baker constitution view of objects and persons, namely, how two "objects" (persons and bodies) are (constitute) one object.[15] Nor by unity do I mean harmony, completeness or absence of multiplicity (complexity). I just mean the "that-one-thing-ness" of the self. Identity over time (and the possibility of re-identification) is not about sameness or qualitative identity, nor about continuity, but about whether it is that one "thing" present at each time. In this I agree with Baxter who argues that the primary issue with numerical identity is not indiscernibility, but being one thing, being a single thing.[16] The "thing" under discussion here is a process, a cumulative network that is changeable and evolving, not a substance or an entity.

The common sense question about the person in the courtroom is not asking whether two different "persons" (viz., person-stages) are connected in some way. Nor is it asking for identity qua indiscernibility, that is, it is not asking, "Is the person in the courtroom exactly similar to (indiscernible from in at least some essential respect) the person who committed the crime as that person was when the crime was committed?" Nor is it asking for a counterpart (*another* person or person-stage) who is similar in some way to the person who committed the crime. Rather, the question is asking "Is this person in the courtroom *the one*, the person, who committed the crime?" When it is, CNM gives an affirmative answer to that question as follows: the person in the courtroom is the self up to this time. It is the cumulative network of traits. The integrity of the process maps onto any subsequent cumulative stage. Each cumulative stage embodies the integrity and is the cumulative self as it is up to that time.[17] It includes its past; it is the self who committed the crime. The self who is sitting here in the courtroom today is the summed up self that includes as one of its traits, its past as the self who committed the crime two years ago.

Rather than starting off with the assumption that there are distinct entities, parts or stages where the problem is to explain how they are unified, CNM posits that there is a structural unity, an evolving integrity. Each stage, each network of traits, is cumulative and the leading edge of the process.[18] At any time, the self at a stage sums up or "expresses" the process as it is up to that time; it includes as one of its traits its history (the prior cumulative network of relations). Whether from an observer's or even the self's own contemporary perspective one knows or can learn about every trait and relation that has constituted that self is a separate issue from its cumulative character.

In asking whether the person in the courtroom is "one and the *same*" person "same" should be understood as a matter of rhetorical emphasis, not literally as invoking indiscernibility or similarity. The person, the self in the courtroom is qualitatively different from the self who committed the crime. But, each cumulative stage just is the self as it is up to and at that time. At any time the self, the cumulative network, is identical with itself as it is up to that time. In contrast to four-dimensionalist counterpart theory, there is not a succession of separate parts or many selves. Rather, there is one self of which each stage is the cumulative whole self at that time. The character of the cumulative network of traits is changeable, but at any time it includes its own past and therefore, is the one self at any time.

The assigning of responsibility and many other experiences depend on some notion of personal unity. For example, Beatty (1970) comments, "in seeking forgiveness of the other, the offender is asserting both that he is and is not the man who committed the offense" (251). Griswold (2007) also notes that the experience of forgiveness depends on a recognizable continuity of the self:

> While I will not here venture into the extremely difficult problems of personal identity, I note that the core of the repudiation in question actually depends on a recognizable continuity of self, else the moral work that the wrong-doer must perform in order to earn forgiveness cannot be undertaken (she would simply say the equivalent of: "it wasn't 'me' who did the wrong, I had a schizophrenic episode," which is to offer no grounds for excuse).
>
> (50)

Here what Griswold refers to as "personal identity" is what I call numerical (personal) unity, the self is one process, such that its past is a constituent of, relevant to, who or what the self is in the present.

Similarly, Schechtman argues that a "person life" is the correct target of forensic considerations, is the object about which responsibility judgments could be made.

> What makes someone the right kind of thing to be held responsible for at least some of her past actions and to have prudential concern

for at least some of her future experiences is not simply some attribute that she possesses at the moment (e.g., self-consciousness or rationality), but the fact that past and future events are actively incorporated into present experience. It is the way in which experience is structured over time that generates the deep connections among different moments of a life that make a person a strongly appropriate target of forensic judgments, and so the attribute of being such a target should not be thought of as something that applies from moment to moment, but rather as something that inherently applies over a stretch of time during which the structure of experience generates a diachronically as well as synchronically unified locus.

(Schechtman, 2014, 102)

A person, a self, changes; therefore, relations between itself at different times cannot be identity (indiscernibility); rather, these are unity relations. Conceptualizing the self as a succession of stages (or counterparts) has the unsettling implication that the self is many selves or, in temporal part theory, never wholly present. Conceptualizing the self as a cumulative network of traits captures the nature of the self as changing and plurally constituted. The question about identity over time is about identifying and re-identifying a changing, plurally constituted network. Re-identification is possible because there is numerical unity.

## 4.1. A Cluster of Conditions

In Chapter 2 I introduced the idea that the self as a network should be thought of as a cluster of conditions, some subset of which is sufficient for its preservation qua a and that self. From one stage the cumulative integrity maps onto a successive cumulative phase of the self. If the self is a structurally unified process, do specific traits have to be present so as to preserve that integrity? It is necessary that a self be a living organized body, where the body itself is understood as an organized cumulative network of traits, although that network of traits can still tolerate extensive alteration.[19] Normally, we also think of a self as continuing in virtue of "psychological" traits, that is, communicative, agential, intentional, semantic, judicative capacities; a continuity of social relations and roles; causal and dependence relations; having a particular origin and a particular social, biological, and personal past. But, the cumulative network of traits may be preserved in the face of a wide range of changes (in biological characteristics, in social, legal, cultural, political, and so on roles) and types of growth and development, as well as loss and deprivation (amnesia, dementia, psychological and emotional trauma, replacement of, loss of or severe alteration in physical parts, physical disability, social roles, and so on). Rather than thinking in terms of a particular set of necessary and sufficient conditions, I have suggested thinking in terms of a cluster or family of conditions, some subset of which may be sufficient for preservation of a self, for the numerical unity of the cumulative network. This does entail the discomfiting conclusion that if there is no clear, single necessary condition or set of conditions, then there may be borderline cases when we can't be certain that it is a self or that particular self.[20]

I don't see any way around this discomfiting conclusion. A self changes and can survive considerable, even drastic change. Discussions of whether someone is still a self or a person, still that particular self or person, often focus on things like cognitive disability or loss of cognitive and memory functions, for example, with dementia or amnesia. However, going back to the person in the courtroom example, re-identification of her or him as the person who committed a crime may not require that s/he have conscious awareness or memory of the deed. Psychological continuity is a normal constituent of the cumulative nature of a self, and may be necessary for *mens rea* and fitness to stand trial, but the latter are different matters from what I am calling numerical unity.

On CNM, some changes are enhancements of a self's abilities and functionality. Others, such as comprehensive amnesia and Alzheimer's disease happen to, are diminishments. They are damage to the bodily/psychological (sub-)network of the self. That damage may have profound effects on other, e.g., social, intentional, communicative, (sub-)networks of the self. Yet those sub-networks map onto the compromised or damaged self. Being in a persistent vegetative state, such as in the case of Terri Schiavo,[21] is a constituent of her; comprehensive bodily paralysis of a quadriplegic or of the physicist Stephen Hawking is a constituent of him; severe amnesia of Clive Wearing[22] is a constituent of him. Each (Schiavo, Wearing, and Hawking) is constituted as that self by the cumulative psycho-bodily network and by networks of kinship, social, legal, biological, and so on relations. Just as bodily mobility may not be, so, too, psychological capacity and memory per se may not be necessary conditions for preservation of the cumulative network of traits. The question is whether we should conceptualize one or the other as the self being disabled or as being in a prolonged process of dying.

With cognitive damage, there may be shedding, so to speak, of many constituting social roles, as in the case of Clive Wearing or as in an Alzheimer's patient, but other social roles may still persist.[23] Participation in communicative, social, and meaning relations, may still be possible and ongoing, however rudimentarily, as it is with selves cognitively disabled from birth. Or, as in Alzheimer's, there may be a threshold after which the process is better understood as one of dying. Or, amnesia or dissociation may be so extreme that we are uncertain exactly how to categorize such a self. Exactly how a process of dying is to be distinguished from disability is not my concern here. My point is only that cognitive disability does not necessarily undermine being that self, that cumulative network, however limiting it may be. That does not entail that it doesn't undermine what is valuable. That a self may be profoundly diminished in its communicative, intentional, discriminative, and meaning capabilities is tragic because such limitation challenges much of the transcendent and inventive value of having such capabilities. But, what we find valuable about various abilities may not set the threshold for being a self at all, and for being identifiable as that particular self, now diminished, disabled, or dying, and deserving of respect and care. The latter might include respecting a self's wishes to not continue care or treatment, or in the absence of knowledge of such wishes, determining that discontinuation of care or treatment might be in that self's best interest.

The main point I want to make here is that a *cumulative* network of traits may be preserved in the face of a wide range of types of growth and enhancement, alteration, or loss and deprivation. What matters is that some sufficient subset of traits map onto a successor stage such that the integrity of the process is preserved. While there may be clear cases when a cumulative network has been destroyed, short of death[24] exactly what that subset is may not be prescribable in advance.

### 4.2. Examples

### 4.2.1. Abandonment or Deprivation of Social Roles

In the film *Cast Away* (Zemeckis, 2000), the character Chuck Noland is a FedEx systems analyst who lives in Memphis, but travels a great deal for his job. He is the sole survivor of a plane crash in a violent thunderstorm in the South Pacific. He survives for four years by himself on a remote, uninhabited island, cut off from all contact with any other human being. He sustains himself psychologically and emotionally in part by remembering Kelly, his girlfriend, and thinking of himself as continuing to be constituted by his relationship to her. He is presumed dead by all his former associates, friends, and family. After four years, he finds a means to venture out on the ocean and is rescued by a cargo ship. When he returns to the US, his former companion, Kelly, has married someone else with whom she has a child. The film concludes with Chuck beginning a new direction for his life.

Chuck's life took an abrupt, unexpected, and drastically altering turn. The cumulative network is reshaped and redirected—and he contributes to its reshaping and redirection by how he responds to and copes with his new situation—in a way that it never would have absent the plane accident. While cut off from all previous social roles, he sustains his psychological connection to Kelly (he treasures a pocket watch with her picture in it), and to his professional role (he keeps an unopened rescued package that he intends to deliver when/if he gets off the island). He has no new social roles unless the relationship to "Wilson"—the volleyball on which Chuck draws a face and to which he talks throughout his four years on the island—counts as a social role. (I think an argument could be made that the interaction with "Wilson" functions as proxy for preserving social and communicative roles of some kind.)

What does CNM say about Chuck? Does enough of the integrity of his cumulative network remain intact that he persists as the cumulative self, Chuck Noland? Or, in light of the drastic alteration in the social role constituents of the cumulative network, does he begin a new self? The bodily, psychological, intentional, agential, and semantic-knowledge sub-networks while affected by the new situation, have not been destroyed, and Chuck, even in his diminished state, exercises to the extent that he can, the communicative and judicative capacities characteristic of his cumulative network, even as he also develops new capacities (e.g., becoming an expert at spear fishing). Thus, CNM says that there is a sufficient set of overlapping traits such that the integrity of the network maps onto the subsequent configuration, in spite of the extensive diminishment in social and communicative sub-networks. I earlier suggested that in the case of a quadriplegic or an amnesiac there may be a sufficient subset of traits such that the integrity of the self maps onto the damaged self and the cumulative network is preserved. The same could be said for Chuck. The aspects of the network that are lost are different from those lost by the quadriplegic or the amnesiac. At the same time, it might be argued that Chuck's comprehensive social and communicative diminishment is a kind of disability or potentially—and had he not been found, it would actually have been—a kind of death (socially at first), or the beginning of a process of dying of the cumulative network.

### 4.2.2. Reinventing the Self

The idea that we can reinvent ourselves and become a new self is a persistent and widespread belief.[25] Among other things, such a belief expresses hope in the future. But, what exactly does reinventing the self mean, especially if, as I have been suggesting, we should conceptualize the self as a cumulative network whereby the past is a trait of the self? If we do not shed our past and if we are constituted by social, biological, semantic, interpersonal, and so on, relations, then can a self really reinvent itself? Basically, CNM says, yes, but it's not literally a new cumulative network, but rather one that has made or undergone radical transformation.

One can imagine reinvention or transformation that goes on routinely, when for example, a self undergoes a spiritual or other conversion, or a self completes college, or another gets divorced. Suppose each "starts over," goes off to a new city, acquires new skills and habits, finds new friends, a job, establishes a new life. We can imagine more radical transformations as well. Suppose a self flees home and family, emigrates to a new country and forges a new "identity" for herself. Or, suppose a self undergoes some biological transformation, for example, sex alteration treatment through hormonal and/or surgical means. In these examples, the transformed self is not literally a new cumulative network, but rather a transformation that is consistent with being a self. The resulting self is not a distinct, new "merely successor" self. Rather, the cumulative network (e.g., biological origin and network, kinship and other social relations, memory, intentional, psychological, agential relations, semantic knowledge, subjective self-reference) maps onto and is preserved in the reinvented self as *its* past. This mapping of the previous integrity doesn't undermine all the social, psychological, and other values and purposes of such reinvention; it's just a logical point if the reinvention is *of* a self.

A self who reinvents herself and forges a new identity could go to some lengths to hide aspects of her cumulative network from others. The self who moves to a new city or country may not share aspects of the self's previous life; a self who transitions to a different gender may not wish to share her or his previous sexual or gender identity. Still in either case, while some aspects of a social and/or bodily network are altered, others are not (biological origin, DNA, and so on); psychological, intentional, and agential networks, and semantic knowledge, communicative, agential, and judicative capacities of the cumulative network are preserved. The newly invented self builds on its own past even as it seeks to alter and redirect its future. Even though facts about the self's previous life may be unknown to colleagues or companions in the newly constructed life, they are, at least in principle, accessible as traits of the self, even if we think they shouldn't be probed, exposed, or outed. That a self might conceal aspects of her cumulative network from others, would not by itself entail that they are not constituents of the network. The past is a trait of the cumulative network, even when many aspects of it are not shared by the reinvented self and can only be accessed and recognized by others with great effort.

Preservation of a cumulative network does not mean that it remains qualitatively the same. It means that the integrity of one stage of the cumulative network maps onto the subsequent stage. The point I am making is that even radical transformation preserves and extends the cumulative network that is that self. The self is still one cumulative network, one self, not two different selves. The psychological, physiological, biological, and cultural changes experienced by *a* self who undergoes some radical transformation are often characterized as being a new self. CNM does not deny the radical change and self-identifications that one might experience in such a case. It just says that these are transformations of one self, of one cumulative network, not literally two selves. All these examples are different from the following type of hypothetical example in which the consciousness (the brain) of one self, one cumulative network, is put into the biological body *of another self*, another cumulative network. The latter is a fusion case, that is, going from two selves to one self. As I will argue in Chapter 4, going from two selves to one self does not preserve *the* cumulative network of either previous self, but is literally a new network. However, the transformation in each of the other examples is a *one-to-one* case and thus is still that one self undergoing alteration. Between the fusion case and the other examples, it is not the scope of the alteration that makes the difference, but the going from two-to-one versus one-to-one.

### 4.2.3. Breakdown and "Identity" Substitution

In the previous examples, there is biological, historical, causal, semantic continuity; a subjective first-person perspective is preserved and maintains narrative unity, even when it is difficult for others to discern that narrative unity. Many views of the self would take the preservation of the subjective first-person perspective—a psychological criterion—as decisive to whether the self is preserved or continues. On many such views, Clive Wearing post-amnesia, and the advanced Alzheimer's patient would not preserve or continue Clive Wearing pre-amnesia or the Alzheimer's patient pre-disease. In contrast, as suggested earlier, on CNM a self may be preserved if there is sufficient overlap of strongly relevant traits and mapping of the integrity onto a successive phase of the self. Preservation of a subjective first-person perspective is a strongly relevant feature of a self and normally does overlap successive phases. But, it's not the only such feature and may not be necessary to numerical unity, even though loss of or damage to such a perspective may seriously undermine many things of value to a self. Whether damage should be thought of as producing disability or as initiating a process of dying is a separate question from whether it is that self (cumulative network) to which such misfortune is happening.

But, what is sufficient? What about a case where there is damage to the subjective first-person perspective in the sense of memory and self-identificatory abilities, *and* breakdown of social roles, semantic and intentional relations, complete severance from a prior life and substitution of a new "identity" and life? Suppose someone experienced such severe trauma that she developed dissociative identity disorder and alter-egos? Or, suppose someone were removed from her life, subjected to extreme isolation, sensory deprivation, and/or other forms of torture and psychological manipulation so as to break down the organized psychological self and substitute another "identity"? Fictional examples might include the character, Jason Bourne from the Bourne[26] series, or Raymond Shaw in *The Manchurian Candidate* (Condon, 1959; Frankenheimer, 1962).

In these cases, the living bodily network and biological origin are preserved, and perhaps that is sufficient for preservation of the self. Some semantic knowledge and abilities overlap, but personal self-knowledge, roles, and intentions do not (or do so in fragmented ways). The overlap that does obtain provides some routes of access to the prior integrity (even if not directly or even if only as a possibility for the conscious self). The question is, is that sufficient to say that the self is preserved in the radically altered self or in an alter ego? On the one hand, in virtue of the social severance and isolation the network has been broken down. On the other hand (and unlike Clive Wearing), if the brain network has not been damaged, there may be dormant capacities for recovery of personal memories and the subjective first-person perspective even in the broken down state. This would be a psychologically and functionally damaged self, but there are also overlapping strongly relevant traits (some psychological, biological, historical, even if not psychologically accessible to the self). The breakdown or trauma happens to that self and it is that, now damaged self, that experiences the damage, including fragmentation of self-understanding. Trauma victims, for example, Holocaust survivors and rape and assault survivors, often experience similar kinds of damage and psychological feelings of loss of self.

One might want to argue that Bourne (and maybe Clive Wearing, too) is a borderline case. That might depend on how important one thinks that narrative unity is to being a self at all. CNM would not disagree with a claim that narrative unity is desirable, and indeed signifies one aspect of a well-functioning self. But, it may not be necessary. It seems to me that the transformations are *of* Bourne and Wearing. Each has overlapping strongly relevant traits such that the integrity of the pre-damage phase of the self maps onto the post-damage phase. Such overlap obtains for each with respect to their origin and bodily networks. For Wearing, there is also overlap of socially constitutive traits, such as a relationship (albeit considerably altered) with his wife, and of some capabilities, for example, some musical ability. For Bourne, there is also overlap of a variety of capabilities and some, albeit fragmented, memories. Imagine the account that an ideal biographer would provide of Bourne. Presumably, it would be the account of one self, one cumulative network that took an abrupt and damaging turn becoming psychologically fragmented in ways that selves do not normally experience. As in an account of Clive Wearing, it would be an account of a self that may not have subjective narrative unity, that had been damaged and in many ways severely disabled. It would not, though, be the account of two distinct selves, but of one self, one process with perhaps atypical constituents of its cumulative network.

## 4.2.4. Recap

As these examples are meant to illustrate, and restating the point made earlier: a *cumulative* network of traits may be preserved in the face of a wide range of types of alteration, growth, development, loss, and deprivation. Rather than thinking in terms of a particular set of necessary and sufficient conditions for preservation of a self, CNM represents the self as a network, a cluster of conditions, some subset of which may be sufficient for preserving its unity as that cumulative network of traits (even when and such that it is *that* self that is dying or that has become disabled). This does entail, as I noted earlier, the conclusion that if there is no clear, single necessary condition or set of conditions for being a self, then there may be borderline cases when we can't be certain that it's not a or that particular self.

In the next chapter, Fusion and Fission, I explore how CNM treats some of the well-known thought experiments in the philosophical literature on persons and personal identity, experiments such as brain (or body) transplants, teletransportation, and the like. Before doing so, I would like to comment on the characterization sense of identity mentioned at the beginning of this chapter.

## 5. Characterization

Sometimes the term "identity" is used to identify the self in some particular way such that it has "an identity." "Identity" in this sense refers to some positive content, often in social-political discourse, for example, some specific gender, racial, sexual orientation, ethnic, religious, social, or cultural set of categories, in terms of which someone or some group of people understands and identifies who she is or who they are, or in terms of which they are so understood and identified by others. "An identity" in this sense—whether cultural, gender, racial, or other some other (typically) social category—is a trait, a feature of the integrity of the self. It is a specific location or cluster of relationally constituted traits ("qualities" or "aspects") of the individual or group of individuals who are constituted in those ways. (I will use scare quotes, as in "an identity" or "identities" to signal this usage.)

Many of these "identities" have been discussed in the context of feminist, communitarian, racial, ethnic, sexual orientation, cultural, and identity politics. Such discussions often focus on the issue of how a marginalized self or a self marked as "Other" constructs and maintains its sense of self "identity," that is, its sense of its own character and integrity in the face of social, economic, and political marginalization or systemic failure to recognize and value such a self in its own terms. Sometimes people are characterized as having and as having to negotiate multiple such "identities." Theorists of identity in this sense have been concerned with how gender, race, sexual orientation, ethnicity, class, and so on, may position and identify one as marginal in society.[27] Former US President Barack Obama has been described "as a successful negotiator of identity margins."[28] The implication is often that such complex, multiple "identities" uniquely characterize those who are "marginal" or different from some reigning cultural "identity."

However, on CNM every self is constituted by multiple locations. In some context or at a particular time, some locations or traits are culturally marked—for example, in the 21st century United States, race, or being Muslim. There may be other culturally marked locations that are particularly freighted at a time and in certain contexts, locations such as gender, sexual orientation, or ethnic, religious or socio-political affiliations, and that pose particular challenges in self-formation and development. And some of these, such as gender and sexual orientation, may be marked in a more global and recalcitrant way, for example, the pervasive "objectification" of women by/for male sexual desire. At one time, in the United States being Irish or Italian and Catholic would have been culturally marked locations that one would have had to "negotiate" and that posed great challenges for selves constituted by those "identities." Those particular ones may no longer be so freighted, but that doesn't mean that they don't entail "negotiation" or don't contribute to the overall integrity of a self. Ontologically, selves with freighted locations are no more complex, no more multiply relationally constituted than any other selves.[29] Rather, some of their locations are more salient and fraught in a variety of contexts than other locations that we take or have come to take for granted. That's not to say that such selves don't face enormous personal, social, cultural, and political challenges; it's just to say that complexity and plurality are characteristic of any self.

In many philosophical characterizations of selves the "identities" that originate from or are dependent on social or cultural locations have not been regarded as essential or natural kind features of a human being, and are often regarded as a matter of convention or happenstance.[30] They have not typically been relevant to most conceptualizations of persons in the context of philosophy of mind (whether those conceptualizations are dualistic or physicalistic) where the focus is on issues such as mental causation and more generally the relation between thought and representation, and the world.[31] Feminists, communitarians, and others have objected to the invisibility of such "identities" in philosophical accounts of persons, and have offered compelling descriptions of socially constituted selves. The CNM model of a relational process self developed here attempts to give a more robust conceptualization of a self whereby these otherwise "invisible" aspects or "identities" of the self are no less features (locations, traits) of a self than those features traditionally treated by philosophical analyses.

## 6. Practical Implications of the Cumulative Network Model of the Self

After discussion in Chapter 4 of philosophical thought experiments concerning the identity and continuity of the self, starting in Chapter 5, I will explore some practical implications of CNM. If selves are relationally, plurally constituted, then practical functions of selves must also be so constituted. The capacity for and exercise of reflexivity and autonomy must also be relationally constituted. Traditionally, something like autonomy has been thought to require independence from social influence. And some social self views challenge the importance of autonomy, arguing that it rests on an atomized view of the self.[32] However, there are many social self views that emphasize the importance of independence and understand socialization as relevant to the development of a capacity for autonomy. Moreover, autonomy also seems to involve the possibility that selves can reshape, shed, and reject social roles, take on new ones, and reinvent themselves.

On CNM as I have described it so far it might seem as if the self is just a process happening, so to speak, in the natural world, without the self acting, or having the capacity to contribute to, reflect on and direct or control the process. If CNM can't account for or isn't compatible with some account of practical capabilities, then it would be a flawed model. An account of the self should make sense from both the naturalistic and the intentional stance. Starting in Chapter 5, I will give accounts of some practical capabilities, in particular, of reflexivity and a first-person perspective, and in Chapter 6, of autonomy. The accounts will explore how a relationally constituted self is capable of reflection and autonomy, in virtue of its relational constitution, rather than in spite of it. I will then (Chapter 7) turn to aspects of the notion of responsibility for a relational self.

## Notes

1. Tan (2001, 303).
2. A "question of which beliefs, values, desires, and other psychological features make someone the person she is. . . . [T]he characterization question concerns identity in the sense of what is generally called, following Erikson, an 'identity crisis'" (Schechtman, 1996, 2). I articulate the characterization question more broadly, in terms of relational constituting traits, some of which are psychological, some not.
3. For example, Williams (1973) (see in particular the papers included in 1973: "Are Persons Bodies?," "Bodily Continuity and Personal Identity," "Personal Identity and Individuation," "The Self and the Future"); Gert (1971), Wiggins (1980).
4. For example, Olson (1997).
5. The person as the target of forensic interpretations is central to Schechtman's person life view of the person. Schechtman (2014).
6. Note that the principle of the indiscernibility of identicals is different from a principle of the identity of indiscernibles. The former says that *if* there is one thing identical with itself, it is indiscernible from itself. It doesn't assert that qualitative sameness guarantees numerical identity [meaning just one thing]. The latter would be a slightly different principle, the identity of indiscernibles, about which there is considerable debate. If properties are universals, or if considerations of identity exclude consideration of what are referred to as "impure properties," then it seems extremely unlikely that indiscernibility of such properties guarantees identity (Forrest, 2006). See Max Black's famous example of two exactly similar spheres in empty space (1952).

7. Parfit discusses the Venus/Evening Star example (1986, 212) in the context of a discussion about reductionism about persons. Parfit's point is different from the one I am making, but he, too, describes Venus as *one* object which can be named, described, as having different traits in relation to different perspectives.

8. This is roughly what Lewis calls the common sense view when "in wondering whether you will survive the battle, you wonder whether you—a continuant person consisting of your present stage along with many other stages—will continue beyond the battle" (Lewis, 1983a, 58–59).

9. One might think of Leibniz. Between monads there are imperceptible differences (perceptible to God) such that each is unique, discernible from every other and indiscernible from itself. I do not subscribe to the Leibnizian view that everything is related to everything else (or that there is an omniscient God), for I think that there is irrelevance. But, on CNM the relational complexity of a self implies that not all of those complexities may be available to my or our discriminative capacities.

10. Thus, for example, that someone has the property of being a-professor-of-philosophy-at-age-45 is a property of that person when she was 30 even though *at 30* she was not a professor of philosophy. Similarly, the person at 45 has the property, of say, being a-job-candidate-*at-30*, even though she is not, *at 45*, a job candidate. I do not further discuss the time-indexed properties view. It entails a somewhat weird view of properties and of the self as having at any time, all the (time-indexed) properties it will ever have. According to CNM, that the self's past is a trait of the self is not the same as having a time-indexed *property*. The self's cumulative past is a relevance condition of the self being what it is.

11. See also Anscombe (1984, 111). She argues that since monozygotic twins are not identical to each other, neither can be identified as the zygote.

12. Even if origin plays a role in normal cases, as we will see in Chapter 4, there may be hypothetical, thought experimental cases in which a network might be said to persist even without satisfying a biological origin criterion.

13. The successor self idea is one held by Parfit (1986); Nozick (1981) holds a similar view with his closest continuer notion of the self over time.

14. Counterpart theory plays a role in the logic of a variety of philosophical issues. In possible worlds analyses of modality, the truth condition for an assertion, "something is possible for me," is that there is a counterpart of me in a possible world who is or does that. In such a case, the counterpart relation is defined in terms of that being which is most similar to me in another possible world (Lewis, 1986). In a four-dimensional stage theory of objects, a counterpart is a temporally successive or prior stage that has the right kind of unity, causal and dependency relations to other stages (counterparts) such as to add up to a four-dimensional object, space-time worm, or person-career (see Lewis, 1983; Sider, 2001). Counterpart theory has been used in the analysis of analogy and metaphor. In the metaphor, "Socrates is a midwife," Socrates is a counterpart of midwife—Socrates plays a role in facilitating the articulation of philosophical ideas similar to the role a midwife plays in facilitating the birth of a child. Here, the counterpart relation is defined in terms of similarity and semantic structural function (Steinhart, 2001b). Counterpart theory is also important to a recent analysis of resurrection (Steinhart, 2008).

15. Baker (2000, 2007). The constitution view conceptualizes an object as constituted by different "primary" kinds of objects—e.g., a statue and a lump of clay, or a piece of paper and a dollar bill—united to be one three-dimensional material object. Extending the CNM approach to objects more generally, it would suggest that there are sub-networks of traits that constitute a single

"thing" (complex)—clay statue, paper dollar bill. Sub-networks are no more "primary" kinds of objects than are the complexes of which they are constituents. That sub-networks in one respect can be complexes in their own right (clay, paper) also does not undermine the unity relations that constitute a superordinate complex (clay statue, paper dollar bill).

16. Baxter (1989, 131). Elsewhere, he argues that "we need to accept that there can be numerical identity without qualitative identity" (Baxter, 1999, 49). See also Baxter (2001). Parfit, too, argued that at least on a reductionist view of persons there is a difference between numerical identity and exact similarity, or qualitative identity (Parfit, 1986, 241–242).

17. I have modified Buchler's articulation of this point. Buchler says, "identity is the continuing relation between the contour and any of its integrities" (1990, 22).

18. Armstrong (1980, 77–78) argues for a relational account of identity through time, based on a causal relation of successive phases (or parts, but in any case, distinct non-overlapping particulars) to one another. He also characterizes the result of this relation as "bond[ing] together different phases of the same thing." This seems to me not an identity, but a unity relation.

19. What matters for CNM is that the cumulative structure of the process continues. Normally and in practical terms that means continuity of the living organism. (See Chapter 4 for how CNM treats wholesale bodily replacement in thought experimental scenarios.)

20. Schechtman (2014) comes to the same conclusion regarding her view about when a person life continues (8; and also her Chapter 6).

21. In 1990 Terri Schiavo suffered cardiac arrest, triggered by extreme hypokalemia brought on by an eating disorder. As a result, severe hypoxic-ischemic encephalopathy developed. For months following, she showed no signs of higher cortical function. Computed tomographic scans of her brain showed severe atrophy of her cerebral hemispheres. Her electroencephalograms were flat, which is indicative of no functional activity of the cerebral cortex. She was diagnosed as being in a persistent vegetative state (PVS), which includes periods of wakefulness alternating with sleep, some reflexive responses to light and noise, and some basic gag and swallowing responses but no signs of emotion, willful activity, or cognition (Quill, 2005). She lived in this state for 15 years, while at the same time being at the center of a long, controversial battle between her parents and her spouse, who was her legal guardian, over the removal of her feeding tube. She died on March 31, 2005, 13 days after removal of the tube.

22. Recall from Chapter 1, Clive Wearing suffers from severe anterograde and retrograde amnesia. See Sacks (2007).

23. In a possibly related vein, considering medical decision-making for the cognitively impaired, Nelson (1995) argues that a person's critical interests may be sustained, or may alter, even when the person is not self-consciously aware of those interests, because the self is not merely a self-contained psychological stream, but is bound up with relations to other selves. I don't know if Nelson would subscribe to CNM, but the idea that relations to other selves may be constitutive of the interests of a self appears to resonate with the network model.

24. And fusion and fission, as I will argue in Chapter 4.

25. Thanks to Don Morse for bringing up this issue to me.

26. Jason Bourne was a fictional character originally created in three novels by Robert Ludlum that were published between 1980 and 1990. There was also a film series loosely based on the books, beginning in 2002, in which Bourne is characterized as suffering from severe memory loss.

27. For example, Alcoff (2006, Anzaldua (2001), Crenshaw (1991), Collins (1990), Lugones and Spelman (1999).

28. Francis Nyamnjoh, quoted in the *New York Times*, www.nytimes.com/2008/11/05/us/politics/05global.html?ref=politics

29. An observation on the complexity (diversity) that characterizes everyone's "identity" was made in a comment on a public comment site about Obama: www.cbsnews.com/stories/2008/11/07/60minutes/main4584507_page4.shtml#: "Interesting [on Obama]. But just as a thought. Both sides of my family were German—but [in] my husband's family one side was Italian, the other Russian & Polish. At one time in history your lineage was traced in this way. Americans and perhaps a good portion of the world is diverse. It is that diversity which makes us strong and unites us. I never really thought of race as anything different than lineage. Everyone's family tree may be diverse in many ways." Posted by future121 at 01:54 PM : 11 Nov, 2008.

30. While some arguments regarding a biological basis for such identities may reify them as "natural kinds," many theorists regard race and gender as political and cultural categories that embody and reinforce power relations. There is a wide range of positions taken by theorists about the extent to which gender and gender norms reinforce relations of domination, too many to enumerate here. See also Haslanger (2012) on the social construction of race and gender.

31. There may be some new developments or shifts occurring in how these issues are treated in philosophy of mind. As pointed out by Ismael, there is now a developing literature in philosophy of mind on the relation between individuals as self-organizing systems, which may also have relations—including in some cases, via self-representational loops—with collectives as self-organizing systems (Ismael, 2007; see in particular her Chapter 6 and 226 ff.).

32. For example, Gergen (2009). This is also one of the complaints about liberalism made by communitarians.

# 4   Fusion and Fission

## Thought Experiments, Persons, and Personal Identity

[F]iction makes us imagine a number of events as possible which are
really impossible.

(Descartes)[1]

## 1. Introduction

The philosophical literature on persons and personal identity is rife with
thought experiments, e.g., about teleporting, brain transplantation, spontaneous biological fission and fusion. They consider such questions as
(1) could two "persons" occupy one body? (2) Could one "person" survive
as two "persons"? (3) Could two different "persons" merge into one "person"? (4) Could a "person" survive in another "person's" body?[2] These
questions can be condensed into the following: could a self be preserved
through either fusion with another self or fission into two or more selves?

Analyses of these experiments attempt to gather support for the self
as essentially psychological or essentially bodily (or animal), or, as with
Parfit, they argue for which relations (psychological, bodily) should really
matter to us. Since the experiments are familiar to many philosophers
who work on the nature of persons, an analysis of them may be useful in
drawing out the difference between CNM and these other views. I have
put this discussion in its own chapter because the thought experiments
may be familiar to and of interest to a more specialized audience than the
broader audience of the book. At the same time, I have tried to make the
examples as concrete as possible so that they are accessible to any reader.

A caveat: while thought experiments can be useful, they also have their
limits. If selves are not the kinds of things that split like amoebas, fuse as
in the brain transplant, replicate in teleporters or come into existence like
Swampman, then the inferences that we do make in the context of the
thought experiments may be of limited use in the broader context of theorizing about selves as they generally really are.[3] Moreover, if selves are
constituted as a cluster of contingent conditions, then a thought experiment may not serve to isolate some single necessary condition which
would account for sameness or continuity over time. It is in part because

the features are contingently related that they can be separated in imagination and thought experiments can even get off the ground. But, then that suggests that for concepts of this kind, the thought experiments may be of limited use or "uninformative of the concept's [strict] application conditions" (Gendler, 2002, 35). However, thought experiments may be useful in helping to reframe a perspective or in bringing to light relevant features in non-thought experimental cases that may have been obscured by assumptions that we make when we interpret actual cases in terms of necessary conditions (Gendler, 2007).

Unlike bodily based theories, CNM suggests that it is plausible to think that in some bodily replacement thought experiments the self could survive when replacement is singular (as in the well-functioning teleporter case) and when the body is not already the body of another self (in contrast to fusion cases). Unlike psychologically based theories, CNM suggests that while it is plausible to think that a self continues in singular teleportation, it is not plausible in duplication or in fusion (e.g., brain transplants between selves). According to CNM, fusion or fission disrupts the network of traits that is the self. Fusion disrupts two networks of traits such that each network is dismantled and parts of each are combined to form a new network. Neither prior network, neither prior self, is preserved. In fission the network cannot distribute over two or more fissioned products, typically bodies. Fusion into one product or fission into two destroys the network; in neither is there a result that is a continuant *of* the self.[4] A narrative approach to the self may allow that some narrative structure could be given to fusion or fission selves, but in my view that wouldn't answer the survival question. Rather, it suggests that whatever survives would, qua self, give itself (or be given by others) a story about itself (or themselves if survival is plural).

## 2. Fusion: Brain Transplant of One Self Into the Body of Another Self

Locke's discussion of personal identity has strongly influenced philosophical treatments of personal identity.[5] His prince/cobbler example—in which the soul of a prince enters and informs the body of a cobbler—introduced the idea that what matters about selves is that they are "persons," by which he meant that they have certain psychological characteristics (such as intentions, memories, a first-person perspective). Locke's thought experiment had a practical dimension to it, identifying "person" as a forensic concept, that is, as someone capable of agential and moral responsibility. Locke argued that the prince's consciousness in the cobbler's body would be morally responsible for the deeds of the prince, because the prince's consciousness *is* the "person" the prince.

Philosophers working from the Lockean psychological assumption have devised thought experiments whereby "persons" are imagined to occupy different bodies and social roles, or split or branch into multiple "persons." These thought experiments assume (a) that the criteria for being a self is being conscious and psychologically continuous, (b) that consciousness—neurophysiologically, the brain—can be transplanted and preserve features such as the first-person perspective, memories, dispositions, intentions, desires, beliefs, and personality, and (c) that doing so preserves the "personhood" of the self from whom the brain was taken.[6] Contemporary, physicalist but neo-Lockean reworkings of that thought experiment envision it as a brain transplant, where consciousness is conceptualized as "going with the brain." Recent neurosurgical developments in head transplants suggest that such a transplant may not be a mere thought experiment (Canavero, 2013). But, even as a physical possibility, the problems I will discuss would still obtain.

In contrast to a psychological criterion for personhood, if more Aristotelian commitments were in play such that a person is an organismic whole and bodily or animal continuity were the criterion of personhood, consciousness transfer or brain transplants would suggest three possibilities: (1) the transfer of the brain would be like any other organ transplant, and the person (self) would be whoever's living, functional body is preserved in the transplant (Olson, 1997); (2) if the brain part is the essential body part, then the case would be better described as a body transfer—the brain (person) has acquired a new body; (3) the form of the body has been so altered by this particular kind of transplant, that it is a new animal entity. The second option (2) is more a purely physicalist, rather than animalist criterion, since the animalist criterion typically involves a whole body (an animal), not just the brain.[7]

In contrast to both the psychological and the animalist theories, CNM says that a brain transplant or exchange between selves disrupts the network of relations such that the result can't be either of the preceding selves. The mapping of the network from one stage to the next has been disrupted such that the resultant self cannot be said to be the next stage of either process. Rather the network of traits that was each self was taken apart, traits rearranged and recombined to make a new network and thus a new self. (Cloning would be somewhat different; see Section 2.5.)

Using Shoemaker's brain transplant thought experiment in which the brain of Brown is transplanted into the body of Robinson to create Brownson (1963, 23–24),[8] suppose Brown were the biological parent of Joe (and not of Jane) and the spouse of Jill (and not of Janet). Suppose Robinson were the biological parent of Jane (and not of Joe) and the spouse of Janet (and not of Jill). What traits map onto Brownson (Brown's brain and psychological features, and Robinson's body-minus-brain)? Is "Brownson," the biological parent of Jane or the biological parent of Joe? "Brownson" would, presumably, think of himself as the biological parent of Joe and not of Jane, but qua body of Robinson would be the biological parent of Jane and not of Joe. If either or both could plausibly map on to

Brownson, then the biological parent relation is different for Brownson than it was for Brown or Robinson. Or, suppose the self from whom the body came had been a parent and the self from whom the brain came had not been a parent. Would the resultant self be a parent (and if so, of whom?) or not?

As a matter of convention, these issues might be resolvable. Perhaps a decision could be made about how Brownson should relate to Jane and Joe going forward; perhaps some legal relation similar to adoption could be established. But, after such a transplant, the relational kinship constituents of the resultant self would match neither prior self. The resultant self would be genetic kin of whomever the body (minus the brain) is kin and at the same time would have psychological and intentional kinship relations to an entire other kinship network.[9] Or, if the brain's genetic heritage also counts, then the resultant self would have genetic kinship origin relationships to two otherwise historically disconnected genetic networks.[10] The brain transplant disrupts biological and genetic, as well as social, relations and traits of selves, such that on the CNM approach this looks to be a new network (self).

Somewhat similarly with the spousal relation. Spousal relations can be altered through legal and social means. But qua brain transplant itself, it seems to me indeterminable of whom Brownson is the spouse. Brownson has married neither Jill nor Janet, nor both. The transplant case is different from one in which a spouse undergoes gender identity transformation and surgical modification. In the latter case, a network with its own history undergoes radical change, which may in turn alter spousal relations. But, in the fusion case, the question is whether fusion of parts of two networks preserves either self. CNM says it does not.

Canavero (2013) charmingly notes these issues as corollary considerations to neurosurgical head transplantation (in the discussion of which he treats the head as the recipient of a recently dead donor body):

> After transplant, body image and identity issues will need to be addressed, as the patient gets used to seeing and using the new body. The patient's perception of the allotransplant should continuously be readdressed by the psychiatrists to ensure that positive, but realistic expectations are maintained.
>
> (341)

And referring to Thomas Mann's novella *The Transposed Heads* and the difficulties involved in determining who in the story is the wife's spouse, Canavero goes on to say:

> This short story highlights the ethical dilemma that must be faced: The HEAVEN created "chimera" would carry the mind of the

recipient but, should he or she reproduce, the offspring would carry the genetic inheritance of the donor.

(342)

On CNM, this is not only an ethical dilemma, but a metaphysical issue. Perhaps that recognition lies behind Canavero's use of the term "chimera" for this new self.

However, Shoemaker suggests that one can imagine a society in which none of this would be problematic:

> in this society going in for a body-change. . . . All of the social practices of the society presuppose that the procedure is person-preserving. The brain-state recipient is regarded as owning the property of the brain-state donor, as being married to the donor's spouse, and as holding whatever offices, responsibilities, rights, obligations, etc., the brain-state donor held.
>
> (Shoemaker, 1984b, 109)[11]

But even if the brain-state recipient has a psychological "memory" of being married to the brain-state donor's spouse, that by itself does not seem sufficient to preserve the spousal relations as constitutive of the self. Jill married Brown. She did not marry the fusion of that brain with the body of another self with a completely different set of social, genetic, physical, and dispositional traits and relations.[12] The psychological criterion stipulates that *memories* of and *intentions* about kinship, spousal, and other relations are sufficient for continuation *of the self*, and thus that the kinship relations themselves are not relevant. CNM is skeptical that those psychological traits alone are a sufficient cluster of traits to preserve the *network* that was Brown; rather, that prior network has been destroyed (as has been Robinson's).

Straightforwardly psychologically defined personhood is also disrupted, for it is not clear how the resultant self should identify itself. Suppose the brain-donor self were female, a mother, a daughter and a spouse, and the brain-recipient self were male, a young boy, prepubescent and unmarried. The resultant self is none of those; *it* is neither previous self. In addition to questions about how "unified" a first-person perspective of such a self might be, what is the self on which it is taking a perspective? Can the "I" refer to itself as a mother or not? As Ismael argues, one could use the direction of fit concept: self-identification goes from self to self-conception ("'I'-thoughts"), not the other way around (2007, 191). In the brain transplant case, the configuration (network) that would *normally* confine self-re-identification to an intersubstitutability context (where "I" uses would not be subject to this break up of tracking the referent) has been destroyed. Therefore, the self cannot self-(re-)identify as one or the other of the selves (network of traits) from which the brain and the body in this new configuration comes. "If enough of the architectural background that supports 'I'-use is broken . . . the notion of a temporally extended self will no longer have application" (Ismael, 2007, 185). I take the broken architectural background idea as another way of describing the destruction of the network of traits.

### 2.1. *Fusion in More Detail*

Pressing the direction of fit point, processes of self-identification and re-identification depend on the constitutive network. If the network is disrupted, if the underlying architecture of either of the previous selves has been sufficiently broken apart, then self-identification doesn't reliably track either one of those selves precisely because it is a new self, a new network of traits.

Communicative, agential, self-referential, and intentional relations are disrupted. Suppose, for instance, that the "person" that came with the brain intends to act in some way that depends on habituated bodily skills involving physical and biological relations (e.g., neurological and physiological pathways, muscle sets, and so on) that the new body doesn't have. For example, suppose the "person" of the brain were an athlete, now in the body of a sedentary person. One might argue that (1) the resultant self, now with the intentional structures of the self from which the brain came, could carry out the intentions of the newly implanted brain (consciousness) to become fit and athletic, and (2) this would be no different from a case of the original athlete intending to get him or herself back in shape, say, after recovering from some illness or accident that rendered her unable to work out for some period of time.

Grant the psychological continuity assumption and that (1) is true. However, this is not equivalent to (2). The resultant self was not an athlete. It has memories of having been an athlete *and* no memories of what are now its (the new network's) own past bodily experiences and capabilities of not having been an athlete (experiences of the self from which the new body network came). The transplanted brain/"person" formulates the intention, "I was an athlete and I remember having been an athlete. I am now going to get (back) into shape." The "I" can not be referring to itself as merely a psychological stream or a brain. A psychological stream or a brain is not and was not an athlete, and does not get into shape. The self who is going to get into shape is the resultant self, a different network of traits. In this example, if the "I" "remembers" having been an athlete the "I" of the memory—*I* was an athlete—would have to refer to the self who had been an athlete. But that network of relations, that self, no longer exists and there is no mapping of those relevant (i.e., bodily) traits onto the new body. Therefore, it's not a memory *of* the resultant self (contra Nagel's[13] and Noonan's[14] views).

The brain transplant situation is different from one in which a self is damaged in some way such that it cannot carry out its own prior or current intentions, for example, because it has become disabled, weakened by illness, paralyzed, or because of some other situation due to which the self's capacities have been altered or compromised. The direction of fit point explains why they are different and why the immunity principle does not help with guaranteeing continuity of self. The immunity principle is the idea that one can't be mistaken about the reference of "I"; that one can't make an error about the person to whom "I" refers when using the term "I." (See, for example, Shoemaker, 1984a.[15]) In the brain transplant case the new network would lack the memory and awareness of all those aspects of the new network that came from the self of the body and would have memories of (bodily) experiences that are not experiences of the resultant network. CNM says that even granting psychological continuity with the self from which the brain came, the transferred consciousness is an incomplete consciousness *of* a new network (self). As far as its present subjective experiences are concerned, it could report and self-refer with immunity to its immediate, present experiences, for instance, "I am lying in a hospital bed" or "I am experiencing pain," or "I am upset that I am experiencing pain." These are non-ascriptive, non-identifying conscious experiences, meaning that they don't assume any other identifying characteristics or properties of the self other than the immediate conscious state.[16] But, if the new network were to refer to itself as "I am parent of x or spouse of y" it would not be immune to error in self-identification. The self lying in the bed is a new network, and therefore, the self who makes such "I" identifying utterances is not the "I" of either previous self. Even a self-reference such as "I believe that I am the parent of x or the spouse of y" seems suspect depending on what the "I" means by "I." If the "I" is assuming the content of parent and spouse as who the "I" is self-identifying, then it is not immune from error. If the "I" is simply reporting or reflecting on itself non-ascriptively as the subject of a conscious experience, then it may be immune from error, but in that case it is not ascribing to itself the trait "being the parent of."

Thus, the "I" can be mistaken about its objective self-reference, even if we grant that the "I" can't be mistaken about itself as subject, as the thing having the thought—I am the one thinking this thought, having this belief, experiencing this pain. A purely subjective use guarantees nothing as far as continuity of the self qua network is concerned. On the network model, consciousness and a first-person perspective do not stand alone (or only with the brain), but are capacities or aspects *of* a self. The subjective report of experiencing pain or of believing x is the report *of* a new network that has such capacities. The having of such a capacity does not mean that the self is the self from which the brain came. Rather, the capacity for self-reference in such a fusion case has to be reoriented and reconstituted. Consciousness and the first-person perspective are constituents of and constituted by the network of traits. "I" goes with and refers to the network of which it is a constituent.[17]

On CNM, the brain transplant would be interpreted as follows: a psychological stream expressed in a brain (a psychological/neurological sub-network) is detached from one network of traits and combined with the bodily sub-network of another self. The transplant creates a new network, a new self. The integrity of neither prior self maps onto the new fusion self. The resultant self doesn't take up the past as such of either previous self as its. Yet, at the same time, *aspects* of each previous self's past are now constituents of it, so it seems that the resultant self also can't just arbitrarily ignore aspects of one of those pasts either. Even on the supposition that psychological continuity of some kind is preserved, the structures of self-referential and self-identifying capacities and of the capacity to form agential intentions are disrupted.

## 2.2. *Compatibility, Isomorphism, or Genetic Similarity*

Suppose one added a "compatibility requirement" such that a transplant would be done only where bodies were isomorphic or at least very similar. Suppose a transplant were between monozygotic twins. Parfit (1986) describes a case involving monozygotic triplets (254–255).[18] Triplets are in an accident and the brains of two of them are destroyed. The third triplet's brain is split into two with each half containing the exact full and same content as the original and each half is transferred into the body of one of the other triplets (a double case of both fusion and fission). Assuming that the triplets are very similar in physical condition, knowledge, and experience, there might not be a big difference in some agential capacities between the self from which the brain came and the selves that result from the brain transplant. However, assuming that each triplet had led its own life, "personal" and at least some "semantic" memories and intentions, as well as social, and personal historical memories would still be disrupted, as would the relations themselves (parental, spousal, social). The first-person perspective of the self from which the brain came would also be disrupted. Therefore, the network of the brain-self would not just map onto the resultant networks. Moreover, we should note that monozygotic multiples are not necessarily biologically exactly similar either. Epigenetic mechanisms and environmental influences can result in the expression of different genes, contributing to such phenomena as different sexual orientations of multiples, or of one being schizophrenic and the other(s) not.

A concession to a more broadly defined compatibility requirement would weaken the psychological criterion by admitting that a wider network of relations [minimally, some network of bodily relations] should be in place and integrated with the brain/consciousness network. It might be argued that a compatibility requirement is irrelevant because it's possible that someone could want or be willing to try out the body of a really different self-network. The point is simply that in either case, it's a new, different self.

## 2.3. The Subjective "I"

A proponent of the psychological criterion would argue that the preceding considerations are irrelevant. What matters in a brain transplant is the preservation of the subjective "I" and that can remain intact on transfer of the psychological stream. Therefore, the resultant self, at least qua subjective "I," is the one from which the brain came. Even if the resultant self is a new *self*, that is irrelevant, because what matters is that the "person," meaning psychological stream, is preserved. (This argument reflects the opposite interpretation of the direction of fit point made earlier.) CNM rejects the view that "person" is to be *identified* with consciousness and that the subjective "I" is impervious to its location. Rather, a psychological stream would be a constituent of a self, of a network of relations, not alone the self. In a brain transplant, a psychological stream would be a constituent of a different network of relations. On the network model, the subjective self is always the "I" *of* something (a network), integrated with, expressive of, and referentially identified with the network. Therefore, it could not simply remain the "person" or "subjective self" of the self from which the brain came.

One of the features of first-person perspective consciousness is the reflexive ability of perspectival self-detachment, and perhaps it is theoretically easy to generalize from that detaching capacity to the idea that consciousness is simply detachable altogether from a particular self. I can see the appeal of projective imagination, of imagining "oneself" in another body, suspending consideration of all other constituents of the self, and imagining it as me "in" and experiencing the world in that body.[19] But, what we can conceive or imagine by tacitly (or explicitly) suspending traits does not necessarily correspond with what is possible for the thing itself.

The attraction of the idea that the thought experiment somehow still preserves me as a "person" or subjective "I" seems to rest on an implicit assumption about the body as being a kind of container of consciousness (or of the brain); that the body is just a matter of geography.[20] Therefore, putting consciousness or the brain in a new container (body) with different properties than the first container is thought of as no different from the first container being altered or damaged (or enhanced for that matter) in some way. The "person" as such would be preserved through such alterations or alternative locations.

According to CNM the body is a constituent of the network of traits that is the self. In the brain transplant experiment, a previously existing body (a bodily network) is a constituent of a network of relations that is one self, just as consciousness (a psychological network) is a constituent of a network of relations that is another self. As constituents of a network, the relations of the network are also constitutive of them in some respects. The brain transplant experiment destroys the integrity of each of those networks of relations. Sub-networks of each network have been extracted and combined so as to form a new self. Those extracted sub-networks (body; brain) don't just suddenly lose all the traits they had, but carry with them *their* pasts as constituents of prior selves, even while they may also lose some relations by being severed from their original network. One might argue that the prior history of the body (albeit not the brain) is irrelevant to the new fused self, but that doesn't seem plausible in light of the architecture of the new network. The resultant combination is a new network of traits, albeit one that has continuity, causal and similarity relations to two *other* selves. That there may be such relations does not establish that one (or the other or both) of the prior selves continues. Neither prior cumulative network maps onto the resultant network. The new self would be causally related to two previous but no longer existing selves, but it would not be equivalent to, or preserve, either one.

### 2.4. Fusion or Body Swapping

It is conceivable that body swapping may not be fusion of *selves* such that the resulting product is neither original self (nor is it fission; see fission discussion in Section 3). Consider the following fictional example from the film *Avatar* (Cameron, 2009). The character Jake Sully, an ex-Marine who is a paraplegic, is remotely hooked up to a genetically engineered hybrid avatar that is both human and "Na'vi," the native species of the planet on which the story takes place. Jake, the human operator of the avatar-body, is genetically matched (whatever exactly that would mean) to the avatar-body, which is dormant until Jake activates it through the remote hookup. The avatar-body returns to dormancy when Jake's hookup is cut off and has no activity, functionality, or conscious life apart from Jake's operation of it. When Jake is operating the avatar-body, Jake's human body is biologically alive, but dormant. The film represents the situation as one in which it is initially Jake experiencing, socially and physically, the Na'vi world through the Na'vi avatar-body. As the story unfolds and Jake identifies more and more with the Na'vi avatar-body and world (a world in which biological humans cannot breathe), psychological and social boundaries between Jake qua human and Jake qua avatar operator begin to blur. At the end of the film, Jake's consciousness is permanently transferred to the avatar-body and the Jake human body dies. (The causal explanation of such a transfer is left unexplained.) We should note that many normal conditions of selfhood have been suspended, and interesting questions about what exactly Jake/avatar is capable of are left unanswered (for example, as a genetic hybrid of human and Na'vi, can avatar reproduce?) But, setting that aside and going along with the fictional thought experiment, what would CNM say about this?

On this description of the case, it seems different from the brain transplant case, because it is not a merging of features of two distinct self networks. Remember, by hypothesis, the avatar-body has no life, no functionality, no agency, no social relations, no past or ongoing life as a self apart from Jake's animation. Thus, in contrast to the previous fusion cases there is not a functional self without Jake's animation of the avatar body. The story is told as if there is one life being lived, and that life develops in an unusual way as Jake/avatar. One way of conceptualizing this situation might be to say that Jake has expanded his network by living a dual life, as Jake/avatar. Perhaps the self-network in such a case might be something like that of a self that "lives two lives," such as the bigamist with two "identities" who shuttles between two families and lives, where each identity is unknown to the other family. With the bigamist there is one body, though, so there are no body-swapping puzzles.

Or, perhaps the situation is something like what might happen in a variation of the teletransportation thought experiment. Suppose Jake is able to travel through teletransportation, such that there are two bodies, Jake B-1 and Jake B-2, each of which is activated when a Jake consciousness hookup is made and neither of which is destroyed but each of which is dormant when the other is active. Suppose one of the bodies were destroyed and teletransportation were no longer possible. This would entail that "travel" would no longer be possible via teleporting. On the teleporting with two bodies analogy, Jake would be "traveling" between two locations by consciousness transfer between two bodies. Then with a permanent transfer of consciousness to the avatar body and death of the human body, such "travel" would no longer be possible and Jake would be confined to one location, the Na'vi avatar-body location.

On the living two lives analogy, the Jake self-network is initially expanded (something like the bigamist's self-network would have expanded to include a second family and life) to become Jake/avatar. When consciousness is permanently transferred to Jake/avatar, there is a contraction of the self-network (permanent loss of the human Jake relations going forward, although they would still be constitutive of Jake/avatar's past) and Jake/avatar would continue by living one of the lives that he had previously been alternating between. The alternating life would still be a constituent of the Jake/avatar's past, just as the past alternating life of someone who lives two lives is a constituent of the self who, for whatever reason, abandons or loses one of those lives. Similarly, when Jake/avatar's consciousness is permanently transferred to the avatar-body and the human body dies, the Jake/avatar network has lost a part of its network, the human part, but the network continues now in a contracted sense. Jake/avatar continues by living one of the lives that he had previously been alternating between.

The tracking of the "I" appears to be consistently maintained and there is a coherent architecture underpinning that "I" (even though the coherence is fictional, not a coherence that is possible for actual selves as they generally really are). Of course, in so far as the avatar example involves two (dissimilar) bodies, it is also not like living two lives, and it may be a stretch to think of it as one self, expanding and contracting in such an unusual way. If such transfer of consciousness could go on indefinitely from one body or species to another, we'd be so far from what selves generally are, that I don't think we could reliably say that there is anything like a self involved at all. It would be a very different kind of thing. The Jake/avatar example as narratively presented, also presents Jake as an unusually disconnected self—no known family relations (except for a twin brother who has died) and a past life as a soldier who was seriously injured. Thus, some of the plausibility of the story depends on Jake having a socially unfilled (and disabled) network such that animating and then ultimately transferring consciousness exclusively to the avatar seems like an expansion and freeing development for Jake. The story also implies that the single transfer to the genetically matched hybrid is stable (in other words, we don't anticipate further transfer of consciousness such that there are indefinitely many branching selves).

Avatar-body is presented as having the capacities and functions *of selves* such that the animation by Jake and then the transfer of consciousness seem plausible. It seems to exhibit both distinctive functions of selves, communicative, judicative, purposive, semantic, moral, some biological (recall there is supposed to have been genetic "matching"), agential and so on, and to preserve Jake's perspective. It doesn't seem plausible to say that a self could be preserved in an insect, for example, since there is no underlying architecture to support anything of what we mean by selves. Science fiction is replete with stories about non-human "things" functioning as if they were selves, things such as insects, aliens, brains, computer operating systems ("Hal" in the film *2001: A Space Odyssey* and "Samantha" in the film *Her*). These involve extensive (often tacit) suspension of traits for the sake of narrative plausibility. For example, with "Hal" and "Samantha" psychological traits are represented as instantiated in computational systems. In contrast to "Hal" and "Samantha," while the avatar-body is physically different from Jake, the story presents it with the underlying architecture of a self. I grant that that assumption could be questioned. And, I admit that I am not completely confident about what to say about the Jake/avatar example. But, it does seem different from the brain transplant example, as it does not seem to be the fusion of two selves. But, if the avatar-body did have an ongoing active life among the Na'vi apart from Jake's remote operation of him such that avatar would be a distinct self-network, then it would be more like the brain transplant fusion example.

## 2.5. Cloning and Body Swapping

Schechtman imagines a scenario sometime in the future in which cloning techniques develop to the point that it is possible to clone entire organ systems and eventually a whole body minus cerebrum such that a "full body transplant" is possible. A cerebrum from a diseased body can be placed into the cloned body that lacks a cerebrum and the diseased body immediately dies. After recovery from the "transplant," the person (cerebrum plus cloned body) resumes the life of the person from whom the cerebrum came (Schechtman, 2014, 151–152).[21] Schechtman says that according to her person life view (PLV) of persons the original person would continue as that original person in the cerebrum transplant. While the cerebrum may provide some biological continuity, the otherwise biological discontinuity (as in the teletransportation example discussed previously, and again in Section 3.2) by itself does not, or at least under these circumstances does not, disrupt or end the person life. Person-related concerns and practices would continue through the transfer (Schechtman, 2014, 154).

CNM would agree that in this example, the clone with the cerebrum transplant would continue the self-network because there is a single network and a one-to-one mapping of the traits of the self between the original and the clone. The clone, alone, qua organism, is not itself a self, a network; it has no history, traits, relations to disrupt. Thus, this example differs from the previous brain transplant fusion examples that involved swapping bodies *of already constituted selves (cumulative networks)*, and where, according to CNM the resulting self is neither of the original selves, but a new self.

While the cloning described in this example, as well as the breeding of the hybrid human/Na'vi avatar-body, are not really how biology works, the example is illustrative of the point that for CNM what matters is that the network continues. Fusion *of selves* does not do that, whereas it is conceivable that under the right circumstances cloning of a body could continue a network.

Schechtman introduces a variant of the case that leads to consideration of fission cases. Suppose the biological organism from which the cerebrum comes survives or is kept alive in a vegetative state. Earlier in her book, Schechtman argued that according to PLV a PVS person is a person. Therefore, it would seem that now there are two persons, both being in some sense the original person. But, this is not coherent and she suggests that our practices would evolve when there are two (Schechtman, 2014, 155).

Schechtman then appeals to the property cluster view, which says that some properties, but not always the same properties are sufficient for a person to continue. She argues that the PVS person has lost so many of the properties that constitute a person that such a person is on the margin, and that whether we regard them as still a person is variable and subject to interpretation depending on a variety of circumstances (156–157). Thus, there is a conventionalist element in PLV that shows up in unusual and a-typical cases, that would not appear in paradigmatic cases.

CNM agrees that context can affect what is determinative, consistent with the cluster approach to traits. CNM says that survival of two selves disrupts the network, just as much as fusion of two into one does. The traits of the network have a one-to-one mapping onto the phases of the network. Therefore, if there are two, neither is *the* network. Schechtman's option for resolving what to do about two surviving is to appeal to the greater capabilities of the cerebrated clone for realizing the full range of personhood functionality. While that may be an attractive and defensible option, my only point is that when there are two bodies that could equally be candidate constituents of the self-network, identification of one or the other as *the* self is unstable, precisely because fission disrupts the network. One solution to restore stability is to eliminate one of the bodies as in the scenario presented by Schechtman. I now turn to a more detailed discussion of fission cases.

## 3. Fission, Teleporting, and Swampman

Now I would like to consider thought experiments involving fission, or branching selves. Instead of, as in the brain transplant, going from two (or parts of two) to one, the issue is, can one self continue as two and in some sense preserve the previous self. CNM says that it cannot.

### 3.1. *Spontaneous Biological Fission*

Suppose that spontaneous biological fission were possible (something like when an amoeba splits into two) such that a fully formed and functioning self with an agential and social history splits. (Williams [1973, 23] imagines such a case.) But, what splits? Whatever biological and causal continuity there would be, what would have split is a body or biological organism. For it to be fission *of a self*, there would have to be splitting and replication of the network. But, for the network to split and replicate, all the relations constitutive of the network would have to replicate, not just the body. But, that would mean that an entire world relevant to, that is, constitutive of the network would have to replicate.

If the network doesn't replicate, but just the body, then we have two biological organisms. Two biological organisms cannot both be the prior self. They cannot both be the first-born child of x, cannot both be the spouse of y, cannot both be the author of a single-authored book z, cannot both be *the* professor of philosophy, or *the* novelist, and so on. They are two new selves. Even if both could carry on philosophical thinking and novel writing, both can't continue and function as *the* spouse, *the* professor or *the* novelist that the previous self had been. The subjective "I" of each would also be disrupted. Each would self-consciously identify itself as "I" am professor of philosophy at university u, first-born child of x, spouse of y, author of novel z, owner of property w, and so on. But, such self-identifications cannot both be right. Such self-identifications refer to one network, map onto one self, not two. One might argue that the fissioned selves could split a job and divvy up tasks, or could write different parts of a book and divvy up the royalties, but that's just to say that the network has been destroyed and roles that the prior network performed assigned to two new selves. Agential and intentional relations are disrupted as well—suppose the previous self intended to divorce a spouse. Which fissioned self would be the self seeking a divorce? Or, would both selves be seeking divorce? Would that make the spouse whom they are divorcing a bigamist? Suppose the previous self had committed a crime— which of the selves should be tried and punished? Or, should both? Neither? Whatever the solutions to these problems, the point is that fission disrupts the network, whatever continuity each fissioned product may have with it, and whatever we end up wanting to say about responsibility.[22] This is a mirror image of the fusion case. Just as a self (the network of traits) is not preserved in a many to one transformation (fusion), so, too, it is not preserved in a one to many transformation (fission). The self as such would not continue but rather there would be two, new selves. And, if selves could begin in such a way—if selves were fissionable creatures like amoebas—they would be a very different kind of thing from what we currently know selves to be.

Fission of selves is different from *in utero* twinning, fission of a blastocyst which results in two organisms that develop into two selves. Incomplete *in utero* fission that results in conjoined twins raises interesting challenges for any theory of the self. Is a set of conjoined twins one self or two? If there is successful surgical separation, has one self become two, or were there two selves to begin with? I'm not sure that any theory can give a definitive general answer; one would have to know the particulars of the case as there are many possible types of conjoined twins. While conjoined twins do actually occur—conjoined twinning is not just a thought experiment—the phenomenon is very rare. If the theory cannot give a clear answer that may just mean that there are borderline cases where membership in the category is ambiguous.[23] What can be said though is that according to CNM *if* there were *one* self when conjoined and two selves upon successful separation, then neither resulting self would be a continuation *of* the prior one self. Each would be a new self, albeit with causal, psychological, and informational continuity relations to the prior one self.

## 3.2. *Teleporter*

Another type of branching case involves the teleporter thought experiment. First, replication without branching. A self enters a teleporter, all information about it is "copied," the physical stuff, the particles, constituting the biological, physical being are destroyed and an exact, particle for particle, replica is produced in the target location. Parfit (1986), taking psychological continuity, or what he calls relation-R, as the feature "that matters," argues that when the teleporter is functioning properly and only one exactly similar physical thing emerges, it is a (psychological) continuant of the "person" that entered the teleporter.

But, now branching. If the teleporter malfunctions and produces two bodies, Parfit argues both are continuants of the "person." Parfit takes the teleporter case to show that what matters is not personal identity, but a succession of psychological states continuous with one another. Personal survival—survival of my consciousness in another body that continues my life, or rather, some life continuous with mine is good enough. Survival need not be singular or unique; continuing in multiple lives is just as good as continuing in one.[24] In contrast to Parfit and others who identify persons in psychological terms, someone who thinks that bodily or physical continuity is necessary to personal survival would regard teleportation as death of the self who entered the teleporter, whatever else might be said about the teleporter emergent(s).

However, according to CNM the story is a bit different. If it is plausible to suppose, as many people do when first confronted with the teleporter example, that the self is preserved when there is only one exactly isomorphic body that emerges from the teleporter, it is because there could be a one-to-one mapping of the constituents of the network that entered the teleporter onto what emerges. Even though there would be all new molecules constituting the bodily component of the network, the entire network would function exactly as if there had been no new stuff. While all the physical stuff was destroyed, going along with the terms of the experiment, the process self of physical and psycho-biological functioning, agency, intentionality, responsibility, communication, and social connection that entered the teleporter could be ongoing. (This is different from fusion because all the physical stuff is "new," not an already constituted bodily and social network of another self.)

But, what if two bodies were to emerge? Suppose a variant of the one-to-many case (similar to one that Parfit considers). A copy is made and an exactly physically isomorphic being emerges in the target location, but the molecules constituting the bodily network of the self that entered the teleporter are not destroyed, and the original bodily network re-emerges in the starting location.

CNM says that duplication *of a self* would have to involve duplication of the network, not just of the body. A one-to-many body transformation cannot preserve the network of relations that had been the self.[25] Either one body is the continuant *of the self* or two new selves (two new networks) begin, albeit each with psychological (causal, and informational) continuity to a previous, but now no longer existing, network of traits. Like with spontaneous biological fission, if selves could begin in such a way, they would be a very different kind of self from what we currently know selves to be.

In the biological fission case, we said it would be arbitrary to designate one or the other fissioned product as the self, as the body onto which the network maps. In the teleporter case, is there some basis on which one emergent would be the clear continuant of the self and the other not? Many people have a strong intuition that the self that entered the teleporter is preserved in the one that emerges in the starting location (assuming no prior teleportation and that it is "the original"). The duplicate is another clone-like self, a similar organism and psychological self, but still a copy and not the continuant of the self. A preference for "a bodily original" may invoke a bodily continuity criterion and perhaps Aristotelian ideas about the animal self and perhaps three-dimensionalist, endurantist assumptions about the persistence of the body. Or, there may be operating something like Nozick's (1981) closest continuer intuition whereby "natural" causal continuity trumps non-natural causal continuity for differentiating the two.

But, could one verify that the original stuff had not been destroyed and is what emerges in the starting location? Imagine that the teleporter is not teleporting to Mars (as in Parfit's example), but locally enough so that swapping of particles is plausible. If two emerge, what would guarantee that there hadn't been some kind of swap of stuff? Perhaps controls and tracking could be set up. But, if the teleporter has malfunctioned, presumably there is a range of possibilities for what could have gone wrong. Suppose, though, that we grant that original stuff has not been destroyed or swapped and that what emerges in the starting location is the original stuff. Should that make a difference? One might argue that since molecular stuff is replaced all the time in the non-fictional, natural case (albeit usually more gradually), wholesale replacement makes no difference. Indeed, this is the assumption of the experiment, and why the singular teleporter emergent is even remotely plausible.

In Chapter 3 (Section 4.1) I suggested that rather than thinking in terms of a particular set of necessary and sufficient conditions, we should think in terms of a cluster or family of conditions, some subset of which may be sufficient for preservation of a self, for preservation of the cumulative network. Thus, while it is necessary that a self be a living, embodied organism, maybe it doesn't have to be the same physical stuff. Hence, the plausibility of the self (the network) being preserved in, or mapping onto, the singular teleporter emergent. However, when there are two emergents, maybe a criterion (natural, biological, bodily continuity) that didn't matter in the singular case matters in this case as a way of differentiating between two otherwise qualitatively similar bodily emergents, such that one is a continuation of the self (the network maps onto or continues with it) and the other is a new self. An argument might be made that natural, biological or bodily continuity matters in this case on the grounds that it better preserves or preserves more of the network of relations. (This would be an animalist or physicalist intuition.) But, another argument could be made for the contrary position, that the intentional aspects of the self are determinative. For example, by entering the teleporter, the self was intending to, was committed to mapping onto the teleported self, and therefore, the teleported body is the one onto which the network maps and is the continuant of the self (a psychological intuition). Some have argued that it could go either way.[26] These are unstable arguments because in either case duplication disrupts the cumulative network of traits.

Suppose another variant of the malfunctioning teleporter, this time that the teleporter damages the bodily network that entered it, makes no copy and something emerges from the teleporter in the starting location. In this case, there is no one-to-many problem. We are left with a garden variety question, how much and what kind of damage can a self survive? Total amnesia? Loss of bodily constituents? Damage to bodily constituents? If a collection of physical particles emerged in no recognizable configuration, the network of relations that is the self is not preserved. If all that emerged were a finger, the network of relations that is the self is not preserved. If a quadriplegic emerged with all other constituents of the network intact, the network of relations that is the self is preserved, albeit tragically altered. If a brain-damaged being emerged with a dramatically altered personality, and damaged personal and semantic memory, but with all other constituents of the network intact, this would be like the quadriplegic case. I had argued earlier that while psychological characteristics, personality, and so on are important, the network of traits that is a self can survive gross alterations in these features. Therefore, with one emergent, albeit profoundly damaged, it *may* be a continuant of the cumulative network, depending on how much of the network is still intact and the scope of the damage.

There are other possible variations on the thought experiment, for example, suppose the teleporter destroys the original and produces two damaged copies. On CNM, while there could be two (or more) similar organisms, or similar psychologically continuous beings, both cannot preserve, or be the continuant *of* the prior cumulative network. Either there is some differentiating characteristic that is sufficient for identifying one as the continuant of the network or neither is. Whether *other* mishaps with the teleporter destroy the self depends on the kind of mishap, what results from it and whether the integrity of the cumulative network is preserved. The network is not preserved if all that is preserved is a finger or someone else's memory of a self. It is also not preserved by psychological continuity alone. It is destroyed by duplication, meaning simultaneous existence and competition for the locations constitutive of the self and where there is no constitutive feature that distinguishes one from the other.

It is plausible to think that it is a continuant *of* the self that "emerges" from the teleporter when only one "body copy" emerges because the single, isomorphic physical product of the teleporter does not seem to disrupt the cumulative network of relations. In so far as the relations that constitute the self are not disrupted, the network of traits continues.

If the teleporter case is plausible as a mode of travel for the self that no more disrupts the self than does anesthesia, sleep, or momentary stopping of the heart, it's because the cumulative network of relations as a locus of physical and biological functioning, agency and responsibility, of communication and social connection goes on apparently undisrupted. The integrity of the network can survive loss and alteration, but cannot be preserved in or map onto two bodies. For duplication to be consistent with continuation of a self, the entire network would have to be replicated. But, that would mean replication of the entire world relevant to the constitution of the self. But, then we are talking about multiple wholly distinct worlds, not replication in this world. World replication is different from the supposition of the teleporter thought experiment.

### 3.3. Swampman

I want to consider one other fictional case, the Swampman thought experiment. In this thought experiment devised originally, and for different purposes, by Donald Davidson (1987), Davidson's body is destroyed by a lightning strike and simultaneously an exact physical replica of Davidson's body, Swampman, is made out of other particles. The Swampman and the teleporter thought experiments differ in that there is informational or structural and ("non-natural") causal relations between the self that enters the teleporter and the body that emerges from the teleporter. In the Swampman case, there is formal exact similarity, but no informational transfer or causal relation between Davidson body and Swampman body. Swampman body is a "stupendous accident."

Davidson had argued that even though Swampman is exactly isomorphic to Davidson at the moment Davidson was incinerated by the lightening, Swampman would not have any semantic understanding of his own psychological states because Swampman would lack Davidson's experience, the causal history involved in acquisition of semantic understanding. But, this would be true of the teleporter duplicate as well. I'm going to bracket this aspect of Davidson's experiment, and assume that Swampman body, like the teleporter self replica, has exactly the same psychological states as the original, and therefore, does have the same semantic understanding. If neither the teleporter nor Swampman body had such understanding, because neither came into being and acquired its understanding in the right sort of way, then in neither case would a self have been constituted.

The teleporter thought experiment loosens normal causal and physical connections by supposing that artificial, human intentional causal relations could be substituted for "natural" self-organizing relations. With the Swampman thought experiment, the question is whether the absence of all causal connections and sudden, accidental but allegedly "natural" self-organizing principles that are normally causally unconnected to the constitution of a biological organism, could constitute a continuant of the self. Many think that causal connection is necessary, although some do not.[27] Whether, nonfictionally, it makes sense to loosen the causal connections such as to alter the way in which nature operates is another issue. But, if the teleporter example plausibly preserves the self, at least in the singular case, then so could Swampman. Even though Swampman body lacks causal and informational relations with the original Davidson, there could be a one-to-one mapping of the network of relations that was Davidson onto the Swampman body. While causal relations and *presumed* understanding about how teleporting works contribute to the plausibility of the teleporter case, perhaps the opposite is true in the Swampman case. Everyone's ignorance (including Swampman's) of what occurred may be one of the conditions contributing to the non-disruption, and hence, preservation, of the network. Swampman would fulfill all the roles and functions, have all the somatic, agential, communicative, intentional, and semantic states and all the social relations that constituted the network, Davidson.

But, suppose such a "stupendous accident" occurs, and it does *not* destroy Davidson, but momentarily causes him to be completely unconscious *and* produces Swampman-body, who is formally, exactly isomorphic to Davidson-body. They both "come to" at the same instant. Davidson and Swampman would believe, think, feel, act, be dispositionally exactly the same, and neither of them could discern who was Davidson and who was Swampman.[28] No one else witnesses the event or can discern any difference between the two. There are two alternatives: (1) Swampman-body is a clone, an organism similar to but not Davidson-body and that doesn't take up the network of traits that is Davidson; the Davidson-body remains a constituent of the network, Davidson; or (2) if there are two, then neither preserves Davidson since the network cannot distribute over two bodies.

The latter, (2), is strongly counterintuitive. First, Davidson is a self as selves generally really are. Secondly, as with the teleporter case, there are probably closest continuer and Aristotelian intuitions about bodily and biological continuity[29] and we are strongly disposed to think that the biologically continuous organism is the one that preserves Davidson, even if one can't tell which one that is. On CNM, for that intuition to have force and for (2) to be rejected, the argument would have to be that natural, biological continuity better preserves or preserves more of the network than Swampman does. Davidson would preserve natural, causal continuity and all historical, informational, and formal relations, whereas Swampman would only have formal relations. Following this thought, if there were two, then Davidson would be Davidson (that process and network continues in its expected mapping from one stage to the next) and Swampman would be some new being. If there were some way to tell the difference between Davidson-body and Swampman-body—or, if someone did witness this stupendous accident and immediately placed indelible distinguishing marks on each of them—Davidson would be Davidson and Swampman another self. (Swampman would be very confused, since he would believe he was, and think, act, and feel exactly as Davidson, and probably very much in need of extensive therapy!)

However, as with the teleporter case, the analysis is somewhat unstable. In the singular case, Swampman could plausibly be the continuant of Davidson, because all the historical, informational, and formal relations of Davidson could map onto Swampman-body and thus Swampman would preserve the network, Davidson. On CNM, at any time the cumulative network includes its past as one of its traits; Swampman could be the body of that same set of traits, including the past of Davidson. But, the structure of the network and its past is not a double body structure. If there were two bodies *and* there were no discernible difference between them, *and* they could not discern any difference between themselves, then it looks like CNM would say that the network of relations that is Davidson would be disrupted and neither body can be the body continuant of the network Davidson.

One might admit that neither would be able to function as the locus of agency and responsibility or to live Davidson's life if they were both competing for it and on every discernible count (including each one's own self-awareness) were apparently equally eligible for it, but still think that underneath, Davidson-body is really the self, Davidson, and Swampman-body isn't. The duplicate body is just a duplicate body and the network self continues as itself. Ontologically, this would be analogous to the chess configurations from Chapter 2, 28a-Cn-Gn and 28a-p, existing simultaneously on two side-by side chessboards. One might argue that in chess when there are two simultaneous exactly formally similar configurations it wouldn't matter which arrangement functioned as 28a-Cn-Gn and were the board on which the game continued, and which functioned as 28a-p. The formal configurations are, for all practical purposes, interchangeable. But, for selves it would matter, because it bears on the practical issue of who gets to live a particular life. In the context of the thought experiment and if Swampman were truly formally isomorphic to Davidson, there seems to be no good practical solution. On the one hand, Davidson-body ought to continue Davidson. On the other hand, Swampman-body has, by hypothesis, exactly the same mental, physical, etc. states, the same thoughts, intentions, hopes, wishes, and desires as Davidson body and would feel, think, act *exactly* as Davidson. On CNM, duplication of the kind imagined would disrupt the network, the self.

Neither CNM's, nor any other resolution is stable. For, in supposing that selves could be produced in such a way, the thought experiment disrupts the framework within which the concept of a self is meaningful while at the same time appeals to our intuitions about selves as they generally really are to attempt to resolve the status of Swampman. If, *contra* the supposition of the experiment, bodily continuity were a necessary condition for being and continuing as *that* self, for preserving the network of traits that is the self (albeit not sufficient), then we should reject the supposition of this and the teleporter experiment as telling us anything useful about selves.

### 3.4. Bodily Continuity and the Cumulative Nature of the Self

The preceding discussion of the teleporter and Swampman thought experiments made the point that body duplication disrupts the network of relations such that there is no stable basis on which to resolve the issue of whether or in whom a self is preserved. I also suggested that when there is a single emergent teleporter body, or only Swampman and no Davidson, a case could be made for saying that the network of relations constitutive of the original self is preserved. An objection to that interpretation would be that it ignores one of the main theses of the theory, namely, that the self is a process. In the teleporter and Swampman cases, the single exactly isomorphic body that emerges from the well-functioning teleporter or that constitutes Swampman is isomorphic only to the immediately preceding body that entered the teleporter or that was Davidson just at the time of the lightning strike. Therefore, the teleporter-made body or Swampman-body is not *really* the *cumulative* process self. For that "natural" causal, biological or bodily continuity of some kind would be required.

But, in the spirit of the thought experiment, consider again, the admittedly limited analogy with chess: suppose, in the middle of a chess game, all the pieces and the board were replaced with exactly physically isomorphic pieces and board, with the pieces located in exact corresponding squares, with exactly the same orientation and placement within a square as the pieces that had been replaced. 28a-p replaces 28a-Cn-Gn. The game—the game as that cumulative process that was being played—could be preserved in the state that it had been and continue as that game. The new physical stuff in the right configuration takes up the past of the configuration up to that point and continues the game, all other things being equal. While the physical stuff (pieces, board) need not be physically continuous, the newly made configuration takes up the past of *that* game such as to be a continuation of *it* because there are other relational constituents of the game (memory, intentions, and strategies of the players, a record of the previous moves, chess relations between the pieces) that sustain the integrity of the game. Therefore, replacement of the physical materials need not disrupt the integrity of the cumulative network of relations that is the game. On this interpretation, the cumulative network of traits can be sustained by other factors besides the exact physical constituents, even if there must be some physical constituents of the network.[30] Similarly with Swampman. In addition to the formal isomorphism of bodies, there are other constituents and relations—social roles and relations, other people's intentions and behaviors—that preserve the network.

Now one might want, at this point, to abandon the thought experimental game altogether, or minimally to argue that a self, unlike the chess game, is not the kind of complex that allows for wholesale bodily replacement. A chess game is a reinstantiable type, whereas a self is not a type but an individual. (But, a particular *playing* of the game is not a type.) The network is not merely abstract information or a type that admits of multiple tokens. Still, one might argue that while the cumulative play of the chess game can be preserved even with wholesale physical replacement, and even a temporal gap in its play, the cumulative network self cannot. The single isomorphic product (Swampman or the teleporter self) would be an instantaneous body[31] and therefore, doesn't have the right beginning that stages of selves are supposed to have. It would not preserve the *cumulativeness* of the self-network that entered the teleporter or that was Davidson.

But, let us imagine another process, say an avalanche. An avalanche is a spatio-temporal physical process organized by snow, ice, temperature, angle of slope, and forces such as gravity, rate of ice and snow melt, and so on. Suppose in the middle of the process of the avalanche unfolding there were a Swampman-like event: there were an instantaneous substitution of isomorphic molecules of stuff such that there were no disruption in the sequence, organization, and integrity of the process. The process as it had been—and as it is unfolding in virtue of what it had been— would continue *as that process*. The cumulative network of traits that is the avalanche would not have been disrupted. Qua process, transformation, replacement, addition, and subtraction, of physical stuff is a normal part of a physical process. Of course, *instantaneous, wholesale* replacement of physical stuff—the occurrence of Swampman-like events—is not how nature operates. But, if we stick with the thought experiment for the moment, which presumes that nature operates differently than it does, and if the avalanche example makes sense, then wholesale physical replacement would not necessarily disrupt the cumulative network. By analogy and in the context of the thought experiment, qua sole survivor Swampman would preserve and continue the process self.

The analysis of fission and duplication has assumed that duplication occurs in the same world, so to speak, such that the cumulative network of traits cannot be preserved when there are two bodies. However, could there be exactly similar selves in different, disconnected worlds? If there were, they would just be two numerically distinct selves in separate worlds. For exact similarity of the self, the entire world strongly relevant to the constitution of that network would also have to be exactly similar. I don't know if it is physically possible, but at least in theory, it is conceivable, that there is another such world with beings in it exactly like each of us. Such worlds would be completely disconnected from one another, and the network that constitutes each self (and anything else) in each world would not be undermined, disrupted or affected by the *ex hypothesi* exactly similar goings on in the other world.

What about fission or duplication in this world, but where the two resultant selves are in two different, disconnected locations, are totally unknown to one another and are unknown as duplicates to anyone else? Suppose, for example, instead of Swampman, there is a thunderstorm on some remote island where a lightning strike created an exact body replica of Davidson, Islandman, with all the memories, beliefs, and so on of Davidson, completely unknown to Davidson, who simply carries on life as usual.[32] Or, suppose the teleporter malfunctions such that the original body is not destroyed, but emerges in the originating location *and* a body duplicate is made and emerges not at what was supposed to be the target location, but on such an island. Further suppose that no one else realizes that this is what has happened and there is no way to trace that there is a body duplicate somewhere. The original emerges in the originating location, assumes that there was a malfunction, but one that failed to transport, and carries on life as usual. Let us also assume that in each case, the body duplicate is marooned in that island location and never establishes any connection to the original and remains unknown to and disconnected from the original. Islandman never leaves the island and could give no causal account of his sudden, isolated existence. The teleporter duplicate might be very confused, but could probably give itself some account of malfunction to explain her or his predicament. The account might be incorrect, for instance, the teleporter stranded duplicate might believe that she or he is the sole survivor, and that the only thing that went wrong had something to do with a malfunction in hitting the target location.

Is each island stranded duplicate something like Chuck Noland in the film *Cast Away* (Zemeckis, 2000) that was discussed in Chapter 3? There I said that while Chuck Noland's life took an abrupt and radical turn, it is still Chuck Noland, that cumulative network of traits that includes its own past. The *Cast Away* character is the self, Chuck Noland, even if he'd never been able to get off the island. But, what should we say about the teleporter stranded body duplicate or Islandman?

The self is the network, and therefore wherever the network is that's where the self is. Think of just the body, for a moment. It is a system, in the language of CNM, it is a functioning network of genetic, physiological, neurochemical, etc. constituents and sub-networks of traits. For some constituents of the system, it is possible to replace them, for example, with a kidney transplant or a prosthetic limb, and the system, the network, continues to function as that network. But, if a duplicate kidney were made and were sustained in some context apart from the network, which continued to function with its original kidney, we'd say that the bodily system continues as that body, and the duplicate kidney is well, just a duplicate kidney. In some context, it could be substituted for the kidney as a constituent of the system, and then it would be a constituent of the bodily network. But, otherwise, it's just a duplicate kidney.

Similarly, with the self. Consider the body as analogous to the self, and the kidney as analogous to the body. The self is a system, a network of bodily, social, cultural, semantic, and so on traits and sub-networks of traits. In some thought experimental contexts (e.g., the teleporter) it is plausible to suppose that it is possible to replace a body as a constituent of the network and the network of relations continues to function as that network. But, if a duplicate body were made and sustained in some context apart from the network, which continued to function with its original body, the duplicate body is well, just a duplicate body.

The teleporter stranded body duplicate can tell itself a causal story for its predicament. It may even think that it is the self, the network, believing perhaps that it is the sole survivor of the malfunctioning teleporter. However, it would be mistaken. Islandman would presumably be quite bewildered. He would believe he is the self of which he is the body duplicate, but would have no causal story to tell himself and no context for orienting himself. Unlike Chuck Noland, there would have been no plane trip, storm and subsequent crash, no events that would explain why Islandman is where he is. Unlike the teleporter self, there wouldn't even be the possible malfunctioning explanation. If we added to the experiment that there were different laws of nature that could explain such an event as Islandman's *de novo* existence, then Islandman might be able to explain to himself that he is a distinct, duplicate body. Suppose an even more bizarre thought experiment and that is that there has been a sudden, complete swap, particle for particle and in the exact bodily arrangement, such that the original molecules of Davidson's body are inexplicably reconstituted as Islandman and Davidson's body has had a complete sudden particle for particle replacement. The result would be no different from the analysis of Islandman. The self is the network, and the network continues to function (just like a body would continue to function if its kidney were similarly replaced).

If nature operated so differently, I'm not sure what we can reliably say about selves. Bodies that could come into existence in such a way and appear to have the capacities of selves would be very different kinds of things than what bodies and selves in general really are. On the network model of the self, formal bodily isomorphism alone is not sufficient for a duplicate body to be a continuant of a self (a network), but I admit that in a thought experiment so far removed from how nature does operate our reasoning doesn't have a firm foothold.

A self as it generally really is, for example, Chuck Noland, unlike the island stranded body duplicates, persists as the self, the network, experiencing an unexpected turn, but one that does not destroy, even though it drastically alters the network. A self can move to a new location and drastically alter its constituents and trajectory while continuing as that one process. There is sufficient functional integrity, causal continuity and so on, even though access to social relations has been cut off. In Chuck Noland's case, the self and the world relevant to the constitution of the self continue to be appropriately related: given the event of the plane crash and the subsequent stranding on the island, that Chuck has no access to his prior social relations just is the way the network has been altered. This is no different, in principle, from a body being radically altered by a plane crash, a bomb, or some other accident or disease condition and the self persisting as that self. What matters is that there is *some* cluster of sufficient conditions that preserve the integrity of the network, and what those conditions are varies.

## 4. Prudential Concern for Future Selves

Discussions about successor selves often appeal to whether a self would have or whether it would be rational for a self to have prudential concern for fission or fusion produced successor selves. In anticipating fission, for instance as a possibility in teleporter cases, an original self might have prudential concern for multiple successor selves. It might have a positive outlook about fission in so far as fission would preserve the possibility that intentions, projects, and other future directed wishes will be carried out, and that aspects of the history of the self will be remembered and preserved, albeit in and by new selves. Or, more perversely, it might regard multiple successor selves as an avenue for escaping responsibilities. But, there are other equally plausible attitudes that a self might have. There might be regret or sadness for aspects of the original self that would be lost or radically transformed, aspects such as kinship or spousal relations. There might be indifference towards multiple new successor selves because perhaps one can't project the same kind of prudential self-concern over multiples. There might be conflict and competition between two (or more) successor selves, such that an original self would fear, dread, or seek to avoid fission. In the aftermath of unanticipated fission—the teleporter gone awry, the Swampman case—it seems just as plausible that there would be conflict and competition as that there would be mutual concern or indifference between the contemporaneous selves. Finally, if fission were a regular occurrence of selves—as opposed to a fictional thought experiment about selves—if natural causal and productive processes were so completely different from what they actually are, we may not have any idea what such selves would think or feel about their fissioned multiple successors.

Our present intuitions about what we think we might feel or think about such successor selves rest on how we feel and what we know about how selves actually are, and that involves uniqueness, singularity, and numerical unity. While there may be some variability in people's intuitions, those probably reflect individual (and possibly cultural) preferences, but still within some general framework of knowledge about selves as they actually are. But, if selves were the kinds of beings that naturally divided, or whose bodies could be instantaneously reconstituted, if brains with all psychological states, intentions, purposes, and so on could be transplanted, or if selves could be duplicated, selves would be quite different from what selves actually generally are. In these scenarios, I'm not sure what the theory of self would be, or what such selves would think, feel or find rational or reasonable to think or feel about themselves and their ancestor and successor selves (see also Gendler, 2002).

## 5. Concluding Remarks

Whether we think that a self persists and what we imagine a self might feel about imaginary fused or multiple successor selves may reflect what we take to be important about selves as they actually are, e.g., psychological capacity and continuity, bodily continuity, social continuity, continuity as a process and with one's history or some combination thereof. If none of the answers given to the thought experimental situations are wholly satisfactory, it may be because the experiments bump up against the limits of what a theory of the self purports to be about. Thought experiments may be useful in drawing out implications of a theory, but there may be thought experiments to which a theory cannot give an unambiguous or wholly satisfactory answer. CNM fares no worse, and in some respects, fares better than rival psychological and biological theories of the self in explaining what might be going on in fusion and fission. That we have unstable intuitions in duplication thought experiments like Swampman and Islandman or that a theory has different answers when there are two emergents from the teleporter rather than one doesn't entail that the theory fails. It just means that duplication is not consistent with that model of the self. If selves as they generally are, are not the kinds of things that split like amoebas, fuse like in the brain transplant, replicate in teleporters or come into existence like Swampman or Islandman, then the inferences that we do make in the context of the thought experiments may be of limited use in theorizing about selves as they generally really are. The thought experiments do not tell us what is possible for selves; their conceivability does not mean that they are possibilities of and for selves. But, what they do perhaps show is that what distinguishes and preserves a self is its cumulative integrity, and that is conceptually distinct from bodily or psychological continuity.

## Notes

1. *Discourse on Method*, I, 6–7, Descartes (1964), Lafleur translation. Most other translations use "fables" instead of "fiction" as in "fables make us imagine many events as possible when they are not." (Descartes, 1988,

Cottingham, Stoothoff, Murdoch translation, 23). The text in French is, "Outre que les fables font imaginer plusiers événements comme possible qui ne le sont point."

2. Where it is more natural to do so, I will use "person" without scare quotes by which I mean the cumulative network self. I use scare quotes to mark other conceptions of the person, for example, when summarizing or referring to views that hold that a "person" is to be identified with the psychological stream.

3. Gendler (1999) provides a concise enumeration of the kinds of cases that I consider (456–457). She argues that while we can make sense of many of these thought experiments, which suggest the conceptual separability of features of persons, they may not provide a firm basis for making reliable judgments about the nature of selves as they generally really are (450).

4. Conceptualizing the self in terms of a cluster of conditions means that there may be variability in the set of conditions sufficient for preserving the self. CNM thus rejects the intrinsicness requirement proposed by philosophers such as Wiggins (1980, Chapter 6; 2001) and Williams (1973, 20). This places the network model in the camp of theories like Nozick's closest continuer theory (1981), although CNM draws different conclusions from his.

5. Locke (1975), Bk. II, Chapter XXVII (Section 15 for the prince/cobbler example).

6. This set of assumptions represents a view known as psychological reductionism, the view that what matters for personal identity are psychological relations. It is a view shared by, among others, Lewis (1983a), Parfit (1986), Quinton (1962), Sydney Shoemaker (1970), and Shoemaker and Swinburne (1984).

7. A brain transplant seems to change who the self is in ways that ordinary organ and bone marrow transplants do not, even though an organ transplant may be strongly relevant to the life of the recipient. Taking immunosuppressants for the rest of one's life may be a strongly relevant constituent of the recipient, but doing so does not destroy the network of traits. That is a brain transplant raises deeper questions about who the resultant person is indicative of the strong relevance of psychological traits to what we normally understand persons to be.

8. Many philosophical discussions of brain transplants take this example as their point of departure (see also Shoemaker and Swinburne, 1984, 108–111). I do not discuss the extensive literature on this example, but only consider its basic premise for the purpose of illustrating a point about my view: that the integrity of the network of traits is what matters. If that is destroyed, then that self is destroyed, even if there may be psychological continuity with another network. For other, animalist critiques of the neo-Lockean analyses of the brain transplant view see, for example, Olson (1997); Shoemaker's review of Olson, Shoemaker (1999), Johnston (1987, 64). More recently, Shoemaker has defended neo-Lockean accounts against animalist challenges (Shoemaker, 2008). I set aside for the sake of argument the biological implausibility of the supposition of this experiment. But, see Steinhart (2001a). Whatever the biological facts may be, the thought experiment illustrates nicely how the view of the self as a cumulative network of traits differs from a view that takes psychological or bodily continuity as the main consideration.

9. Note that this is different from the transformation in parental relations that might happen if a parent were to undergo a sex change. In such a case, the history and genetic relations map onto the subsequent stages of the self even if qualitative features of sex-specific parental roles were to alter.

10. With artificial reproductive technologies an assortment of biological and genetic kinship relations is possible. In surrogacy, a fetus could have DNA from two genetic sources who are distinct from the gestational parent whose metabolism may influence the epigenetic program of the fetus. These possibilities for an organism's genetic origins are different from the question of whether an organism's biological and genetic origins can be swapped out in the midstream life. On the network view of the self, if it entails wholesale disruption of an existing network and organization into another network, then the answer is no.

11. See also Shoemaker (1984c). Similarly, CNM finds implausible Quinton's claim about a 6-year-old girl displaying Winston Churchill's character, if by that is meant that Churchill's brain and psychological content is embodied in a 6-year-old girl such that *Churchill* is preserved (Quinton, 1962).

12. People do sometimes say that their spouse has become a different person from the one they married. This could be for any number of reasons and involve a wide variety of transformations that selves can undergo. But, in these cases, they are transformations of *a* self, a one-to-one transformation, not a fusion of components of two selves.

13. Nagel (1971, 1986) argues that most of us have false beliefs about the intended referent of "I" when we use the term, suggesting that we believe ourselves to be entities of some kind (perhaps something like souls?) who remain the same "thing" through time. In contrast, Nagel argues that "I" refers to "whatever *in fact* makes it possible for the person to identify and re-identify himself and his mental states" and that, he says, must be the brain. (Quote is from Parfit, 1986, 469, referring to a then unpublished manuscript of Nagel's.) Nagel develops his argument for the "objective identity" of the self in the intact brain, which is more than just its own psychological content, in greater detail in Nagel (1986, see esp. 40–41). Even granting that having a brain of the kind that human selves have is a necessary condition for the capacity for reflexive self-reference, identification, and re-identification, the brain is not the self, is not itself the daughter of x, the doer of a deed, the citizen of a nation, the philosopher, and so on. Therefore, it won't do to say that the *self* to which "I" refers is the brain. The brain alone does not suffice for preservation of the self or for a coherent account of the preservation of a first-person subjective experience.

14. Noonan argues that the concept "object of self-reference" should be substituted for "person" and a distinction should be made between *"I"-user* and *referent of "I."* Noonan's frame of reference is Lockeanism versus animalism and the issue is whether the animal that has the new brain is the person from which the brain came or not. Noonan argues that the animal with the new brain is the *"I"-user.* The *referent of "I"* by that user is the "person" (which in this example would have to mean the brain/consciousness). I confess to finding this incomprehensible. I don't understand what it would mean that there is an animal that is an *"I"-user,* but that the *referent of "I"* by such a user is a brain/consciousness. The referent of "I" is the self, not a brain. Noonan (1998); see also Noonan (2001) in which Noonan responds to Mackie's criticisms of the Lockean approach to the problem (Mackie, 1999).

15. I leave aside whether cases of mental illness, such as schizophrenia, in which the subject believes that she or he is not the one thinking the thoughts in her or his mind, would challenge the immunity principle.

16. See Strawson (1987) for a possibly related point regarding a Kantian non-denotative significance of "I."

17. McDowell's arguments against Parfit's reductionism make this point as well (McDowell, 1997).

18. Parfit also considers compatibility or exact similarity in the context of making a different point, when he suggests that obsession with the body of someone could be transferred to the body of an identical twin, presuming their similarity or "compatibility" (Parfit, 1986, 295).
19. I agree with what I think Velleman (2006, 180–181) is suggesting, that is, that projective imagination is a process in which I imagine what it's like to be x, e.g., Napoleon Bonaparte, or I imagine myself as being that person (however faintly), rather than, as Mackie (1980, 56) proposes, a process in which the imagined subject (Napoleon Bonaparte) is imagined to be the subject of my present experiences.
20. This language is sometimes found in discussions of pregnancy. While the issues in pregnancy are very different from the ones being discussed here, I suspect there are similar underlying assumptions about the body that, regarding reproduction, are intermingled with religious beliefs and limited understanding of biology.
21. Somewhat similar to a thought experiment imagined by Shoemaker (1976, 112–113).
22. Whatever the solutions to these problems, they will not rest on preservation of the prior cumulative network. Parfit, too, considers these problems in a discussion of desert. I discuss responsibility in Chapter 7.
23. The Hensel twins, dicephalic parapagus twins, are a case in point. There are two heads. Physiologically, some functions are distinct—each has a stomach—but lower tract digestion and excretion are singular. There is one set of reproductive organs. There is one pair of arms and hands, one pair of legs. "They" are referred to as two selves, but agentially (swimming, bicycling, driving a car) function as one self. ("They" have two driving licenses.) Even when one twin authors a school paper or an email message, the organism as a whole acts to produce the product (write, type on a keyboard), although they are evaluated as if each twin has produced distinct work. "They" are often discussed as being two completely distinct persons in one body. Presumably, that means that there are distinct psychological streams and personalities (although the extent of non-verbal communication and coordination that appears to take place raises some doubts about how distinct such streams really are).
24. A film short, *The Un-gone* by Bovey (2010), explores the scenario of a malfunctioning teletransporter, with rather more chilling results than Parfit's cheery thoughts about continuing on as two.
25. Or, at least as two simultaneously functioning, conscious and agentially active selves, in contrast to the discussion of *Avatar* involving two bodies where one was dormant when the other was active.
26. Braddon-Mitchell and West (2001) put the point as a matter of relativism: "It turns out that what properties must be preserved for a person's survival may vary from person to person or culture to culture" (59). According to Braddon-Michell and West, persons can have (personal and cultural) practice-based preferences for what counts as survival, and there may be no fact of the matter as to whether a successor stage is a continuant of a person or a new person. It will depend on how cultures (and persons) organize person-directed practices (80).
27. Others who have considered this question and concluded that causation is not required include Campbell (2005), Kolak and Martin (1987).
28. There is a moment in the film *Multiplicity* (Ramis, 1996), immediately following duplication, when the two emergents have no idea which one is original and which the copy. Both think they are the original. As represented in the film, only a third party, the doctor who allegedly performed the copying, is

able to identify which is which, using a bodily continuity criterion and treating the copy as a fully formed clone.

29. In spite of the fact that many people are also willing to regard the single, exactly isomorphic body that emerges from the well-functioning teleporter as the "same self" as the one who entered the teleporter. Perhaps some have the idea that the material of the body has somehow been transported and bracket the thought that the body that entered the teleporter is destroyed. Or, some may have dualist assumptions, whereby an immaterial soul has been transferred to another material, happily isomorphic, location. Neither of these notions is actually relevant to the terms of the teleporter thought experiment. Many philosophers, like Baker, Johnston, Olson, and Van Inwagen, all have Aristotelian and biological visions of the self as a human being (Johnston, 1987), human animal (Olson, 1997), or human organism (Van Inwagen, 1987) and thus would reject the notion that the teleporter case could preserve such a self.

30. The physical constituents could be those of a software program in chess played virtually.

31. In a related vein (but for different reasons, as noted previously) and in a critique of the method of using puzzle cases to test the intuitions of wide psychological reductionism, Johnston claims "no human being could survive teletransportation or like cases of complete body transfer" (Johnston, 1987, 64).

32. Something like the case that Shoemaker imagines of a psychological duplicate created in a faraway place (Shoemaker and Swinburne, 1984, 130–132), a type of case enumerated by Gendler (1999, 457).

# 5  First-person Perspective and Reflexive Selves

If, in short, there is a community of computers living in my head, there had also better be somebody who is in charge; and, by God, it had better be me.

(Jerry Fodor)[1]

The view I'm interested in . . . gives up the idea that there is just one self per head. The idea is that instead, within each brain, different selves are continually popping in and out of existence. They have different desires, and they fight for control—bargaining with, deceiving, and plotting against one another.

(Paul Bloom)[2]

One's sense of self is not the result of an inner perception of a core of being. One's sense of self is compounded of one's appreciation of one's singular locations in one or more of a set of locative manifolds. In order of socio-historico-cultural diversity there is a manifold of physical places (one sees and acts upon the world from "here"), of temporal moments (one acts and speaks "now"), of moral positions (one is responsible to or for this or that person or persons) and of social positions (one has this or that social standing vis-à-vis these others). While embodiment is everywhere singular, there is diversity in temporal indexicality, yet more diversity in the positions one may occupy (even simultaneously) in various moral orders, and even more diversity in one's social relations to various others. Who is the "one" who thus senses his or her positions in these manifolds? Of course, the embodied person!

(Rom Harré)[3]

## 1. Introduction

As I have laid out the view thus far, the self is a cumulative network, a process constituted by the interrelatedness of multiple traits, biological, social, cultural, semantic, intentional, and so on. It might seem as if the self is just a process happening in the natural world, without the self acting, contributing to, reflecting on, directing, or controlling itself in any way. The question arises, how is it that a cumulative network is an agent with the capacity for independence and autonomy? How does a network choose, reflect on itself, become responsible? Does CNM present the self as too fragmented to be *a* self, or to have a first-person perspective? Having the capacity for self-representation and self-identification as well as for autonomous agency, are important and distinctive self functions. CNM, therefore, needs to give some account of how a relational process self actively contributes to its own individuality, to the character of its own constitution and direction, and is capable of self-representation, identification, and other reflexive functions.[4]

An active self-conscious self has often been thought of as non-relational, a substantial "thing" or perspective that remains constant in conscious experience, the executive decision-maker of the self, standing independent in some sense from the self. Perhaps it is a widespread desire to regard some aspect of the self as distinct from the vagaries of the world and even of its own constitution (part of the sentiment expressed by the Fodor epigraph at the opening of this chapter). However, on the approach being here developed, a non-relational, substantial inner self or central controlling module would not make sense. Rather, the reflexive activity of a plurally constituted, but also unified singular self will have to be conceptualized in relational terms as, I suggest, a functional capacity for communication among self-perspectives.

There have been many critiques of the notion of a substantial inner "self" as an independent subject[5] as well as a long tradition of regarding the self, even with respect to subjective experiences, as internally differentiated and multiple. For example, there is Plato's tripartite theory of the soul that converses with itself; Augustine's reflections on himself in *The Confessions*, in which he distinguishes between "I," my soul, the eye of my soul, and mind;[6] Freud's tripartite system of id, ego, and superego; James's notion of the self as consisting of material, social, spiritual selves, and an ego;[7] and Mead's characterization of the self in terms of internalized social roles ("me's") and a capacity for spontaneous response ("I").[8] More recently, in psychology Bloom (2008) has argued that the first person is actually plural perspectives, that the self is a community of selves (expressed in the Bloom epigraph at the opening of this chapter).[9] The idea of split or multiple selves or self-perspectives (and distinguishing between higher and lower "selves" or "natures") is sometimes invoked to explain problematic or dysfunctional experiences, such as self-deception, *akrasia* (weakness of will), and irrationality.[10] Much contemporary research in neuroscience suggests that "I" functions are dispersed and not the activity of a single modular unit let alone a unitary subject.[11] According to CNM, the self is the unity of a plurality. It functions as a unitary subject in so far as its constituents are unified, integrated or coordinated. The self can take a comprehensive, unified perspective on itself (e.g., I-as-a-whole), or function reflexively through specific constituents and perspectives (e.g., I-in-a-role).

I am not going to provide an account of consciousness, of how the brain operates, or of how it is possible in terms of neurobiology and neurophysiological mechanisms for such reflexive activity to occur. My aim will also not be phenomenological description of experience. Rather, I am interested in developing a model, a set of categories, for conceptualizing a network self's activity and perspective. If the self is not just a passive recipient of sensations and perceptions or a series of associations to which it has made no contribution, but is active, agential, in its own constitution, how ought we conceptualize that?[12]

## 2. Pragmatic Reflexivity

Traits or locations of the self can also function as perspectives, such that the self can take a perspective on itself, and actively contribute to itself. The reflexive process will be conceived as communication among self-perspectives. I borrow from philosophers in the American pragmatic tradition, specifically from Mead's notion of the "I," the "me" and the generalized other (Section 5), from Royce's notion of interpretation (Section 6), and from Buchler's notion of reflexive communication (Section 7). Mead and Buchler have explicitly relational views of the self and were concerned with the nature of "subjective" experience and with how to conceptualize self-constituting activity in a naturalistic framework. I supplement with an important transitional concept (interpretation) from Royce.

Mead argued that social roles constitute the self and its capacity for agency in social contexts. That capacity depends, according to Mead, on the self having internalized, and made its own, not only its own social role, but the system of relations between social roles. It is only by having internalized the system that one would be able to fully participate and enact a particular social role. Royce developed the notion of interpretation as a distinct cognitive process by which meaning is created. Buchler proposed that the capacity of the self to communicate with and create meaning for itself be conceptualized as what he called reflexive communication. I freely borrow from (and modify) their work as I develop the idea of reflexive activity and a first-person perspective for the cumulative network self.[13]

## 3. Self as Reflexive Community

The self is a cumulative network constituted by the unique interrelatedness of its traits. But, it also actively contributes to its own constitution as an individual. I suggest that for this purpose the self, the network, be thought of as a community of perspectives, stripping "community" of any honorific associations.[14] What do I mean by community and how does it apply to the self?

### 3.1. Community

Community is not meant to invoke any communitarian notion of social, cultural, or tradition-based locatedness. Nor by community do I mean something normatively valuable (as in a "spiritual community") or self-consciously chosen (as in "a community of activists") or intimate and unmediated. I mean that there is an *experiential* parallelism, conscious or not, between the members.[15] What distinguishes it as community (rather than simply physical, biological or social coincidence) is that the parallelism prompts signifying activity for each of the members in relation to a common object or condition for mutuality (even when selves are not in communication with one another). By signifying activity, I mean that the individual, in response to the common object, begins communicating with herself about it (Buchler, 1979, 30). For example, a community of opera lovers. Even if they do not necessarily know or communicate with one another (although most probably do communicate with some other opera lover[s]), they share some experience of opera in the same respect and that experience prompts signifying or interpreting activity in each experiencer; they have experiential parallelism with respect to that common object, opera. Or, the community of New York City subway riders, whose common object is the experience of riding the subway. Or, the "LatinX community," individuals who experience being LatinX in the same respect and as significant in some way.[16] Or, the community of "Gadgetiers," a segment of media consumers who are early, active adopters of new technologies.[17]

Community (experiential parallelism that prompts signifying activity) does not require, but is a pre-condition for communication between selves.[18] Communication can occur between members within a specified community (opera lovers, Gadgetiers) or between members of different communities in virtue of a more encompassing community (a community of music lovers, of public transit users, of technology users). (I define communication more precisely subsequently.)

Community—experiential parallelism—prompts signifying activity, that is, members of the community use signs to interact with some common object. But, not all "common objects" prompt signifying activity or are a condition for community. For example, while all human beings breathe oxygen, it is doubtful that there is an "oxygen breathing *community.*" Breathing oxygen is necessary for our continued existence, but does not typically prompt signifying activity. On the other hand, those who experience respiratory compromise—e.g., asthmatics or emphysema patients—may constitute a community because breathing prompts signifying activity. Or, in a context in which basic conditions of existence were stark or compromised, community might emerge, e.g., alpinists sharing an oxygen supply at altitude, front-line recipients of ecological disruption, degradation, or pollution who become political activists or members of a diaspora. These examples might suggest that community is formed when there is a problematic situation, something that Dewey might endorse. But, that is not necessary as the earlier example of opera lovers illustrates. Community or experiential parallelism does not require that a common object be experienced as problematic.

What is common in the environment may or may not be a basis for community. For many of us soil probably does not function as a basis for experiential parallelism. But, members of a community of farmers or gardeners experience soil in a similar respect and their interaction with that common "object" generates signifying or interpreting activity for the farmer or gardener. Members of a community do not share all perspectives, but in so far as they form a community, they share some common perspective or contribute (consciously or not) to a common, overall direction (e.g., a community of neighborhood watchdogs contribute to a safe neighborhood) or experience something in common (e.g., a community of farmers, a community of slaves) that prompts signifying activity. A community of slaves experiences slavery in the same respect, different from the respect in which a community of slaveholders would, although both would also be members of a larger community, a slavery permitting society.

Experiential parallelism—having a common object of experience in some respect—does not entail having the same interpretation. Members of a community may have different interpretations and disagreements about their common experience. Imagine, for example, a community of scientists investigating some common object, but disagreeing about its classification or explanation. Or, legislators considering legislation (a common object) about which they disagree, perhaps even vehemently oppose one another. The members of a community need not all communicate with one another; for example, religious believers or political activists may not all know one another or communicate with every other. But, there is signifying activity within and among members in relation to the common object, whether they are all communicating with one another or whether the signifying activity is harmonious, edifying or not.

In a similar vein, Young (1986) argues that theorists of community have mistakenly tended to privilege face-to-face and unmediated intimacy as the paradigm of community; this is a "metaphysical illusion" (15).[19] Rather, she argues, all human relations are mediated:

> Even a face-to-face relation between two is mediated by voice and gesture, spacing and temporality. As soon as a third person enters the interaction the possibility arises of the relation between the first two being mediated through the third, and so on. The mediation of relations among persons by the speech and actions of still other persons is a fundamental condition of sociality. . . . The greater the time and

distance [of expanded societies] . . . the greater the number of persons who stand between other persons.

I take "mediation" as analogous to what I am calling "signifying activity" of the members of a community in relation to a common object. In contrast to Young, however, reciprocal communication need not be taking place for there to be community. Rather, community (experiential parallelism that prompts signifying activity) is a pre-condition for such communication.

### 3.2. Reflexive Community

For community as I have just described it, experiential parallelism is social, that is between individuals. But, the concept can be adapted to the self. The self-network is a community of self-perspectives: constituents of a self function as perspectives between which there is experiential parallelism. Reflexive community or experiential parallelism is not simply an internalization of some aspect of social community. Perspectives are not separate modules or partitions in the mind or self. Rather, perspectives are aspects of the network, of the self, respects in which the self can function or view itself. To take a perspective on itself means that the self in one respect acts on, communicates to or with, interprets itself in another respect in relation to a common "object"; and, the common object can be an aspect of itself. In so doing the self functions as an "I" or as "I's." We can think of perspectives as "I-positions," for example, I-as-spouse, I-as-philosopher, I-as-desirer-of-x, I-as-passionate-about-y. From I-positions a self may act, choose, judge, interact, and communicate with others, and reflexively with itself. The self may constitute a perspective on itself as a whole at a time, I-as-I-am-up-to-this-stage, or, as reflecting on its past, I-as-I-was-or-acted-at-t, or less comprehensively, for example, I-as-desirer-of-something, I-as-female, I-as-feminist, I-as-spouse, I-as-rationalizer, I-as-philosopher, I-as-English-speaker, I-as-anxious, I-as-optimistic, and so on.[20]

I-perspectives may also share some common perspective. For example, I-as-feminist and I-as-political-participant may share a wider perspective, e.g., I-as-progressive or I-as-conservative, a wider self-perspective from which the self regards a variety of social, economic, and political issues. Or I-perspectives may contribute to a common, overall direction, for example, I-as-spouse and I-as-feminist as two parallel perspectives from which the self contributes to and seeks to define her marriage. Or, more comprehensively, the self as she is up to this stage interpretively projects herself into the future. Or, as an intense emotional but temporary experience, I-as-griever-at-the-death-of-my-parent and I-as-sibling may contribute to how I conduct myself in navigating the disposition of my parent's estate. Experiential parallelisms can overlap with respect to their common object. For example, the I-as-daughter, sister, cousin, mother, aunt, feminist may be perspectives from which the self experiences family relationships. Or I-as-Huntington's-Disease-Carrier and I-as-prospective-mother may be perspectives on biological reproduction.

In order to model this idea of the self as a community of perspectives, a metaphor might be helpful. Imagine multiple lamps, perhaps of different illuminating strengths, connected by wires. Each lamp illuminates objects in its field of illumination including some other lamps in the network and in a different way from the other lamps that, when on, also illuminate that area. Each lamp may not illuminate each of the areas illuminable by other lamps in the network of lamps, even if its illumination field overlaps fields of some other lamps.

Applying the metaphor to the self, the connected lamps represent the multiple constituents of the self. The wires stand for relevance relations between traits of the network. Lamps of different illuminating power represent the idea that some perspectives may be more dominant, or organizing for other perspectives. Not every lamp is connected to every other lamp; not every trait of the self is connected to every other trait. But, just as there are connecting routes of access between lamps, there are mediating routes of access between traits or perspectives. When turned on the lamps represent the self in some respect(s) being active as, functioning as an I-perspective (or perspectives). I-as-feminist may function as a perspective on itself in another respect, say, I-as-spouse. In third-person language, aspects of the self are objects for one another; in first-person language, I in one aspect of myself reflect on (and may communicate with) I in another aspect of myself. I-as-network-up-to-this stage may self-consciously take stock of who I am overall, and perhaps engage in introspective imaginative projection of how I want my life to go for the next decade. Or, in taking stock of myself overall I may also reflect on myself in a given respect, for example, by redefining for myself what being a feminist means to my overall self-direction.

From a subjective experiential point of view, it might feel as if there is one thing, "the I," that moves from one location in the network to another, or that stands "above" or "outside" each aspect, sort of like an interior panopticon or spotlight—or, in the language of the metaphor, as if there were one lamp that is independent of and illuminates different aspects of self. On the network view of the self, the one "thing" is a community of perspectives, any one of which may function as, be active as an "I." Perspectival activity belongs to one network. Subjective experiences are the experiences that they are in virtue of their being the constituents of the network of which they are constituents and in virtue of the relevance and mediating (i.e., signifying and communicative) relations among them.[21]

That the self is a community does not necessarily mean that it is harmonious within or completely transparent in every respect to itself. A self may also communicatively partition off aspects of itself, as for example, it might do in self-deception. Or, a self might be conflicted, at war with itself, indecisive. Or there could be more serious cases of fragmentation, such as dissociative identity disorder.[22] The plurality of constituents or perspectives of the self and the possibility of partitioning, conflict, indecision mean that communication is not always positive; perspectives of the self can act incommensurately or not communicate with one another or communicate in combative or other potentially unhelpful ways. None of that entails that there is not a self that is the agent and potentially responsible for its acts and attitudes.[23]

On the network model the self is no different in principle from other complex, organized systems, such as a living, organized body. The body acts and functions as one body through the coordination and synchronization of multiple bodily systems, even though there may also be redundancy and much that works sub-optimally. To the extent that a body experiences its own bodily systems, it normally experiences them as belonging to and constituting one body. Similarly, the self normally acts as one self through the coordination and synchronization of multiple perspectives and experiences itself as one self. Even a self that experiences itself as conflicted, disordered, impulsive, in turmoil or "out of sorts" still experiences that disorder as its own. A body that doesn't function well as a unitary whole or that engages in involuntary movement (e.g., in Huntington's Disease or Tourette's syndrome) or that fails to engage in voluntary movement (e.g., in stroke or other forms of paralysis) is still a body, and these conditions are explained by disease conditions or other causes of breakdown in bodily coordinating systems. Similarly, in addition to the dissonances of everyday life, a self may have difficulty functioning as a unitary agent or fail to act on its own best judgment (e.g., as in *akrasia* or weakness of will). But, it is still a self, one where there may be disordered desires and impulses, or more seriously, disease or other conditions of breakdown or difficulty in coordination of or conflict between the constituents or perspectives of the self. The point is only that in undesirable or dysfunctional cases (e.g., self-deception, self-conflict, impulsivity, dissociative identity disorder) failure or disorder is still that of one network, the self. In answer to Harré's question in the epigraph at the beginning of this chapter, "Who is the 'one' who thus senses his or her positions in these manifolds?" CNM says, "Of course, the cumulative network!"

By introducing the notion of the self as a community of perspectives, the idea is that if the self is a unified plurality of traits, then so, too, is the "I." It cannot be something that stands outside or "above" the network as an independent, executive self module or entity, "an I" that stands apart from and decides between first-order and second order desires or interests.[24] "The I" on the latter model is active and integrates (or not) desires and interests, but is modeled as an observer or decision-maker standing apart from other constituents (desires, interests) of the self.

As represented in Figure 5.1, "I" may endorse desires or interests selecting from among them and perhaps attempting to integrate those selected. Selection, endorsement, and integration could be thought of as temporally progressive, but "I" seem to remain something apart from the desires integrated. Another model which posits a central "I" is Dennett's (1991, 1992) where the self is "an abstract center of narrative gravity."[25]

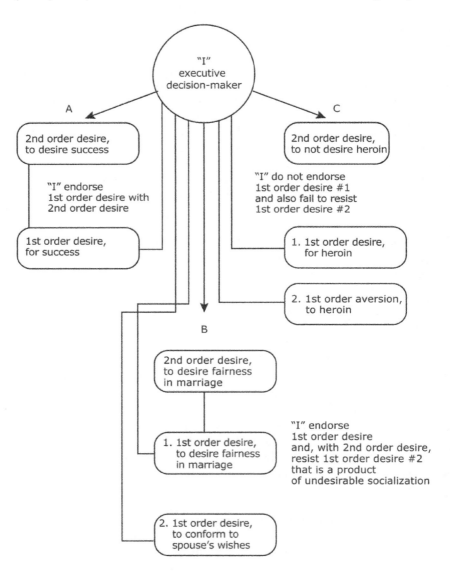

*Figure 5.1* Executive "I" Model of Self.

(This figure appeared in Wallace, 2003, 184.)[26]

In contrast, according to CNM, the self is differentiated and perspectively located: "I" is the self in some respect functioning in a particular way. That particular way, I am suggesting, should be modeled as perspectives communicating with one another. Suppose while working on this essay I-as-emotionally-or-mood-constituted become discouraged, so discouraged that I have trouble continuing to work, while at the same time I-as-philosopher want to get on with it, articulate the ideas, and finish the essay. Maybe I also feel the pull of wanting to read a novel (I-as-desiring-to-read-novel) as well as the pull of obligations as a spouse (I-as-spouse). The self, from a broader perspective, may also be, in some sense, observing its own conflict, feeling the pull of these conflicting "I's," I-as-discouraged, I-as-desiring, I-as-willing-to-complete-work, I-as-restless and maybe even "talking itself" out of a funk and getting back to work. Figure 5.2 shows this modeling in terms of the self as a network or community of perspectives.

The point that I (I-as-philosopher) am making is that functionally, an "I" is always perspectivally located, albeit not restricted to any one location or perspective. In addition, I-as-philosopher is just one of plural I-perspectives. "I" am not observer, evaluator or "super-perspective" apart from the locations of the self. Multiple perspectives—"I"-positions—are the activity of and belong to one network; I in my plurality am myself (the network is itself) functioning perspectivally.

As noted earlier, the idea of a self as a community of perspectives is not a new idea, although it has been appealed to perhaps more often to explain problematic or dysfunctional experiences, such as self-deception,

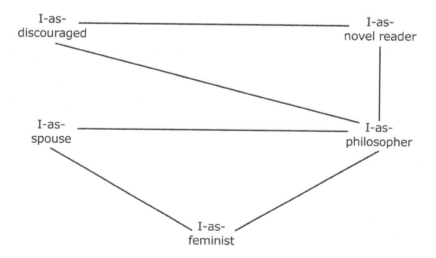

*Figure 5.2* Relational "I" Model of Self.

(A similar type of figure appeared in Wallace, 2003, 185.)[27]

*akrasia* (weakness of will), and irrationality, than "normal" experience. However, according to CNM, functioning as multiple perspectives is *normal* reflexive activity and self-representation. Whether reflexive activity is one or the other ("normal" or dysfunctional) depends on the kind and degree of integration or commensurateness between the different traits or perspectives of the self.[28] This is not to say that a self can't be conflicted or at war with itself; battling I-perspectives is probably a normal aspect of human experience. A self can experience itself as an I, as the center of experience, both reflexively (when it takes itself as an object of its own awareness) and simply egocentrically (when the self is aware of its perception as from its own, egocentric visual perspective, or in proprioception, or when the self asserts itself as the subject of a thought or action). The point is that however else a first-person perspective should be described, subjective experience is being modeled as communicative relations of the network, as a community of perspectives.[29]

The plurality of the self does not necessarily undermine experiencing the self as a single actor or perspective. Such experience can be the result of coordination of perspectives or actions. The self experiences itself as functioning in particular ways, just as in physical activity, say riding a bicycle. "I am riding the bicycle" means "the-network-functioning-as-bicycle-rider is riding the bicycle." My legs are pumping, my respiration and heart rate are up, and so on. Aspects of the network can become prominent in self-awareness; for example, I-as-rider am conscious of, have a perspective on, I-as-leg-pumper. Still, it's the whole body that is riding the bicycle, not just the legs, and the self can experience itself as a whole agent engaged in that activity. Specific activities (legs pumping) belong to the coordinated action of the whole. Similarly, when I experience some present state of activity or consciousness as the experience *of being me* doing that activity or in that state of consciousness, I am experiencing the belongingness to or continuity of that activity or awareness with the network qua conscious, that is, with the community of perspectives.[30] In cases where there is some kind of breakdown in normal conditions of reflexive activity or self-consciousness, for example, in extreme sensory deprivation, or comprehensive amnesia, the self (I-as-amnesiac, I-as-sensory deprived) may be self-aware. The disorientation that accompanies such awareness would express damage to or failure of feedback in the network and of communicative relations in the community of perspectives.[31]

## 4. Reflexive Communication, Preliminaries

Reflexivity—for example, Frankfurt-like second-order evaluations of first-order desires[32]—requires being able to detach from and take a perspective on oneself. On the network model of the self, the internal differentiation of the self as a community of perspectives is a condition for the possibility of self-detachment. A self can (partially) detach from a perspective precisely because it is multiple perspectives, and can experience or "view" itself in one respect from itself in another respect. At the same time, the self can also integrate or transform perspectives and in so doing contribute to its own integrity and direction.

I call the process of communication between self-perspectives "reflexive communication."[33] Experiences such as self-criticism, self-identification, self-discipline, self-representation, self-conflict, self-deception, are all species of reflexive communication. Reflexive communication between self-perspectives can go well or badly with respect to what is rationally, morally, or in other respects desirable. While there are differences between specific reflexive experiences and their effects, my focus now will be on a general model of the underlying activity of reflexive communication.

At this point, the reader could go to Section 7 for an account of reflexive communication. But, I want to briefly review the work of two other philosophers, George Herbert Mead (Section 5) and Josiah Royce (Section 6). This review is in part an examination of the genealogy of the concept that was helpful to me, and perhaps it will be to other readers, in clarifying reflexive communication. However, these sections could also be skipped and referred back to as the reader's interest dictates when reading Section 7 on reflexive communication.[34]

## 5. Relational Self as Active: "Me" and "I"

Mead (1934) argued that the self consists of a "me" and an "I." The "me" is the self as the generalized other. The "me" is the attitude of the community, the internalized attitudes of the social roles that make up the community in which the self is located. Mead suggests that a self internalizes social roles and attitudes while at the same time generating its own responses to them. In so doing the self reshapes those roles and makes them uniquely its own. Thus, internalization is active. The self is not reducible to social roles or conventions, but contributes to the shaping of its own "socialization." This is the well-known combination, for Mead, of the self as a "me," reflection of the social roles, and an "I," the responsiveness of the self. Social (and more broadly, relational) constitution not only does not preclude but provides a constitutive base for reflexive activity. It is a process whereby a self or "I" contributes to its own constitution, not as something sitting apart from it, but from within its own constitutive locations. These notions of the "me" and the "I" provide a starting point for understanding how relational constitution is a basis for, not an obstacle to, self-definition and self-direction.

The organized community or social group which gives to the individual his unity of self may be called "the generalized other." The

attitude of the generalized other is the attitude of the whole community. . . . If the given human individual is to develop a self in the
fullest sense, it is not sufficient for him merely to take the attitudes
of other human individuals toward himself and toward one another
within the human social process, and to bring that social process as
a whole into his individual experience merely in these terms; he must
also, . . . take their attitudes toward the various phases or aspects of
the common social activity . . . in which as members of an organized
society . . . they are all engaged; and he must then, by generaliz-
ing, . . . act toward different social projects which at any given time
it is carrying out.

(Mead, 1934, 154–155)

The "I" is the response of the individual to the attitudes of others. It is
the self aware of itself as acting in or through a social role, even though
the "I" cannot be captured or defined as such. According to Mead, this
initiative of the self is an activity that initially is distinct from the structure of the internalized generalized other and then is subsequently incorporated into the "me."

The "I" reacts to the self which arises through taking the attitudes of
others. Through taking these attitudes we have introduced the "me"
and we react to it as an "I". . . . It is because of the "I" that we say
that we are never fully aware of what we are, that we surprise ourselves. . . . As given, it is a "me," but it is a "me" which was the "I" at
the earlier time. . . . It is what you were a second ago that is the "I"
of the "me." It is another "me" that has to take that role. You cannot
get the immediate response of the "I" in the process. The "I" is in a
certain sense that with which we do identify ourselves.

(Mead, 1934, 174)

The "I" is his action over against that social situation within his own
conduct, and it gets into his experience only after he has carried out
the act. Then he is aware of it. . . . He had in him all the attitudes of
others, calling for a certain response; that was the "me" of that situation, and his response is the "I."

(Mead, 1934, 175–176)

The self is not reducible to social roles or expectations because the
"me" incorporates the responses of the "I." The notion of the "I" is
intended to capture the functional spontaneity of a self to the social roles
through which the self acts and expresses itself. The self as an "I" is not
necessarily bound by convention but is also capable of expressing itself
beyond the given social roles of its present community.

At times it is the response of the ego or "I" to a situation, the way in which one expresses oneself, that brings to one a feeling of prime importance. One now asserts himself against a certain situation, and emphasis is on the response. The demand is freedom from conventions, from given laws. Of course, such a situation is only possible where the individual appeals . . . from a narrow and restricted community to a larger one, . . . one appeals to others on the assumption that there is a group of organized others that answer to one's own appeal—even if the appeal be made to posterity. In that case there is the attitude of the "I" as over against the "me."

(Mead, 1934, 199)

This framework of the "me" and the "I" characterizes a self as socially constituted ("me"), but not reducible to given or fixed social roles. Mead claims that the "I" can act independently of a given social convention, but that it can only do so in relation to another organized community. That community could be one that is imagined, or projected as a possible future community.

Mead aims to preserve the idea that a self is active in its own constitution, while at the same time acknowledging its social locatedness and constitution. Self-consciousness and reflexivity are social in nature but the self is not reducible to its social roles. Reflexive activity includes the capacity of an individual to take the attitude of an other toward herself. Thus, self-constituting activity involves the self taking multiple perspectives on itself. However, on Mead's account, the "I," conceptualized in terms of spontaneous responsiveness to immediate situations, remains elusive and undefined.[35] Mead's interpretation of the self as having a capacity for self-awareness and as actively contributing to its own self-constitution is both somewhat episodic and limited by being a modified version of a stimulus-response model. But, the self is not only responsive to what is socially given, but is capable of self-direction in mediate and future directed ways. The notion of a first-person perspective (or perspectives) and the capacity for actively reshaping the overall direction of the self calls for a more robust structure whereby the capacity for self-control, awareness, and self-direction is not restricted to a spontaneous kind of reaction in the immediate present.

## 6. Reflexive Activity as Interpretation

The Roycean theory of interpretation, offered in *The Problem of Christianity* (1968), and influenced by Peirce's theory of signs, suggests a more structured model for conceptualizing self-direction and self-mediation. For Royce, interpretation is a social and interpersonal process. I will lay out in very schematic terms Royce's account of interpretation as I understand it and then suggest how it might be extended to understanding the reflexive process *within* a self.

Interpretation is logically or formally triadic (see Figure 5.3); psychologically it is social (Royce, 1968, 294). An interpreter interprets an object to another interpreter, that is another self (305). Interpretation is communication that can take place in action, not just in linguistic exchange. As a process by which selves "pass from blind leadings to coherent insight and resolute self-guidance" (308) interpretation is both self-revelatory and self-defining. Consider Royce's example of "way in which two men who row in the same boat regard the boat and the oars which they see and touch, and the water over which they fly":

> Each man views the boat and the oars and the water as objects which he experiences for himself. At the same time, each of the two men believes that both of them are experiencing, while they row together, the *same* external facts, . . .
>
> The boat which each man finds, sees, touches, and feels himself pull, appears to him as verifying his own ideas. The common boat, the boat which each man regards as an object not only for his own, but also for his neighbor's experience, is essentially an object of interpretation. . . .
>
> Each rower verifies his own idea of the boat. Neither of them, as an individual, verifies the other's idea of this boat. Each of them, as interpreter, . . . believes that their two individual experiences have a common object. Neither can (merely as an individual) verify this idea. . . .
>
> If the common interpretation is true, then the two oarsmen actually form a community of interpretation, . . .

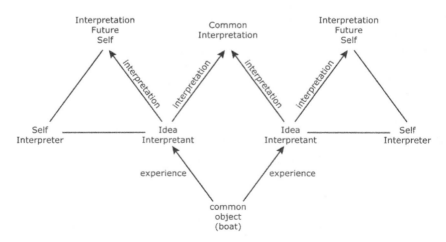

*Figure 5.3* Triadic structure of Roycean interpretation.

They constantly interpret themselves as the members, and their boat as the empirical object of such a community. And they constantly define what could be actually verified only if the goal of the community were reached. By merely rowing they will indeed never reach it. . . . For such a goal is essentially the experience of a community; the success . . . the final truth of each idea, or of each individual person, that enters into this community is due . . . to its essential spiritual unity in and with the community.

(Royce, 1968, 327–329)

Royce's account of interpretation suggests that a self partially detaches itself from its own experience and identifies itself with a common object of interpretation. At the same time, each self, each interpreter is aware of the other as an interpreter of the common object. In relationship to the common object, interpreters direct themselves toward a common goal (itself an interpretation, albeit not necessarily an explanatory one). The interpretative relationship is one in which selves form a "community of interpretation" through the common interpretation. In this process they also give themselves self-definition and self-direction. See Figure 5.3. Moreover, every interpretation can become the basis for another interpretive process, allowing for revision and redefinition.[36]

In Royce's analysis, interpretation takes place in an interpersonal community of selves (interpreters). Through that interpretation selves project themselves into a common future and thereby forge interpretive unity as a community.[37] Royce also suggests that interpretation is a process that goes on within a self, whereby a self mediates between its past and present self to give direction to itself qua a future self. While Royce himself does not characterize the self as a community, this "internal" differentiation of perspective would suggest that the self is a community of selves (or perspectives), (1) the Present Self (Interpreter) interpreting an idea of (2) the Past Self (Interpretant) for (3) the Future Self (Interpretation). In so doing the (Present) Self interprets itself, lends itself control and self-direction as it moves into its future. It is a process in which a self partially detaches itself from its own perspective and identifies itself with a common object and interpretation.

While Royce did not develop the model of a cumulative network self that I am proposing, the nascent idea of a self as a community of perspectives expresses the idea that an "I" or a first-person perspective is not a distinct observer or evaluator. "I" is a reflexive function, by which the self as a network of traits evaluates or mediates from or between its location(s). The self is a community of first-person perspectives.

## 7. Reflexive Activity as Reflexive Communication

I found the work of Mead and Royce helpful for how to think of a network self as having an active, reflexive, subjective perspective (or

perspectives). On Mead's account, the self does not reduce to its socializa-
tions, because there is self-initiated action or response to a situation (the
"I"). And the Roycean theory of interpretation offers a structured way
of thinking about the reflexive perspectival functioning of a self whereby
the self partially detaches from a given role to generate meaning. Now I
want to develop the notion of reflexive communication, a concept that
I borrow and adapt from Justus Buchler (1979) and that was, I believe,
influenced by the Roycean idea of interpretation dissociated from the
honorific, spiritual, and mentalistic terms in which Royce framed it.[38]

### 7.1. Communication

Communication can be thought of in two basic ways, as communication *about*, *to*, or *from* and as communication *with*. In the former, communication is unidirectional or asymmetrical; in the latter, bidirectional,
reciprocal, or symmetrical. (It could be multidirectional, if there are
more than two communicators involved.) An example of asymmetrical
communication:

> To communicate is to cause other persons to have thoughts (and
> beliefs) or feelings (and attitudes) of a kind one wishes them to have.
> In the former case we have informational communication, and this is
> candid informational communication if one causes another person to
> apprehend, although not necessarily to believe, what oneself believes
> or is thinking about. To cause one's hearers to come to believe what
> one believes is the ultimate goal, and if attained, the crowning suc-
> cess, of candid informational communication. For the most part,
> however, one must be content with causing one's hearers to believe
> that one does believe or to think what one *says* that one believes or
> thinks.
>
> (Castañeda, 1977, 165)

This description of the nature and purpose of communication characterizes it as something that most likely takes place in speech or by linguistic
means, and is unidirectional or asymmetrical, from speaker (communicator) to hearer. The recipient is not also communicating to the speaker.
Thus, this is not communication *with*. It also suggests that the purpose
of communication is to stimulate apprehension or to persuade in some
sense (cause belief). According to this definition, it appears that success is
required for communication to have taken place. If hearers fail to appre-
hend what one wishes them to, then something else, not communication
has occurred.

While communication could be a process of transmitting information
or of causing belief or apprehension of what one says, or of causing

someone to feel what one wants them to feel, this definition even of just asymmetrical communication would be too narrow and set the bar too high. Consider a painting. Perhaps the painter intends thereby to communicate something about either the subject of the painting, or to communicate by arousing particular feelings or reactions in others. However, the painter's product may not have its (the painter's) intended effect nor may it impart to others what the painter herself thinks, believes or feels (even when viewers attempt to attribute intentions to the painter). But, it (and the painter through the painting) may still communicate something to others, for example by generating interpretations that the painter hadn't consciously realized herself. The purpose of communication need not be information transmittal or persuasion (belief causation), although it could be. Communication could be exploratory (by aiming to provoke exploration of possible meanings in viewers) or deliberative (e.g., a political statement that aims to provoke public debate about some issue) or to evoke an emotion or feeling. Communication should be understood more broadly as a process of meaning generation through signifying activity. Meaning may not be antecedently clear, but may emerge from the process.

I borrow from Buchler (1979) in the following characterization of communication as a process of sign generation in and by an individual. A sign is "that which serves to represent or interpret a natural complex [or object] and which itself is interpretable" (1979, 54). A sign need not be linguistic, but could be a drawing, a gesture, a facial expression, an emotion, an action (think of how betting functions in a poker game), a musical phrase. Minimally, communication requires that some kind of signifying activity take place in the recipient. Castañeda's description then would correctly locate where an effect has to occur in order for something to count as communication, even if the particular effect (apprehension or belief formation) is narrowly construed. Buchler's construal of the effect is broader, a move which Buchler thinks is important to doing justice to the full range of human communicative experience. The intent is to encompass all, including artistic and aesthetic, experiences, and modes of communication. I think the intent is also to characterize communication as a pervasive and in some way rudimentary process in human experience, and not only something that occurs when we explicitly set out "to communicate" by transmitting information, persuading or instilling belief.

Asymmetrical and symmetrical communication are then defined as follows:

*Asymmetrical communication* occurs when in response to an object a self begins to generate signs (or meanings). An object can be anything—an idea, an utterance, a physical object, a performance, a policy, an action, a feeling, an emotion, a person. For example, a politician communicates asymmetrically when she gives a speech to constituents with whom she does not mutually interact to produce an interpretation of the speech or of herself. Such interpretations may themselves consist in emotions and interests that are aroused or piqued, and which function as meanings. Constituents may take the speech or the politician or both as the object. An artist may communicate asymmetrically (for herself, or to viewers, critics, posterity) when she produces a painting or a poem (the object) that generates signs in viewers with whom the artist does not mutually interact to produce meanings. A critic may communicate asymmetrically by writing a review of the painting (the review is another, related object) that is read by art lovers who do not mutually interact with her, the critic, to produce meaning. At the same time, a viewer of the painting or a reader of the review may communicate with herself about the painting or the review, and when she does so, she engages in *reflexive* communication. More on this shortly.

*Symmetrical communication* (communication *with*) occurs when selves generate signs in relation to a common dominant object *and* the selves are also objects to or for one another in some respect.[39] For example, two people communicate symmetrically when they view the painting (common, dominant object) and discuss it with one another. Or, the members of a poetry group communicate symmetrically when they read and discuss the poem. Or, in performance, the members of a string quartet communicate symmetrically, but non-verbally, with one another and about the music. Royce's rowers, discussed in Section 6, communicate symmetrically, also non-verbally. Symmetrical communicants are generating signs, meanings, about the object (painting, poem, speech, performance, piece of music, rowing a boat) *and* about each other. Not all communication is salutary. Exerting power through gesture, language, action or violence could be an instance of symmetrical (or asymmetrical) communication. A self being an object for another is not what is sometimes meant by "objectification" (although it could be).[40] Being an object for each other just means that in symmetrical communication each self is a sign or meaning-generating object for the other. In the symmetrical communicative context, in so far as the participants do recognize one another *as communicators*, it might be said that the participants recognize each as being in or as being a self with a first-person perspective.[41] Table 5.1 summarizes the differences between asymmetrical and symmetrical communication.

## 7.2. Reflexive Communication

Minimally, communication is a process in which an individual or individuals generate signs or meaning. This characterization of communication describes it as occurring either asymmetrically, for example, when an individual (or individuals) is communicated to, or symmetrically, as when

*Table 5.1* Asymmetrical and symmetrical communication

| Asymmetrical Communication[42] (Communication to or from) | Symmetrical Communication (Communication with) |
|---|---|
| (1) an object is a dominant object for a self; and | (1) an object is a dominant object for each of the selves involved in the communicative process; |
| (2) object generates meaning for a self for whom it is a dominant object. | (2) object generates meaning for each self; and |
|  | (3) each self is an object (meaning generator) for the other self. |

individuals mutually generate meanings, that is, when they communicate with one another and in some sense about one another as well as about the object or content of communication.

Similarly, communication occurs reflexively, that is, within a self. Aspects or perspectives of the self communicate about, to or with one another. *Reflexive* communication can take either form, asymmetrical or symmetrical.

Asymmetrical reflexive communication would be when the self responds to or engages in generating meaning without necessarily doing so with a self-awareness of itself as doing so; in other words, without the self also being an object for itself. For example, when the self is caught up in a process, such as in a surge of feeling, of outrage for example, in response to an offense, or in the flow of action or of producing something, say, a painting. In such a case, a self is generating meaning in relation to a dominant object (the offense, the activity, the painting) but doesn't necessarily thematize *itself* as an object.

In *symmetrical* reflexive communication, one self-perspective would be an object for another self-perspective (and vice versa) in respect to a common dominant object. This is easiest to imagine in an example of deliberation, but I want to emphasize that this could take place in much less articulated forms, as when emotional or desiring I-perspectives are communicating with and are objects for one another. For the deliberative example, suppose, I-as-philosopher want to finish my manuscript and I-as-novel-reader want to read my novel: the two I-perspectives communicate with one another about whether to continue working or to read the novel. Each self-perspective is generating meanings about what to do and about each other. This can be diagrammed as follows (Figures 5.4–5.7):

(1) The I-perspectives, I-as-novel-reader, and I-as-philosopher experience a common object, e.g., a choice about how to spend one's time. A choice situation has an impact on (IO) each I-perspective.

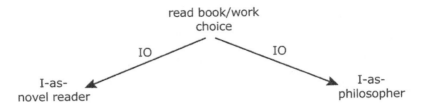

*Figure 5.4* Reflexive communication, Step 1.

(2)  In response to this impact, each I-perspective starts to generate signs
about (GSA) the common object,

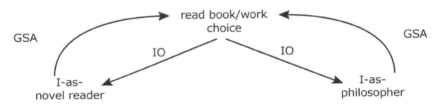

*Figure 5.5* Reflexive communication, Step 2.

(3)  while at the same time, each I-perspective is also an object for (has an
impact on—IO) the other I-perspective, and in response to that each
I-perspective also generates signs about (GSA) the other.

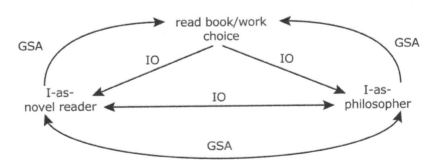

*Figure 5.6* Reflexive communication, Step 3.

(4)  In this process, the I-perspectives generate "an interpretation" of
the choice (e.g., a resolution or decision about what to do) as well
as interpretations about each other or even about an integrated
I-perspective, e.g., I-as-novel-loving-philosopher.

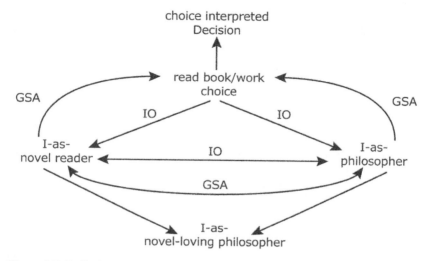

*Figure 5.7* Reflexive communication, Step 4.

In reflexive communication, the self may be aiming to persuade itself to believe or do something (whether transparently or self-deceptively), but it may also be engaged in processes that are not a matter of belief formation at all but could involve emotional self-development, or even repression. Communication is not always felicitous or orderly. Or a self could be engaged in a revelatory or transformative process. Using the example of self as feminist and self as spouse, suppose the self aims to articulate for itself how to be a feminist and a spouse in relation to each other. A communicative relation is established between the self qua feminist and the self qua spouse. Let's say that the dominant object for each is marriage and that the self in each respect generates signs (communicates to itself and to the other about marriage). In doing so, each perspective of the self functions as an I. Each, I-as-feminist and I-as-spouse, is object for the other I. In the process of reflexive communication these two aspects of the self may simply express the nature of each role or more deliberately, may forge a third I or self-perspective, let's say, I-as-feminist/spouse. Each I-perspective is related to (is an object for) the other I-perspectives. In addition, each I-perspective is related to the other in virtue of its sign-generating relation to the common, dominant object, marriage, and may generate an interpretation of marriage, for instance, marriage-in-light-of-feminist-concerns. See Figure 5.8. That an I-perspective can be an object for another I-perspective means that a self can partially detach itself from any of its perspectives. This capacity is crucial for the ability to articulate for itself a new self-perspective, one that is partially constituted by what's "given" and partially constituted by the self's own communicative processes.

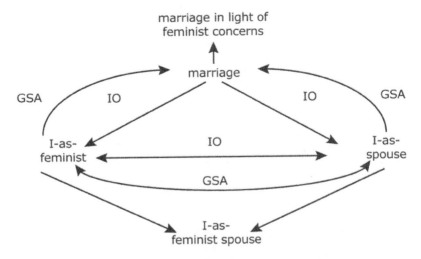

*Figure 5.8* Reflexive communication, feminist-spouse example.

   The process of reflexive communication could take place in a very general way or in some specific respect of the dominant object and its interpretation, e.g., marriage-in-light-of-feminist-concerns could consist in an act of self-governance, articulating normative guidelines for oneself such as whether to wear a wedding ring, or under whose name to file a tax return. The process could take place in action itself (e.g., how one negotiates with one's spouse about childcare) and not only as a (prior) mental self-assertion of how one is going to behave or present oneself. Recall Royce's rowers example in Section 6. Their interpretive relation was not linguistic, but was realized in action. Since feminism and marriage are dimensions of the self that have larger social and historical determinants, the process could also have a dimension of communicating with others, e.g., other feminists, other spouses, one's own spouse.
   The initial reflexive process in turn might lead the self to initiate *another* process of reflexive communication between the self qua daughter and the self qua feminist. Suppose, for instance, that the issue of whether the self will change her family name after marriage produces tensions in family relations or in relation to being the "good" daughter or one's own sense of oneself as the "good" daughter leading to both social and reflexive symmetrical communication. Or, suppose a self qua daughter and qua feminist reconstructs for herself (and perhaps subsequently with her sibling) expectations (that have social and familial roots) about who will be the primary caregiver for their aging parent. Thus, the self is a community of its locations, (spouse, feminist, daughter, sibling) and may be active in determining its own "internal" self-constitution. The self might

also communicate with itself more generally when for example, I reflect on where I am in life (the self as it is up to this time) and how I want the next year, say, to go.

Reflexive communication can be thought of quite broadly, and is not necessarily about reason giving per se or about linguistically articulatable self-conscious awareness. Rather each of these would be species of reflexive communication, which in its most encompassing sense is about how a self actively contributes to its own self-constitution. This of course could, and often does, include giving oneself reasons and engaging in rational deliberation. But, it could also include day-dreaming, emotion modulation, warring with oneself, battling an addiction, experimenting with self-representations,[43] simply exploring the meaning of something, say a painting or a piece of music, or pushing oneself to improve athletic performance.

I've presented cases of reflexive communication that might make it seem that it is a very orderly and smooth process. But, that was largely in order to clarify the concept. Reflexive communication (just like social communication) need not and may not be at all orderly. Arguments, disagreements, conflict, civil war between I-perspectives, indecisiveness, incoherence in action, emotional modulation, anxiety management, being overwhelmed by passions or desires, akrasia may all be ways in which the multiple I-perspectives of the self interact with one another and communicate reflexively with one another. Reflexive communication, as much as social communication, can be miscommunication; it can fail to achieve a well-functioning interpretation; clarity may be elusive. Just thinking of the example used earlier of the self-as-discouraged and the self-as-writer; reflexive communication between these I-perspectives may just be muddling, with desultory results.

Whatever one thinks of a more encompassing view of reflexive communication, the main point in introducing it is to provide a way to conceptualize some notion of reflexive, I-perspectives for a relational and plurally constituted self. For CNM, reflexive activities and the first-person perspective have to be conceived in relational terms. The first-person perspective is a community of perspectives. "I" in the reflexive (and not merely egocentric) sense is a perspectival function whereby the self in one respect takes a perspective on itself in another respect. The reflexive function or activity may be characterized in its most general terms as reflexive communication.

## 8. Looking Ahead: Reflexive Communication and Autonomy

The process of reflexive communication that I have described is one in which the self functions in a location (self-perspective). At the same time, it may partially detach itself from a location and in doing so generate the possibility of a new location or perspective (recall the feminist, spouse, feminist/spouse triad). The communicative process involves both author-ship and detachment. In creating a new location (or "space") for itself the process allows for the possibility of self-invention, self-direction and self-control.[44]

Through reflexive communication a self can project itself into the future by articulating self-perspectives. Its future is its, not because it is unrelated to or undetermined by its social and other locations, but because in reflexive communication it has the capacity to partially detach itself from some perspective(s) in some respect and articulate another perspective for itself. This is the root of the capacity for self-governance or "self-rule," the literal meaning of autonomy. The extent to which autonomy is achieved may vary of course; it may be a matter of degree or it may be something which one exercises in some self-respects and not others, or it may be something which the self as a whole exercises, for example, in relation to the classic idea (and ideal) of articulating and executing a "life-plan" for oneself. Reflexive communication provides a way of understanding some of the capacities thought to be essential to the possibility of autonomy—creativity, interdependence, self-control, collective articulation, detachment, revision—while recognizing without reducing the self to its locatedness. But, not every instance of reflexive communication constitutes autonomy or self-rule. Rather, with autonomy or self-rule, *rule* implies normativity, and *self*-rule implies that the self in some respect is the source of the rule (as inventor, validator, endorser or in some other capacity). Thus, while reflexive communication provides a way to conceptualize perspectival *self*-communication and is necessary for autonomy, by itself it is not sufficient. In the next chapter, I explore the notion of autonomy as self-*rule*, whereby the process of reflexive communication is the root of rule or norm-generation.

## Notes

1. Fodor (1998). In this piece, Fodor reviews *How the Mind Works* by Steven Pinker and *Evolution in Mind* by Henry Plotkin.
2. Bloom (2008).
3. Harré (1995, 371).
4. In this I am in agreement with Strawson (1959, 37).
5. For example, critiques offered by Anscombe (1975), Dennett (1991, 1992, 2001), and Wittgenstein (1972, 66–67).
6. "These books reminded *me* to return to *my own self*. Under your guidance *I* entered into the depths of *my soul*, and this *I* was able to do because your aid *befriended me*. I entered, and with the *eye of my soul*, such as it was, *I* saw the Light that never changes casting its rays over the same *eye of my soul*, over *my mind*" (my emphases). *St. Augustine*. 1961, Book 7, sec. 10, p. 146.
7. James (1950, 292).
8. See Section 5 on Mead.
9. Bloom (2008). While I'm not so sure about the idea of *selves* popping in and out of existence (Bloom's expression), I will pick up on the idea of selves negotiating (communicating) with one another.

10. Among philosophers, see, for example, Davidson (1982), Hare (1963, e.g., 81), Pears (1984, 87).

11. See also Dennett's (2001) use of neuroscientific research to develop his multiple drafts view of consciousness.

12. The idea that the self is active in its own constitution is in some ways a Kantian idea, although the activity need not be conceptualized in Kantian terms. See Blackburn (1997).

13. These three philosophers may not be the ones that immediately spring to mind when one thinks of pragmatism. Royce is often thought of as an idealist. But, he himself acknowledged the influence of Peirce and James on his thinking, and characterized his own work as an absolute pragmatism. Mahowald characterizes Royce's work as "pragmatic": the guiding question of the pragmatic method—what practical difference would this idea make?—"illustrates a common and essential accent on future experience as the criterion for human judgments. Such an emphasis marks the properly pragmatic attitude for both James and Peirce. While other philosophies may also stress future experience, none claims this as its defining characteristic . . . [this emphasis] will likewise define the pragmatic element in our study of Royce" (Mahowald, 1972, 24). Buchler eschewed a pragmatist characterization of his work, even though he was inspired by and his work emerged from the pragmatic tradition. He explicitly acknowledges this in a letter to Beth J. Singer (in Marsoobian et al., 1991, 13–14). Buchler also acknowledges the importance of the sign-studies of Peirce, Royce, and Mead, and the powerful work of Dewey (Buchler, 1985, 9). I discussed Mead, Royce, and Buchler in an earlier paper that was a preliminary working out of some of these ideas (Wallace, 2003).

14. James at one point characterizes consciousness as "this community of self" by which he means the continuity of the stream of thought (1950, 239).

15. I have adapted Buchler's definition by eliminating his particular terminology of proception and substituting the adjectival form of "experience." Buchler intends his term "proception" to supplant, for technical, philosophical purposes, the term "experience." Buchler's terminology is unfamiliar to many readers and this is not the place for exposition of the Buchlerian system. My adaptation serves the purpose here well enough. But, see Buchler (1979), especially the Introduction, for a critical analysis of the concept "experience."

16. Even though there may also be many differences between specific LatinX communities.

17. Berman (2011, 32ff.), referring to work done by the IBM Institute for Business Value, identifying technology users as sub-communities of "Gadgetiers," "kool kids," and "massive passives."

18. Although it is also possible that community, what is experienced in common, could prevent communication.

19. Young is arguing for freeing the concept of community from personal, small town, decentralized, honorific associations so that it can encompass phenomena such as urban community and broadly defined social and political communities.

20. The self taking on or viewing itself *in a role* might be more familiar terminology for this idea, but I don't limit the notion to roles per se.

21. I have been influenced by William James in my thinking. See James (1971) and James, "The Stream of Thought" in *The Principles of Psychology*, vol. 1 (1950).

22. This is not the problem of multiple selves or persons associated with four-dimensionalist views of the self discussed in Chapters 2 and 3.

23. A worry expressed, for example, by Sartre in his criticism of Freud (1956, see Chapter 2, 203–211).

24. See, for example, the work of Frankfurt. A signature piece would be Frankfurt (1971).
25. Dennett (1991, 1992). Gallagher (2000) provides a nice figure of Dennett's model and contrasts it with a more "distributed" model of the self, the latter very similar to the model that I propose (19).
26. *Journal of Speculative Philosophy*, 17, no. 3, pp. 176–191, Autonomous "I" of an Intersectional Self. Kathleen Wallace. Copyright ©2003. The Pennsylvania State University Press. The figure from this article is used by permission of The Pennsylvania State University Press.
27. By permission of The Pennsylvania State University Press, as in Note 26.
28. I don't know if this was Davidson's intention, but it seems to me that he is expressing a similar thought in his defense of the idea of some partitioning of the mind into semi-autonomous structures between which there may be nonlogical causal relations. "A theory that could not explain irrationality would be one that also could not explain our salutary efforts, and occasional successes, at self-criticism and self-improvement" (Davidson, 1982, 305). On the normalcy of this idea of the self as a reflexive community, see, for example, Ainslie, on a self as a "community of interests," a kind of center or alliance produced by negotiation among important interests (Ainslie, 1986, 1992).
29. Natural explanations for how the felt intimacy of being a subject may have developed biologically would be the work of psychologists and neuroscientists.
30. This may be similar to what Gallagher and Marcel (1999) refer to as embedded self-awareness. "When one is aware of one's actions at the time of acting, one experiences them as owned, as one's own" (291).
31. Some thought experiments (e.g., the brain in the vat) suggest that self-consciousness and the sense of "I" could be had even if the brain were not properly connected to a normal human body. I (I-as-philosopher) am not sure what the network model of the self could say about this other than to reiterate the point made earlier that a brain by itself is not a self, however important it may be as a constituent of a self.
32. A desire to eat chocolate would be a first-order desire, a desire or assessment that I ought to resist that desire would be a second-order desire or evaluation of the first-order desire. See Frankfurt (1971).
33. Buchler (1979, 29–57). See Section 7.
34. Earlier versions of the sections on Mead and Royce first appeared in Wallace (2003).
35. Mead is aware of this; he says that he is interested only in identifying what must be a feature of conduct. Baeten (1999) makes a similar criticism of the "I" and elaborates and builds on the basic structure suggested by Mead.
36. Royce argues that interpretation is a cognitive process distinct from perception and conception, both of which he tends to conceive on a dyadic and correspondence model. Interpretation is selective, is the construction of signs and meaning, and is necessary for knowledge to be achieved. Knowledge is an ongoing process of interpretation as communities of selves move into the future. Royce's theory of interpretation was influenced by Peirce's sign theory and the notion of the community of inquirers. See Royce (1969a, 740ff.).
37. For Royce, community is achieved through interpretation (communication), the reverse of what I suggest, that community is a *pre-condition* for communication. Roycean community could be a kind of community, one that is more explicit and self-aware qua community to its members and probably more honorific than what I intend by experiential parallelism.
38. Buchler's style is more discursive than is congenial to many contemporary philosophical habits of exposition. I will abstract the definition of reflexive communication, which I think was developed from the insights of Mead and

Royce (and probably Peirce's sign theory), and use it to develop an account of self-constituting activity and first-person perspectives.

39. "Dominant" just means predominating or experientially prominent. It doesn't necessarily carry any political or power connotation, although something could be a common dominant object of communication because of political or power-based conditions.

40. "Objectification" could be an undesirable form of this aspect of symmetrical communication, or, an undesirable form of asymmetrical communication.

41. Habermas, discussing Mead, says that in a communicative context, the participants are always in a first-person perspective. Habermas (1992, Chapter 7). I'm not sure how that would be the case with asymmetrical communication. But, it might be a way to describe the feature of symmetrical communication whereby selves are also objects for one another.

42. Communication must involve a self, a sign, or meaning generator, but asymmetrical communication could occur without a *communicator* having initiated the process of meaning generation for a self. For example, the Milky Way on a clear night where there is little ambient light may communicate to a viewer its vastness and in response to it, the viewer generates meanings. But, the Milky Way does not communicate to a rock or another galaxy (qua galaxy, setting aside the possibility of other communicators in another galaxy). This is a broad way of understanding communication. Buchler admits that the distinction between mere impact and communication may be difficult to draw (Buchler, 1979, 29–30). Most of the time we are probably interested in communication in so far as it involves communicators, meaning selves who function as initiators or recipients or both. But, communication is a species of a more encompassing natural process that selves undergo and contribute to. I won't press this point, as it is not germane to the issues I want to pursue.

43. For example, in practicing my self-presentation for a job interview I-as-job-seeker am communicating with myself, I-as-prospective-interviewee.

44. In Roycean terms, creating a new "space" might be thought of as "providing a unifying interpretation" (i.e., one that unifies one to a larger spiritual community). I am abstracting from the mentalistic and quasi-religious aspects of the Roycean perspective.

# 6 Autonomy and the Network Self

It was a frightening pleasure, but one she never again could be made to indulge in. She also made and doggedly kept other rules. . . . She asked no questions about Lymond . . . and set herself to finish quickly the tasks which had drawn her to the Loire, and then to leave for the coast and a ship for the Tyne before anyone could prevent her.

(Dorothy Dunnett)[1]

He belongs to himself and is at his own disposal. Or else what are we? . . . We are . . . at least no less than the animals. We are members of a race, and of a kingdom and of a family. The world has borrowed his strength often enough; can we not lend him ours when he needs it?

(Dorothy Dunnett)[2]

The idea is that such self-governance essentially involves, not the intervention of a little person in the head, but rather guidance and control by attitudes that help constitute a sufficiently unified point of view, a point of view that constitutes the agent's relevant practical standpoint.

(Michael Bratman)[3]

## 1. Introduction

Autonomy, or self-governance involves some capacity for acting independently of natural and social conditions. Thus, the question naturally arises, if a self is socially constituted can it be autonomous? Alford expresses a general sort of worry about whether a "socially constituted" self could "really" be autonomous, "capable of self-development" and of "an inner life":

The real enemies of the self are those who write of a need for a socially constituted self, as though this answered anything or meant anything other than the obliteration of the self [and not deconstructionists such as Lacan who seek to show that self is a neurotic symptom]. To write of the socially constituted self addresses none of the questions we want to answer, such as how we can protect and foster a rich inner life while overcoming the isolation and fear that leads monadic individuals to substitute wild self-assertion for self-cultivation. To write of the contribution of self-development achieved through meaningful political participation, identifying with the group, and so on is, in this context, not so much wrong as meaningless.

(Alford, 1991, 181)

While Alford's view expresses a worry that is sometimes had about social constitution and autonomy, other thinkers have pointed out the importance of social conditions and socialization to developing the capacity for autonomy. Feinberg (1989) points out that no one can be "literally and wholly self-made" (33), G. Dworkin (1989) that "all individuals have a history . . . develop socially and psychologically in a given environment with a set of biological endowments, . . . mature slowly and are, therefore, heavily influenced by parents, peers, and culture" (58). A self gets a great deal of causal help from others; selves are what Baier (1985) and Code (1991) call "second persons." As Meyers (1989, 2005) and others have pointed out, competencies, such as critical self-reflection that are often taken to be central to the capacity for and exercise of autonomy, depend on socialization, that is, on training and shaping of personal habits and skills as well as on a social environment which encourages and rewards the exercise of those skills.[4] Of course, social norms, institutions, practices, and relationships can also limit the range of significant options available and constrain the agency and freedom of the self.[5] Socialization and other social relations and conditions, such as being in prison, may be autonomy inhibiting, just as physical ones, such as being quadriplegic or schizophrenic, may be. Social and other conditions are not in principle autonomy inhibiting; some are, but some are autonomy enabling and enhancing. Christman (2009) argues that a theory of autonomy should acknowledge the fundamentally socio-historical nature of the self, and in doing so, recognize the ways in which social constitution can be both enabling and restricting. For Christman, the autonomous person is one who can reflexively and coherently navigate, integrate, critically evaluate and so on the social norms of one's social location.[6]

On the other side, some theorists argue that the notion of autonomy should be jettisoned altogether as representing a false ideal[7] or that its value should be qualified because it ignores the reality and importance of relationships and of dependency relations in particular.[8] But, more commonly, in Western thought, autonomy has been reconciled with socialization by conceptualizing autonomy in terms of a capacity for critical reflection and endorsement, or a capacity for integrating, for making principles, beliefs, wishes, and desires one's own, even if beliefs, desires, and so on have originated in a process of socialization and enculturation. I don't disagree with the importance of critical reflection and endorsement. However, since I have suggested that a self is not only "socialized," that is, socially influenced or caused in a variety of ways, but is socially, as well as biologically, physically, and so on, constituted, I would like to explore how self-definition and self-governance can be understood within the framework of the cumulative network model (CNM) of the self. I am going to suggest that autonomy (1) be conceptualized as a species of what I previously called reflexive communication that (2) is engaged in generating and acting on norms for self-guidance or self-rule. The notion of independence from social and natural conditions is reframed in terms of the reflexive communicative capacity to partially detach from such influences.

CNM might be thought to present a difficulty in conceptualizing who or what *the* self is in autonomy or *self*-determination. As a process the self is a changing and changeable network of relations and there seems to be no distinct, constant self or agential point of view. The self just is a network of multiple physical, biological, social locations; there is no self over and above such locations. It might then be thought that whatever preferences, values, desires, and norms that the network expresses are just internalized features of social roles, rather than expressions of genuine *self*-determination (via endorsement, choice, deliberate adoption, decision, or whatever is the preferred way to describe self-determination).

However, I have suggested that this difficulty can be bypassed by conceptualizing the self as an active network or system of perspectives capable of (reflexively) communicating with one another. The self has multiple "I" perspectives that communicate with one another (e.g., I-as-spouse, -feminist, -philosopher, -moody, -moral-chooser, -opera-lover, or as -angry, -desiring, -loving in some respect). The self can also take a "summed up" perspective on itself, e.g., I-as-I-am-up-to-this-time, a perspective from which the self can communicate with itself in one of its specific perspectives. Reflexive communication between I-perspectives is essential for self-understanding. I now want to suggest that it is the underlying mechanism by which a network self realizes autonomy.

Autonomy is a species of reflexive communication in which the self not only communicates with itself, but takes a normative or regulative perspective on itself. In reflexive communication, a perspective or perspectives of the self generate, enact, and assess a norm, rule, policy, principle, or guideline that regulates, guides, or directs the self synchronically (at a time) or diachronically (over time). Autonomy or self-rule does not require independence from social locations or self-perspectives, but rather, in reflexive communication, involves the capacity to partially detach from one role or perspective, to perform a legislating, executive, and assessing (and re-assessing) function with respect to it, to other aspects of the self, or to the self as a whole. Autonomy is not incompatible with assimilation of social norms. Rather, they may be normative conditions not only for the possibility of some activities, but for self-legislating, execution, and assessment; their assimilation may be a phase in the process of becoming autonomous in some respect. Nor is autonomy incompatible with relying or depending on others. Rather, there could be instances in which a self-generated norm is a rule to do just that, i.e., rely on others in some respect.

This approach means that autonomy is not only a process of making values, preferences or desires one's own. As self-*rule* or regulation autonomy itself has a temporal structure; it presupposes a temporally extended self, a process. Rule or regulation takes time and usually implies the possibility of recurrence, repetition and re-enactment, and reference to a normative stance. Self-rule or regulation can be changed or modified in its content. It might also mean that at a particular time a self could follow its own rule and by doing so be autonomous (self-ruled or self-guided) even if at a time, the self is not actively endorsing the rule, as might be the case, for example, in some pre-commitment arrangements.[9] In giving itself normative guidance, the self may enhance its narrative unity.

CNM rejects the notion that there is single perspective, controlling location, or transcendent self in the mind that is the seat of control and hence of autonomy, arguing instead for a community of first-person perspectives (Chapter 5). Others have rejected a single perspective notion as well. As noted in the previous chapter, in aiming to explain irrational behavior such as weakness of will, akrasia, and self-deception, it has been suggested that some partitioning of the mind seems to be required, and that the mind is a web of beliefs or attitudes, or that the self is a system of interconnected parts or functions. Pears (1985a, 1985b) suggests that agency should be attributed to a subsystem of independent mental states. Davidson (1982, 1985) argues that there may be boundaries between conflicting attitudes and semi-autonomous, overlapping territories in the mind. Others have also viewed the mind as a system. Watson (1975), in an early criticism of Frankfurt, adumbrated the notion of the self's agential standpoint as constituted by an evaluational system (216). Bratman (2007, 2012) characterizes agency in terms of a planning system of self-management and governance. Ekstrom (1993), borrowing from epistemology, argues for a notion of autonomy as coherence among mental states. Sneddon (2013) follows a line of argument similar to Ekstrom's in accounting for what he calls autonomy of persons (in contrast to autonomy of choice). Sripada (2014) proposes that self-control can be best understood by a divided mind account, suggesting that the exercise of willpower involves a deliberative regulatory system that is distinct from an emotional or conative system of the mind. The network model of the self and the account of autonomy developed here would be in the company of theories that consider the self as a system with the capacity for agency, self-control, and autonomy.

In the rest of this chapter, I will try to flesh out what I mean by normative self-guidance or self-rule, re-examine reflexive communication as the root capacity for autonomy, and explore a variety of ways in which the cumulative network self can be understood as autonomous or self-ruled. I will draw on and borrow from other thinkers to help develop my own view (and less as a matter of dialectical or critical engagement with their views).

## 2. Autonomy as Self-rule

The term "autonomy" connotes a cluster of related concepts, among them self-governance, moral self-governance, independence from others, free will, authenticity, ownership, and authorship of oneself, self-assertion, and critical reflection.[10] I understand autonomy in its most literal and etymologically original sense as meaning self-rule or self-governance. Mele (1995), too, takes this as the root meaning of autonomy.[11] And, G. Dworkin (1989) argues that "the central idea that underlies the concept of autonomy is indicated by the etymology of the term: *autos* (self) and *nomos* (rule or law)" (57). The concept was first applied to a state that was able to make its own laws rather than be under the rule or power of another state. In extending the idea to individual persons Dworkin says that persons are autonomous when "their decisions and actions are their own" (57).

> My suggestion is that it is the broader notion of autonomy that is linked with the identification of a person with his projects, values, aims, goals, desires, and so forth. It is only when a person identifies with the influences that motivate him, assimilates them to himself, views himself as the kind of person who wishes to be moved in particular ways, that these influences are to be identified as 'his.'
>
> (Dworkin, 1989, 60)

In distinguishing autonomy from freedom, Dworkin characterizes freedom as a "local concept, autonomy a global one":

> The question of freedom is decided at specific points in time. He was free to do such and such at a particular time. At a later time he was not free to do that. Whereas the notion of autonomy is one that can only be assessed over extended portions of a person's life. It is a dimension of assessment that evaluates a whole way of living one's life.
>
> (Dworkin, 1989, 60)

I don't disagree with much of Dworkin's characterization. Identification with and endorsement of projects, wishes, goals, desires, and so on can be aspects of self-rule. And I agree that there is a distinction between freedom and autonomy, and with Dworkin's point that freedom is neither necessary nor sufficient for autonomy (Dworkin, 1989, 60). However, the notion of identification and Dworkin's formulation emphasize the "self" part of self-rule, an authenticity condition and a central feature of autonomy. But, just as central is the "rule" or governance part. As Bratman (2005) puts it, some normative content is a distinctive feature of self-governance:

> [t]he very idea of governance brings with it, I think, the idea of direction by appeal to considerations treated as in some way legitimizing or justifying. This contrasts with a kind of agential direction or determination that does not involve normative content. And this means that the higher-order policy-like attitudes that are cited by the hierarchical theorist should in some way reflect this distinctive feature of self-governance.
>
> (43)

Autonomy involves not just that motivations come from the self or are endorsed by the self, but that the self, like the state in the original etymological meaning of the term, legislates, generates a rule or norm for itself, executes, that is, conducts itself according to its own norms, and assesses (and re-assesses) its own norms and conduct.

While my purposes are different, in company with Plato and Aristotle,[12] I want to explore an analogy between the individual and the state, in my case in order to bring into relief the notion of self-rule.

## 3. Self-rule: Individual and the State

An autonomous State would be one that has the sovereign authority to legislate and to govern itself and that actually does so govern itself. An autonomous State determines its own laws (by whatever mechanisms are in place, democratic or otherwise) without interference from others. As such it exhibits de facto autonomy and sovereign authority, two of four closely related meanings of autonomy identified by Feinberg: (1) capacity to govern, (2) the actual condition of self-government or de facto autonomy, (3) an ideal of character, or (4) sovereign authority (1989, 28). De facto autonomy, which is roughly what I mean by autonomy, presupposes capacity. The concept of sovereign authority suggests that the State has a right to absolute authority over itself within its own boundary or territory, a right to freedom from interference. However, sovereignty is no guarantee that a State will exercise its authority wisely or govern itself well. When it governs itself poorly others may or may not interfere, depending on whether there are negative repercussions to themselves (e.g., the effects of civil war bleeding into another territory) or whether there are morally heinous aspects to its mode of self-governance (e.g., apartheid) such that other States or collective actors exert moral and economic pressure through boycotts, or military pressure, and so on. (There could also be ways in which a State governs itself poorly that do not lead others to rise in protest or interference, and sovereignty remains intact.)

The concept of sovereignty may be analogous to Dworkin's notion of freedom for the individual in so far as both seem to be about non-interference, a right to exercise authority over one's own affairs (however well or poorly one does so). Applying this concept to an individual, a self would have sovereignty in so far as it has authority over itself and a right to non-interference, however well or poorly it actually governs itself. Qua sovereign, the self freely engages in voluntary, intentional behavior, but is not necessarily autonomous if the core of autonomy also involves the notion of self-governance or self-rule (Feinberg's sense of de facto autonomy).

An entity has de facto autonomy when it regulates and governs itself. A State may be more or less successful in governing itself, and thus more or less successfully self-ruled. For example, if a legislative body were paralyzed by internal conflict such that it were unable to pass legislation, and thus the nation which it is supposed to govern were to drift into situations in virtue of the legislature failing to act or allowing laws to expire, then such a State would not be or would be less autonomous than one in which there were a robustly functioning legislative body that was able to purposively direct and regulate its national affairs. The example is meant only to be illustrative of a case where self-governance might fail in some respect. Inaction, as in a sunset provision that allows a law to expire, could be a deliberate strategy or pre-commitment device in self-governance, too. Not governing well could result in or be a failure to govern at all, and thus be a failure to achieve autonomy or self-rule. Similarly, a self would be de facto autonomous when it actually (at least somewhat successfully) rules itself, that is, is able to generate or legislate rules or norms for itself, conduct itself according to its own norms, and assess its own conduct and norms. Governing itself badly could result in diminishment of or failure to achieve de facto autonomy or self-rule.

Autonomy understood as self-rule involves assessability of norms and observance of its own norms. The functional characterization of norm guidance developed by Railton articulates the point:

> Agent A's conduct C is guided by norm N only if C is a manifestation of A's disposition to act in a way conducive to compliance with N, such that N plays a regulative role in A's C-ing, where this involves some disposition on A's part to notice failures to comply with N, to feel discomfort when this occurs, and to exert effort to establish conformity with N even when the departure from N is unsanctioned and nonconsequential.
>
> (Railton, 2006, 13)

Assessability means not that autonomy necessarily requires perfect alignment with a norm, but that what one does, how one acts, or lives can be assessed as approximating or fulfilling with varying degrees of success the norm(s) that the self (or the State) has legislated for itself. It also means being able to assess the norm itself and whether compliance with it contributes to flourishing or should be modified or even abandoned and a new norm generated. A person who eats vegetables every day because she likes and desires vegetables is not autonomous even though she freely and authentically eats vegetables (the desire is genuinely hers and she is not coerced into eating them). If she doesn't eat vegetables one day, there is no normative judgment or assessment of her behavior as not keeping with a rule. However, the person who legislates a rule for herself, "eat vegetables every day," can evaluate her own conduct as complying or not with the norm she has set for herself. The latter norm governed case would be an instance of (local) autonomy and the former case would not. Of course, there could also be another norm that in some instance takes priority over an "eat vegetables" rule, in which case the assessment dimension of autonomy would also be in play. A self can assess whether a norm ought to be complied with. Suppose a self, who has endorsed some socially conventional gender norm, assesses conformity to that norm as not conducive to the self's flourishing. The self reflexively communicates with itself, and may modify or abandon that norm and generate a different one, with which it then aims to realign itself. Norm-generation and assessability allows for transformation of as well as self-governance by norms.

Autonomy involves (1) the defining, evaluating, generating, or endorsing of norms, policies, rules, standards by which to guide oneself (the legislative aspect), (2) the capacity or power to enact or execute those norms and the enacting of them (the executive aspect), and (3) assessability and re-assessability (a sort of judicial aspect). In practice, these aspects of autonomy may be functionally entwined, imperfectly realized and not necessarily present in the same degree. For example, a quadriplegic might be autonomous with respect to (1), but less so with respect to (2), or at least not without a lot of aid from others. Mele (1995) makes a similar distinction, such that a quadriplegic, for example, might lack executive autonomy or autonomy with respect to action, but, in Mele's terms, have "psychological autonomy" or autonomy with respect to mental/verbal possibilities, i.e., beliefs, values, decisions (even though they cannot be enacted, or not without a great deal of help).[13] This example also shows that autonomy does not necessarily entail needing no assistance or support from others, or preclude establishing a norm that one seek or rely on aid.

Autonomy is a process of self-governance in either a local or global sense. A self may be autonomous with respect to a specific type of choice or action (local) or it may be autonomous in terms of shaping itself as a whole (global). In either case, the underlying process is one of reflexive communication wherein the self generates norms or guidelines that guide its conduct, synchronically, and diachronically. In executing and complying with its own norms and in assessing itself as having done so or not, the self is communicating among its multiple perspectival capacities.

One might ask what the basis is for an entity having the authority, so to speak, to be self-governing. With regard to a State, there are usually founding documents, agreements, customs, and in some cases, sheer seizure of power that establish its authority, as well as ongoing political mechanisms for exercising it. Some ways of establishing authority might be more legitimate than others. With regard to a self, the basis is most commonly thought to reside in or derive from the rational, reasoning, intentional, planning, and inventive capacities of a self. Autonomy capacities should be conceived more broadly than how rationality generally tends to be conceived, but for now the point is just that having autonomy capacities is a sufficient basis for establishing an authoritative stance for a self. Realizing those capacities is part of what makes for a flourishing and rewarding life, a kind of Aristotelian argument for the basis of and importance of autonomy. A more Kantian argument might be that rationality and with it the capacity for autonomy entitle selves to respect, and that is fundamental to the very possibility of morality. In either case, in so far as a self is capable of autonomy, it ought to be regarded as having it, protected in its exercise of self-rule, and encouraged to develop "autonomy skills."[14] Even when a self doesn't develop autonomy skills or doesn't exercise self-rule or exercise it well, we still tend to think that possession of the capacity means that we should respect the sovereignty of the individual and encourage or facilitate the potential for development of autonomy skills.

## 4. Reflexive Communication as Root of Autonomy

I said earlier that autonomy can be understood as a species of reflexive communication. Reflexive communication is a way of broadening our understanding of autonomy capacities to include norm-generation, execution, and assessment, that is, self-rule.

In Chapter 5, I discussed the notion of reflexive communication, as the capacity by which a network self can be thought of as perspectives in communication with one another. Autonomy conducing communication is (symmetrical) reflexive communication. In reflexive communication, one I-perspective is an object for another I-perspective (and vice versa) with respect to a common dominant (salient) object *and* each I-perspective generates signs both in relation to the other I-perspective and to the dominant object. Extending the concept of reflexive communication to autonomy:

(1) That a self-perspective can be an object for another self-perspective means that a self can partially detach itself from a perspective. This

means that a self is not just determined by, but can be (partially) independent of, its locations or perspectives. Reflexive communication is the ability to articulate a new self-perspective, one that is partially constituted by what's "given" and partially constituted by the self's own communicative processes, which may transform or supplant what is "given." A self guides itself not because it is unrelated to or undetermined by its social and other locations, but because it has the capacity to partially detach itself from a role or perspective(s) in some respect and communicate with or about it from another I-perspective.

(2) The sign-generating activity of reflexive communication is now one of generating, executing, and assessing norms by which the self guides or rules itself.

Recall the discussion in the previous chapter of I-as-feminist and I-as-spouse. In reflexive communication constituents of the self are not merely passive locations, but perspectives through which the self contributes to its own formation. When the self does so by generating, executing, and assessing norms or guidelines for its own conduct and direction, it is self-governing. The I-as-feminist and the I-as-spouse communicate with one another and generate a norm (or norms)—e.g., a naming norm (retain name of family of origin, adopt spouse's family name, create a new name)—by which the self navigates the marital relationship and its identity as both feminist and spouse.

Reflexive communication can take place in other modes as well, and so, too, can norm-generation. An athlete may generate and assess in the course of action norms by which to regulate or guide the self's movements. The self communicates with itself, this time in action (reflexive communication in "the mode of active judgment"). An artist, experimenting with colors and shapes, may establish and assess a color palette that serves as a normative framework for a series of paintings (reflexive communication in "the mode of exhibitive judgment").[15] The artist may re-assess the color palette in the process of painting itself or with respect to future painting. Or, in making a moral choice, I-as-empathic may communicate with I-as-committed-to-a-principle to generate or assess a norm to guide one's conduct, and this communication may occur both in action and in verbal articulation of a norm.

Autonomy as self-governance involves generating norms for self-guidance and assessing one's compliance with them as well as re-assessing norms themselves. These processes need not be formal or highly articulated. For example, in mastering a dance, a self sets norms of movement and in movement assesses and re-assesses its approximation to those norms. The capacity for autonomy should be understood not just in terms of reasoning capacities, but in terms of reflexive communication between perspectives of the self that can occur in a range of modes of judgment. Autonomy as self-governance suggests that a self has a kind of subjective authority, which earlier was identified as having a kind of sovereignty or right to govern itself. But, a question might be raised about whether there is a or some perspective(s) that is (are) authoritative. In the examples discussed thus far, perspectives are treated as on a par with one another. But, are some of a higher order than others? Ought some perspectives take precedence or are only some perspectives capable of being norm-generating perspectives? Are only some authoritative?

## 5. Autonomy, Hierarchy, and Subjective Authority

Frankfurt (1971) suggested that autonomy involves hierarchy whereby higher order or second order desires endorse lower or first-order desires. Frankfurt came under criticism for this (e.g., Watson, 1975) and later modified his view to say that autonomy involves agential satisfaction, identification with or wholeheartedness with respect to what the self endorses or cares about (Frankfurt, 1988, 1999). Sneddon (2013) suggests that taking a higher order stance towards one's own thought processes is crucial to being able to take control of one's choices and actions (although doing so need not involve explicit reasoning [60]). Bratman (2007) argues that there is pressure towards hierarchy in the self-management of the multitude of conflicting first-order desires (242). This creates a need for subjective authority in establishing priorities and order, both synchronically and diachronically, and thus the need for what Bratman calls planning agency (Bratman, 2007).

Autonomy involves the ability to take a perspective on oneself in at least some respect. Whether the distinction between higher and lower is the best way to think about this depends on what is meant by "higher order." The idea of higher order functioning is concerned with two things: (1) the nature of the capacity, capacities, or "causal power(s)" involved in autonomy and (2) the issue of the self, or an aspect of a self, having an authoritative perspective on itself, or exercising a kind of subjective authority. Authority implies being above or higher than that over which authority is exercised, or having justified power or control over something. In social settings, authority may be a function of power, or the holding of an office, or, it could be an expression of expertise or knowledge, or some other quality that in some context bestows authority on someone or some group. For a self, higher order functioning is usually conceptualized in terms of the exercise of rational and deliberative capacities, or, with Bratman (2007), in terms of planning ability and the engaging in justificatory reasoning for choices and policies, or, with Sripada (2014), in terms of the deliberative system (essential to the exercise of will power and a different "causal power" from the desiring or emotional system).

Autonomy can depend on the exercise of such rational capacities, but for CNM it need not. Rather, for CNM the capacity for norm-generation, execution, and assessment can occur in many different modes. The perspective from which a self establishes a norm functions as subjectively authoritative for the self in that respect. This could involve rational deliberation in legislating a norm, but it could also involve active or exhibitive inquiry, as, in our previous examples, when an athlete or a dancer determines in action the optimal placement of the foot for executing a particular movement, or when an artist experiments with paint to form a color palette that provides a normative framework for a series of paintings, or when a moral chooser navigates between empathy and principle. A perspective could take priority over another in some context(s), but that priority might not hold for all contexts. CNM by itself would be neutral on the relative priority of rational and emotional perspectives for generating moral norms. The account of why, and in what contexts and respects, one or the other should have priority would come from moral theory, not from some intrinsic superiority of one perspective over the other.

Establishing a subjectively authoritative perspective could be a local or global matter. For example, suppose as environmentalist, the self legislates a norm for itself to not own a car and to organize one's mobility around other modes of transportation. This would be an instance of local autonomy, by "local" meaning autonomy in a specific respect (even if in an automobile-based culture it could have far reaching effects). Or, more globally, the self as a writer sets a norm that writing is the highest priority and organizes one's life, social relations and obligations, other activities, and so on, around this priority, expressed by legislating more specific norms such as a rule, "write every morning for two hours," or "check email only once a day at 3 p.m."[16] In this example, the self qua writer functions as subjectively authoritative for the self as a whole, that is, for establishing an overall direction and set of priorities for the self. Such norms can be re-assessed, of course; periodic re-assessment is a recurrent aspect of being autonomous.

Not only may the scope of a perspective's authority be local or global, but the locus of subjective authority may shift depending on context and purpose. The process of norm-generation through reflexive communication could occur in any one of many I-perspectives, I-as-feminist, I-as-housewife, I-as-spouse, I-as-parent, I-as-philosopher, I-as-moral-chooser, I-as-moody, or I-as-a-whole-self-as-I-am-up-to-time-t. As in the previous examples, the self could be autonomous locally in some respect(s) or context(s) and not in others. Or, the self could take a comprehensive perspective on itself as a whole and reflexively articulate a new direction or normative policy for itself as a whole or with respect to its overall identity (global autonomy or autonomy of person, or what Meyers [2005] calls "the unified self"). Autonomous redirection of the self may occur when a self steps back, so to speak, and takes stock of its life as a whole, for example, asking, "how shall I organize my priorities for the next ten years of my life?," "what directions and guidelines shall I set for my life?," "do I accept or reject the values of parental upbringing?," "my cultural or religious socialization?" Or, it might be more specific, for example, "what norms can I set for myself *qua* feminist and *qua* married?"

Whether autonomy concerns a self as a whole, or a self in specific respects (or perspectives), it does not consist in *the* higher level self viewing, critically reflecting on and/or controlling *the* lower level self. Higher and lower are not fixed locations, but rather functions that are expressed in different perspectives. Autonomy consists in I-perspectives reflexively communicating with one another to generate, execute or assess a norm or norms by which to regulate or direct one's conduct, behavior or choices in some respect(s). What perspective(s) counts (count) as authoritative for the self will depend on the organization of the network, on context, and on the scope of a norm. The plurality of perspectives does not rule out constancy in self-organization and self-rule. A self may have a strong moral compass; a self may have a firmly established direction and orientation. All CNM says is that for any of this to come about or be sustained there need not be a single, ruling perspective.

A couple of worries might arise at this point. One, how does the self resolve conflict among perspectives if there is no single authoritative I-perspective or "executive I"? Second, if there are multiple I-perspectives, where is the one "true self"? Third, if there is no single authoritative I-perspective, then wouldn't the self risk degenerating into "brute shuffling," Bratman's memorable phrase (2012, 81), between ever shifting perspectives, contexts, and preferences?

I will discuss "brute shuffling" in Section 6. Here I briefly comment on the other two points. A single, authoritative I-perspective is not necessary for autonomy. Rather, self-governance can be achieved and conflict resolved through communication (think, negotiation) among perspectives. A resulting resolution of conflict or establishing of priorities might be thought of as constituents of the self cooperatively organizing themselves accordingly. I am not saying that self-conflict is easily or always resolved. Conflict resolution could be less than autonomous. It could be very messy, involve less than reasonable processes and normative outcomes. Or it could not be autonomous at all and perhaps be simply dominance by an aspect or perspective of the self. Suppose a powerful emotion or irresistible desire dominates or overcomes other considerations, a case perhaps of intemperance or incontinence. That selves are not always autonomous is a feature of selves no matter what theory of self or of autonomy one has. But, there is no reason why CNM's way of conceptualizing autonomy is any less autonomy than a model that says there is a single, directing or ordering perspective that keeps the rest of an unruly self in order. What matters is that the self is the source of its own normative guidance, and CNM can give an account of that.

Regarding the "one true self" idea: One version of it suggests that through some transformative experience—such as, religious conversion, or sex reassignment surgery—one can discover or is able to "be" one's real self. Or, another version might be that there are aspects of a self accessible to or known only to and by the self that remain invisible to others and that are highly valued by the self. There may also be aspects of a self that are repressed or rendered unrealizable by circumstances, by others, or by other aspects of the self. There may be beliefs, thoughts, feelings, desires, moods, intentions that a self doesn't reveal or share, and that a self may feel are more "true" or authentic than what is revealed. It's often said that one can never truly know another person, particularly when someone does something unexpected or that doesn't seem to match what one previously knew about the person. But, nothing in any of this implies that such aspects are necessarily more "truly" the self (even if in some cases, they might be highly valued aspects of a self and, in some of these examples, valued at least in part because they are not shared or revealed). All that CNM says is that any such aspects of the self are nodes in or functionings of nodes in the network, even if routes of access to those aspects of the self are closed off to others (and maybe even to other aspects of the self). Autonomy or self-rule may be directed toward governing such aspects of the self, either by managing their hiddenness or by determining how to realize or express them.

## 6. Autonomy, Authenticity, and Identity

Self-rule or normative self-guidance would seem to involve some commitment to coherence, consistency, and coordination of multiple and possibly conflicting dimensions of the self. A self-*governed* life is different from a life of "brute shuffling," a life that drifts or shifts from one thing to another with no apparent reason or coherence. To be normatively guided means to have some organization and coordination among one's conative states, to have and be guided by priorities among one's different traits or "identities." In the language of CNM, through norm-generating reflexive communication, the self strengthens some self-relations, weakens others, introduces new locations or perspectives and aims to establish their relative importance.

The demand of self-management for coordination or ordering suggests that there is pressure towards some version of orthonomy, that is, good or right governance. In other words, if bad governance tends toward, or risks, being not governance at all, then there is some pressure toward right governance. If that demand is only a demand for *some* ordering, coherence or coordination, then what might count as "good" or "right" governance could be pretty variable, and hard to prescribe in detail or in advance for any particular self (*contra* the highly prescriptive treatment of orthonomy given by Pettit and Smith, 1993).

There might be a tension between self-governance and authenticity, that is, a tension between demands for coherence and coordination on the one hand, and the fact that the self as a process develops and changes over time on the other. What might be a compelling form of self-governance at one time may be disavowed at a later time, what may at one time be something that authentically reflects and expresses the goals and commitments of a self may at a subsequent time feel alien to a self. Examples could range from radical changes in gender or professional identity or experiences involving religious or political conversion to more local examples such as someone committed to a marriage experiencing a change of heart or a change in commitment in the context of agreements concerning the disposition of frozen embryos Matsumura (2014).[17]

If autonomy ought to reflect the self as it is, then as the self changes, authenticity seems to demand that self-governance allow for change, replacement, and supplanting of self-generated norms. Assessment and periodic re-assessment of one's own normative stance is a dimension of autonomy. At the same time, a couple of cautionary observations are in order. First, the disposition(s) of a current phase of the self could be temporary. A current state could be *un*representative of the authentic character and dispositions of a self and a stronger guiding tone or character of the self may be probative or reassert itself after having temporarily receded in self-awareness. This is the underlying insight behind at least some pre-commitment strategies, whereby the self takes steps in advance to protect itself from temporary (or even recurrent), potentially strong, but unrepresentative or unendorsed conative states and dispositions. Second, since a process self is always subject to further change in the future, the identification of authenticity with whatever is a self's current state may be precarious.

According to CNM, the self is a process, not an isolated time slice or discrete temporal part. The self who seeks to disavow or to transform *is* the cumulative upshot of the one process self who may, at an earlier phase, have generated, executed, and assessed norms, agreements or commitments. These are authentic constituents of the self, even if the self in a present moment may feel psychologically alienated, temporarily or permanently, from previously generated norms or prior agreements and commitments. Authenticity or identity is not a momentary phenomenon, characterized solely in terms of a present disposition, conative state, or even deliberative state. As a process, its past is constitutive of, relevant to, who the self is even as it may change going forward. At the same time, the processual nature of the self may exert a pressure towards disavowal, reinvention, and new norm-generation. This is in part why assessment and periodic re-assessment are dimensions of autonomy. Still, disavowal or reinvention is always from a particular, determinate stance or phase of the process, not the stance of a wholly new, in that moment *de novo* self. Recalling the discussion in Chapter 3, the integrity or character of the self may develop and change over time, indeed as a process it would have to, even as the process persists as a unity.

Moreover, at least some forms of self-governance involve committing oneself to something in the future. In self-governance one is contributing to the shape of one's own future, even if, as the process continues and develops, the self may revisit, assess or change its normative stance. Of course, as the self develops and transforms, some commitments or norms may be difficult to change. Because the future is uncertain, this is a risk of any self-governance. To be governed by a norm with which one in one's present state no longer identifies by itself does not necessarily imply either non-autonomy or inauthenticity.

Return for a moment to the analogy to a State. Suppose a State passes a law that later becomes outdated or no longer reflects the public will. Is the State no longer autonomous, *self*-governed, with respect to such a law? The law is a product of the State's own normative processes. While the State is governed by the outdated law, it doesn't thereby cease to be self-governed (autonomous). There are presumably (political and legal) mechanisms by which the State can change or repeal the law, although there may be some laws or commitments (some treaties, for instance) from which, even with a change of public will, it would be extremely difficult for a State to withdraw. That does not mean that the State is no longer self-governed. It means, rather, that some normative choices or commitments are riskier than others in the sense that the ability to revoke or repeal them may be limited or possibly non-existent in the future. The capacity to re-assess, revoke, and reinvent norms ameliorates the risk of becoming bound to outdated, ineffective or inauthentic norms, but still, it is a risk of any governance.

We probably accept as part of societal governance that laws become outdated, or, as products of political compromises or bare majorities, are imperfect expressions of public will. But, a demand for ongoing authenticity seems more compelling for an individual self. Even acknowledging the importance of authenticity, at least some forms of self-governance involve commitment into the future and thus entail the risk of generating a norm that one may in the future want to disavow. The processual nature of the self and the sheer change and contingency in the world may result in some inevitable tension between authenticity at a time and autonomy. In addition, the plural constitution of the self also means that authenticity is not simply realizing one's *one* true self, but rather may involve living with multiplicity that is not perfectly integrated. For example, I-as-feminist and I-as-spouse, I-as-moody and I-as-energetic could be authentic perspectives and constituents of the self. Even though the self might seek to integrate them, there might also be a persistent tension between equally authentic aspects of the self.

While transformation and change may often be accommodated by the self's capacity to normatively transform and integrate its multiple constituents, there may also be consequences of self-governance that are not so easily changed, disavowed or abandoned and aspects of the self that are not perfectly reconciled or integrated with another. Some commitments may remain constitutive in at least some sense of the self going forward. Some may continue to be binding simply because the nature of the commitment and the temporal structure of the process don't allow for going back to undo a choice made or a norm generated. One can't undo having become a parent. There are of course many social and legal norms that make it difficult to renounce that choice and commitment. It is also a commitment that when one makes it, carries with it a commitment into the future. Selves have walked away from such commitments, and sometimes on the grounds of personal self-realizations and new commitments. But, the fact that some normative choices are supposed to bind one in the future doesn't mean that the self who finds itself bound by but wishing to disavow such choices is thereby inauthentic (even if unhappy) or no longer self-governed. Rather authenticity may involve recognizing the self as a process, and that its identity, that is, its character or integrity, is as much wrapped up with the cumulative force of its history as it is with a current state or with how it projects itself into the future.

It is not only from the risk of degenerating into "brute shuffling" that autonomy or self-governance may involve some pressure towards coherence and conservation of norms. It is also because its past is a relevance condition of the self at any time. It is no doubt complicated in any given case to sort out what can be coherently transformed and what can't, and between cases where the self has given up self-governance and cases where the self continues to be self-governed even when it disavows and changes norms. In contrast to the State where there may be fairly clearly specified procedural rules for changing norms and the following of which ensure that the State continues to be self-*governed* (and is not merely exerting power or whim), for a self, the process is not so mechanical or publicly rule governed. A self may not follow formal procedural rules that mark the process as governance. Still, the notion of *validatable* norm change (validatability follows from the assessability feature of autonomy) seems central to change that is an expression of self-*governance*. The tension between stability and transformation, between autonomy and authenticity, between (a) the commitments of prior self-governing and (b) disavowal and new legislation is endemic to a process self. One of the tasks of an autonomous self is to navigate that Scylla and Charybdis.

## 7. Autonomy, Social Norms, and Socialization

Not all normatively guided activity is autonomous. A self could merely internalize or be "in the grip of" (Gibbard, 1990, 60) a variety of social norms and unreflectively act according to them. And even when reflexive communication is involved, it could result in self-deception, or adaptive preference formation and mere reproduction or reinforcement of internalized oppressive, addictive, limiting, or destructive patterns. For example, suppose a self aims to become a professional colleague, but merely internalizes, imitates, and reproduces "old boys club" patterns of behavior. Such an example would be parallel to the housewife example discussed in some feminist literature, whereby the self internalizes and enacts socialized gender patterns and roles without generating norms of its own. Of course, in the housewife case, the idea is not only that a given social role is simply reproduced, but the role is itself subordinating and therefore autonomy inhibiting in other ways. The latter points to ways in which norms, whether self-generated or merely unreflectively internalized, could inhibit, suppress or discourage the development of autonomy skills, as well as have an impact on restricting the range or scope of self-rule (both locally and globally). But, the immediate point here is the nature of the reflexive process rather than the content of the norm itself. The same mere internalization process could take place with respect to politically or socially challenging positions as well. For example, someone could be a feminist or socialist or social conservative in so far as one simply assimilated and reproduced the position, similar to the process wherein a traditional role is simply reproduced, a kind of mimicry rather than self-rule.

However, in another respect a "good-old-boy" or a housewife could be autonomous. Each could articulate and authorize those norms as their own, as norms that each sanctions or approves or even modifies in some way, and invests with validity for him or herself. Such a process could itself be shaped or influenced by adaptive preferences, although by itself that doesn't necessarily mean that a self has not exercised its own judgment, evaluated and authorized for itself what, given its situation, should be the norms by which it will be guided.[18] To say that such a self could be autonomous, doesn't mean that the scope of the self's autonomy is ideal. It could be widened, the self's options improved, and the self's autonomy skills improved. But, endorsement of an existing social norm, even one that is less than ideal for the fullest possible human flourishing, may count as autonomy or self-rule. Self-rule can occur under many, including less than ideal, circumstances.

Turning now to the content of the norm, is there a difference between authorizing, choosing, or endorsing a social role that is by definition subordinating and one that is not? Could someone deliberately choose slavery *and* remain autonomous?[19] Or, choose to submit to monastic rule, or to the authority of a husband (the housewife example), or to military rule by enlisting in the armed forces, and still be autonomous? What about choosing to join a cult and submit to the authority of a cult leader? Are these cases of renouncing autonomy?

On the one hand, one might be autonomous in some sense because one self-legislates in so far as one endorses a norm (e.g., "obey the master/

spouse/leader/abbot/superior officer"). One might also still assess and re-assess whatever demands or rules are made by the authority under which one lives, even if one's executive ability is circumscribed. Or, one might develop norms of resistance that one enacts even in and as one conforms to rules and authority. On the other hand, one might be so beaten down that none of that is possible. And it is a risk in any of these examples that even when there are good reasons for choosing subordination, and when doing so realizes a normative commitment, such submission could undermine the capacity for autonomy.

Still, there might be some global norm that one expresses one's commitment to through submission to a rule defined and administered by an authority. This might particularly be the case for commitments that can only be realized through coordinated, collective action. For instance, the soldier who is committed to the norm of defending her country in the face of attack, or the nun or monk who joins a monastic order in order to commit her or himself to participation in a communal order dedicated to God or to serving moral goals, such as, ministering to the poor.

There might be some differences here though, between cases where one simply submits to the will of another and where one submits to a system of rules administered by another (e.g., as in monastic or military rule). The latter has a normative structure to it, whereas the former does not. Still this might not be a well-defined boundary since an authority could devise and impose rules, however arbitrary.

In the monastic or military case, it seems that the individual could be taking a normative stance by choosing a rule or set of rules, and identifying with them as his or her own norms. The nun/monk or soldier renounces many personal concerns and commits to following the order of the community as the guide and basis for self-regulation. In defining one's self-identity through membership in such a community, the individual explicitly endorses as norms of that self-identity the rigors of monastic or military rule. Thus, the individual would have the appropriate intentional, ongoing, authorizing relation to them qua norms. In someone choosing subordination to the will and authority of another, e.g., a husband or cult leader, it seems that the individual is not choosing, endorsing or identifying with a norm, but is submitting to the will of another. Perhaps such a case is something like the intemperate person who acts on her own whims and desires, while in subordination the self is subject to the whims and desires of another. In contrast, the nun or monk (or soldier) appears to meet the functional characterization of norm guidance developed by Railton referred to earlier (Section 3) that nicely captures its regulative character.

The person choosing subordination may be choosing a way of life that the person may even continue to value, and in some cases, it may even be courageous to do so (see the example in Note 19). Sneddon (2013) argues that such a life therefore counts as autonomous (69). On the account of autonomy as self-rule, the process of living that life would not count as autonomous if the individual is unable to generate, follow or assess norms. But, if there are some respects in which the self has such a capacity then in those respects, the self would be autonomous.[20] It therefore may be difficult to generalize about these kinds of cases, since whether and to what extent they impact autonomy seems to depend on the particulars of each case.[21]

Not all social norms or their internalization is oppressive or limiting. Assimilation of social norms may play a constructive role in autonomy, such as when norms are constituents of a starting point or phase in the process of becoming autonomous. For example, a tennis player or a dancer who in submitting to a training regimen masters basic skills and capabilities and thereby develops the capacity for inventiveness and self-determination as a tennis player or dancer. Or, as a driver one learns the rules of driving, in practice makes them one's own and endorses them as the normative conditions for exercising self-control as a driver and for making driving possible in a social setting. Once one has become proficient, following the rules may be largely automatic. By itself that doesn't mean that one is not autonomous. In fact, proficiency, wherein one doesn't need to reflect on or think about the rules, may enhance one's autonomy in the sense of being able to act in a self-guided way (Mele's "executive autonomy," referred to earlier). It may also make one over-confident or careless, but the point is just that autonomy is not incompatible with, and may be achieved in part through, the assimilation of social norms and by the development of "autonomy skills."

The self not only assimilates social norms but makes them its own, such that a norm may be partly the product of the self's own reflexive activity. In this sense endorsement or reaffirmation (as opposed to knee-jerk reproduction) of oneself as "a good-old-boy" or as a housewife could be an instance, with the qualifications noted previously, of autonomy. Autonomy does not require abandoning assimilated social norms, although it could involve rejecting them and developing new ones, or modifying and transforming them in significant ways.

## 8. Autonomy and Power

I'm not addressing political theory in this book, but there is a line of thinking about selves, identity, and autonomy in contemporary critical theory that I very briefly want to comment on. A deeper worry about norms and socialization as disabling of autonomy comes from a Foucauldian line of thought, namely, that all social norms and processes of socialization ("normalization") are embedded in, are expressions of, and means of reinforcing power relations and institutions. The self is intractably shaped by mechanisms of power. If that is the case, there is no independent or transcendental standpoint that the self can take to critique, transform or reject any norms, because every such position is itself pervaded by power. The very idea of a genuinely autonomous self is illusory. On this line of thought, though, the very argument itself would be intractably shaped by mechanisms of power and therefore, would be suspect as a perspective *on* power relations. I think, therefore, that Allen (2008) is right when she argues that Foucault's point is, or at least should be, not that rationality can never operate critically, but that we need to recognize and be critical of the ways in which power operates and shapes subjectivity and our political positions and critiques.

The fact that power relations are pervasive seems indisputable. But, that doesn't entail that every social location is or is merely a power relation. The fact that we are necessarily constituted by forces and conditions, social, and otherwise, does not mean that such constitution is a totalizing determination. Rather, relations of dependence and interdependence are distinct from submission and subordination (Allen, 2008, 84). Moreover, social constitution and social norms can be enabling of autonomy—for example, as a source of autonomy skills. According to CNM the multiple constitution of the self means (1) that no single perspective or location of the self is wholly determinative of the self, and (2) that each self is a unique network of perspectives and locations. Their unique interrelatedness is not merely reducible to the social (or biological or whatever) origins of any of the perspectives and locations. Even with the operation of power relations, the reflexive activity of the self is not merely a reproduction of its underlying social sources.

CNM says that there are many ways in which social constitution shapes a self and some of those ways may be autonomy enabling, rather than subordinating or oppressing. Some ways in which the self is socially constituted may not be about, or primarily about, power. Even in less than ideal circumstances, even in circumstances when a self has less power than another self or when a self is powerless in the face of social and political structures and institutional arrangements, a self may still have the possibility of self-rule in at least some respect(s) partly because the self is plurally constituted and as a process, incomplete. This is not to deny that there may be important considerations about the scope of power, about equity and opportunity. I don't mean to downplay the possible effects of power, but they shouldn't be overdrawn either.

## 9. Examples of Autonomy as Self-Governance Through Norm-Generation

I want to consider some additional examples to show how this approach is inclusive of experiences (such as navigating relationships, athletic action, and caregiving) that are not often thought of as autonomous.

In the spouse/feminist example from Chapter 5, a self might articulate a norm for being a spouse/feminist as an extension of feminist judgment and of self-transformation for its own sake. Or a self might articulate a policy with respect to achieving some particular goal, for example, a norm guiding daughterly conduct for the sake of sustaining or transforming some constellation of family relations. Norm-generating reflexive communication may take place in a very general way or in a specific respect, for example, marriage-in-light-of-feminist-concerns. It could take place in an action or active judgment (e.g., under whose name to file joint tax returns) or in an arrangement of jewelry (e.g., wearing or not wearing a wedding ring), an exhibitive judgment, and not only as a mental or linguistic assertion about how one is going to behave.[22] Feminism and marriage as dimensions of the self have wider social and historical determinants. The process of legislating a norm for oneself may thus have a dimension of collaborating with others, e.g., other feminists, other spouses, one's own spouse. The policy might also lead the self to initiate another process of self-definition, e.g., with respect to oneself as daughter or with respect to one's participation in social and political activity. In the good-old-boy example, a self might authorize being a good-old-boy as a norm of self-identity for its own sake, or as a useful norm for corporate advancement. Autonomy can take different forms, where norms may function as ends in themselves or instrumentally.[23]

As mentioned earlier, norm-generation need not be only the product of (rational) deliberation. A well-trained athlete develops norms in physical action, norms by which she is able to self-direct her movements. Imagine the athlete assessing the distance between herself and a hurdle and adjusting her pace so as to clear the hurdle. In the act of running, she also partially detaches from the act to assess and adjust her pace. The assessment is a form of reflexive communication, even if is not articulated in linguistic propositions and even if it occurs in split-second timing. The norm regulating bodily movements is validated in the successful action and the capability to repeatedly, and sometimes inventively, do the action. This would be a kind of autonomy (self-rule) developed and expressed in physical activity. Sneddon also includes some athletic activity as autonomous:

> [O]ther actions that are immediately controlled by specific mechanisms will also be amenable to the influence of more centralized capacities. This could be through training only, leaving the online performance of these actions under the control of the specific mechanism. However, the mechanism might allow for online intervention by, for example, explicit thought. The skilled movements of athletes are good examples for these sorts of action. They are the result of lots of training. Some are performed automatically—they must be, given the speed at which one must stop a puck or return a serve. However, athletes are often capable of intervening in the performance of their entrenched habits on the fly. This is at least part of what makes

creativity in sport possible. Either way, actions performed under the control of these sorts of mechanisms can be, but need not be, autonomous. *The crucial issue is not whether conscious thought is involved, but rather whether a choice (action, etc.) is made under the control of oneself.* This, the hierarchical theory contends, is a matter of the psychological arrangement of the production of the action.

(Sneddon, 2013, 24; my emphasis)

Training and practice themselves could constitute a process by which a self establishes norms for self-rule—self-control, in Sneddon's terms—during play and performance. Thus, the athlete could be autonomous even when specific actions during play are automatic, as well as when the athlete is able to invent in the process of play.[24] The point I am making is that the norm-generating process takes place in action itself—in the attentive, repetitive practice—as the self develops the capacity for self-governance with respect to a particular type of action. Just as in some contexts autonomy depends on the development of a skill such as critical reflection, in another context (action) it depends on the development of motor skills; in the one context autonomy may involve articulating in words a norm or a rule, in the other context, embodying or being able to articulate in action a norm. Similarly, a carpenter may invent and execute methods in the process of crafting woodwork, which serve as norms for her self-governance as carpenter. Each, the athlete and the carpenter, generates norms which are self-directing; each is engaged in a process of reflexive communication in the mode of active judgment. Neither may state in words or assertions exactly what the norm is, but each authorizes it and is able to articulate it qua norm in action, enact or exhibit it as a norm.

Autonomy can also develop in and guide social interaction. A parent interacting with her infant experiments with different ways of holding the infant. In her actions, she communicates with herself and with the infant, and in so doing develops norms by which she recurrently directs herself in the ongoing care of the infant. Such an interaction could also be purely reactive or impulsive (just as a carpenter's activity could be largely mechanical). But, it need not be; it can be attentive and reflexively communicative. When it is, a self is engaged in self-directing norm-governed caregiving.[25] The parent's reflexive communication is intertwined with interpersonal or social communication with the infant. (It could also be intertwined with communication with other caregivers.) She invents ways of responding to the infant that she authorizes as norms for comforting, communicating with, and succoring the infant. Such norms evolve over time as the infant grows and the parent's relationship to her child develops, but the point is, that this too can be autonomous and no less so for being parental and social than more typical, paradigm examples of autonomous action, such as a person making a career choice.

Similarly, a self could be autonomous in virtue of having developed a norm in consultation with others, or by having as a norm, that one consult with others. For example, suppose I-as-power-of-attorney for my aging parent legislate a rule for myself to always consult with my siblings before making a decision concerning my parent. The self is not less autonomous in legislating and following this rule than it would be if it set as a rule to never consult one's siblings. Perhaps one would authorize this rule for oneself because one thinks that it will help one make better decisions by gathering as much information as possible. Or, perhaps one authorizes the rule for oneself qua sibling in order to maintain good sibling relations. In any case, a process of reflexive communication among I-perspectives of the self (I-as-power-of-attorney, I-as-daughter, I-as-sibling) generates a norm for self-governance. We could also think of this as a composite I-perspective, I-as-power-of-attorney-daughter-sibling, whereby the multiple I-perspectives negotiate a common integrated perspective for authorizing and enacting a norm.

Suppose in setting up the power of attorney, an aging parent, a self and her siblings together develop the norm that two siblings shall have power of attorney, but neither one can authorize expenditures over a certain amount of money without the approval of the other. This would be an instance of reflexive and social communication operating together to generate a norm, a policy, in this case one that is legally binding. This is probably an instance of each self using social communication as a resource for reflexive communication *and* an instance of group or we-planning. The latter, we-planning, is not necessarily incompatible with individual autonomy.[26] In so far as each self communicates reflexively to establish this as a norm for herself each self would be autonomous with respect to the power of attorney. Other instances of negotiation between selves could also be instances of autonomy whereby even when compromise is involved, selves are still self-governed and therefore autonomous. What these examples also suggest is that while self-assertion, critical evaluation, setting some distance between one self and others may be necessary for at least some kinds of autonomy, other modes of social interaction, such as listening to, assimilating the views and experiences of others, might also be desirable as autonomy skills, especially when autonomy involves social collaboration and the development of norms as a member of a community or in relationships with others.

A self may also take a more "global" perspective and communicate with itself with regard to how to regulate or guide itself into its future or how to shape its self-identity with respect to its guiding values and norms. Autonomy in this sense concerns whether or to what extent a self has control over its life as a whole, its general direction, values, and goals. This is usually thought to require having at least some local autonomy or autonomy of choice, as well as self-knowledge, and the ability to shape oneself (Sneddon, 2013); or, having authorship of one's own narrative

(Velleman, 1996); or being able to be and enact one's "true self" (an authenticity requirement, e.g., Taylor, 1992); or having achieved integration, unification (e.g., Meyers' unified self, 2005), or coherence (Ekstrom, 1993, 2005). Some of these, such as requirements of wholeheartedness or integration or coherence, set the bar too high. It seems to me possible for a self to be autonomous, even if it is under duress or in less than ideal and enthusiastically (or wholeheartedly) embraced circumstances. Exercising autonomy might precipitate a family schism. For example, a self might communicate with itself about the values and norms according to which the self has been raised and transform or reject them, replacing them with other values and then regulating or ordering one's life in light of them.

In thinking about this global sense of autonomy, or "autonomy of the person," the question arises, are there norms, or ways of life that are incompatible with autonomy? Norms or ways of life that appear to be freely chosen, but that shouldn't count as autonomous or genuine self-rule? Classic examples that raise the question might include the house-wife or slave examples mentioned earlier. One that we haven't considered yet is that of the willing addict.

## 10. Constraints on Autonomy

I have suggested that norm-generation through reflexive communication could take many forms and be wider or narrower in scope. But, are there some choices or norms that just can't count as autonomy? A classic example in philosophical discussions about autonomy is the case of the willing addict. Does freely choosing to become an addict or to be ruled by an addiction count as autonomy? Dworkin suggests that it does: the willing drug addict is autonomous because "his actions express his view of what kind of influences he wants to motivate him" (G. Dworkin, 1989, 61)

On the notion of autonomy that I've proposed, if the willing addict were to engage in a process of reflexive communication such that the addict generates a rule or guideline for her behavior, e.g., "seek drugs whenever possible" or "prioritize drugs above all other goals and activities" or some such regulative rule, the addict may be autonomous with respect to the initial choice, for it seems to involve authorizing this as a norm for the self. But, if the ongoing addiction then becomes a compulsion over which the addict no longer reflexively communicates or exercises control or in which the addict loses the capacity to authorize, or the self is simply driven by desire or need, then the originally willing addict may no longer be autonomous.[27] (Other accounts of autonomy might put it in terms of the addict who is not responsive to reasons or whose reasoning is not autonomous.) If the addict's norm is that she become ruled by addiction, by something over which the addict cannot generate a norm or withhold or grant assent, then the addict has generated an autonomy denying norm. Being ruled by addiction may also involve deterioration of autonomy skills and compromising of the capacity to generate [other] norms.

But, it is also conceivable that a willing addict does remain autonomous. Consider the character, Lymond,[28] who is unwittingly made an opiate addict by a traitorous master of his household lacing his food with increasing amounts of opium. When he realizes what has happened, he is quite dependent on opium, although functional in life. He does not wish to be an addict; he does not endorse drug addiction as a global norm for his way of life. But, Lymond willingly perpetuates the addiction—he authorizes it as a norm instrumentally—because the urgency of a task in which he is engaged doesn't allow him to take the time and experience the physical disability that withdrawal and detoxification would require. He postpones detoxification, knowingly risking deterioration, disability, loss of the capacity to overcome the addiction, and even death. He puts his own future autonomy capacity at risk. (He does undergo detoxification once the urgent task is completed.) In this case, Lymond engages in norm-generating reflexive communication, authorizing as his norm "take opium as needed and continue as an addict," enlisting the aid of one of his men to help him regulate the dosage that will keep him functional. The addiction is a necessary evil, authorized not for its own sake or as a way of life, or for the pleasure of the drug, but as a rule he chooses to follow in order to realize the larger, urgent goal that he has set for himself. In this case, Lymond is a willing addict, but is autonomous because while he sets addiction as a rule (an instrumental, and temporary one) he also preserves his capacity for norm-generating reflexive communication, albeit under highly risky conditions.

What about a willing addict who generates as her norm addiction for its own sake, knowing full well that in doing so she will severely compromise or even lose her capacity for norm-generation and thus, in effect, abandons autonomy? Can one autonomously abandon autonomy, that is, generate a norm to abandon self-rule? Such a deliberate choice seems irrational and implausible, but conceivable. It also seems to be a different sort of case than one such as the intemperate person drifting into addiction, or than the case of someone who against her own better judgment or against a prior resolution can't resist a desire that leads to addiction— the incontinent or akratic person.[29] Neither of these has the appropriate intentional relation of authorizing the addiction as a norm for her self-rule and future direction whereas in the case we are imagining, the willing addict would have such an authorizing relation. At the same time, there also seems to be something inconsistent or contradictory about such a moment of self-rule, that is, taking as one's norm that one gives up or seriously inhibits the capacity for self-rule. One might want to argue that generating as a norm that one will abandon norms, or abandon the capacity to generate norms, doesn't qualify as a proper norm. A norm, or at least a prescriptive, action guiding norm by definition functions as future-guiding. Autonomy supposes that norms are consistent with the continuation of the capacity to generate norms. In that case, the willing addict who is willing to compromise or destroy that capacity would not be acting autonomously.

But, to press the point, could one be addicted, not, as in the previously discussed Lymond case, but for its own sake, and still be self-ruled? The novel *Leaving Las Vegas* (O'Brien, 1995) gives an account of a willing addict, an alcoholic named Ben, who decides to abandon himself to alcoholism and drink himself to death. The novel describes Ben as quite resolute and methodical in arranging the circumstances of his life (he moves to Las Vegas because one can purchase liquor there 24 hours a day) so as to carry out this plan, indeed to make his choice nearly irrevocable (a pre-commitment strategy). At the same time, when asked by a prostitute, Sera, with whom he forms a friendship, why he's killing himself, he answers that he doesn't remember, but knows that it's what he wants to do. What's not clear is what Ben wants, to kill himself (and drinking is a way to accomplish that) or to drink (and killing himself comes with drinking).[30]

That the character is already deeply alcoholic when he makes the decision renders questionable whether it is a genuinely reflexively generated norm at all rather than a strong compulsion towards drink or self-destruction. But, if we suppose that it is voluntarily made (and the author goes to some lengths to present it as if it is in a darkly existentialist sense), and that the character retains the capacity to plan and execute a plan (which involves ongoing, norm-generating reflexive communication among self-perspectives), there would seem to be some measure of autonomy or self-rule.

Another possible interpretation might involve distinguishing between "free" or "voluntary" meaning uncoerced, witting, and intentional, and "autonomous," meaning governed by a reflexively generated rule or norm. Then we might say, that the willing addict *voluntarily* but not autonomously chooses addiction. Similarly, the incontinent or intemperate person might act voluntarily, but not autonomously.

Even if being compelled by his desire—to kill himself through drink or to drink even if it means killing himself—should not count as autonomous, he might be autonomous in a more restricted sense. He is repeatedly able to plan and to reaffirm his choice. He explicitly resists efforts by others to dissuade him or to interfere with his choice. While this could be sheer stubbornness or the effects of addiction or cognitive impairment, it is also conceivable that he has a sense of what counts as observance or not of the plan and rules that he has set for himself.

It is possible to autonomously choose self-destruction. That is the premise of assisted suicide and the death with dignity movement, in which the individual's judgment about the value of continued living is the guiding. norm.[31] Is the willing addict analogous to this kind of judgment and therefore autonomous? In our *Leaving Las Vegas* example, suppose Ben's process of reflexive communication were something like the following. I-as-I-am-up-to-this-time communicates with I-as-alcoholic along the following lines: "This is who I am (an alcoholic). I embrace myself as such. I ought to be who I am and therefore, I will live it to its logical conclusion, namely, my own death." This stance seems to have normative content in that it posits a mode of self-rule, albeit a destructive one, and as one that should be followed because it represents who or what the self authentically is: this is who I am and who I ought to be to the fullest, however self-destructive that actually is. This seems to reflect some kind of norm-generation and thus, autonomy. But, suppose, Ben's stance were something like this: "I like to drink with abandon and will continue to do so simply because I like it, even if doing so leads to my own death." This seems to make no appeal to a rule or a norm, but is simply the assertion of a preference or desire (intemperance), without apparent normative content.

I am not really sure how best to interpret Ben's behavior. But, if it is possible for a self to be autonomous albeit in self-destructive or self-limiting ways, then that suggests that while autonomy is usually thought of as positive and desirable, it is possible for self-rule to take a self-destructive form. Generating as one's norm that one ought to renounce the authority to continue to have that authority (and ability) may render suspect the extent to which an individual is genuinely self-governed, for who, if they are capable of self-governance, would choose to give it up? But, it seems possible, even if unlikely.

If on the other hand, autonomy requires that norm-generation and assessment itself be substantively normatively guided, that is, that there are standards or norms for what counts as a genuinely autonomous norm, then autonomy would be restricted, perhaps to norms that are autonomy conducing or more generously, to norms that are consistent with the continuation of that capacity. This is what is referred to in the literature as strong substantive autonomy. In that case, autonomy would involve two levels of normativity, that the self be normatively guided and that a norm itself meet certain standards. I hesitate to pursue this path for it risks conflating autonomy (self-rule) with orthonomy (right-rule).[32] While it seems right to think that self-rule could become so poor as to fail to count as governing at all, the range of possible norms by which a self could reasonably be said to be self-governed is quite wide.[33]

Independently of the substantive content of norms, distinctions could be made regarding the degrees of autonomy possessed by selves. Possessing some range of skills (such as capacity for empathy or capacity for critical reasoning) could enhance one's capacity for norm-generation. And, one's relative position in society and access to resources, cultural conditions, and existing social norms could enhance or restrict one's scope of action or one's capacity to execute, to act on, one's reflexively generated norms. Thus, some selves could be more (or less) autonomous than others due to the possession (or lack) and development of certain skills and capacity, or because the scope of the exercise of their capacities is wider (or narrower), or because they have more (or less) authority and power, or because they can be efficacious in a wider (narrower) range of circumstances, and so on.

## 11. Autonomy: Contemporary Discussions

In this section, I briefly canvas some of the approaches to autonomy in the contemporary philosophical literature, in order to contrast and locate my approach in the field.

There are a variety of approaches to autonomy in the contemporary literature. Some characterize it negatively, that is, as a right to non-interference in defining and leading one's own life;[34] others posit that the possession of certain capabilities[35] or the aiming for or realization of certain kinds of goals[36] constitute the substance of autonomy. Some accounts of personal autonomy argue that it depends on developmental, historical, and social factors that are external to the agent. Other accounts argue that genuine autonomy is not ultimately explained by anything external to the agent [e.g., education, peer pressure, the state of the world prior to the agent's birth or development as an adult agent] but depends on the possession by the agent of particular [mental] abilities, values, beliefs, and dispositions, regardless of how they were acquired. Feminist capability accounts, as well as Sen's account, would be categorized as "externalist" accounts of personal autonomy, that is, accounts that argue that autonomy depends on factors (developmental, historical, social, and so on) that are external to the agent. On an "externalist" account, the history of an agent's development matters to whether the agent is autonomous.

My approach treats autonomy as the realization, to at least some degree, of a kind of capability, of norm-generation, execution and assessment through reflexive communication. While I have mentioned some of them, I have not given an account of the conditions or skills themselves that might promote such a capability and its realization, but have instead explored the application of this broadened account of autonomy in a wide range of contexts. I would like to reject the internalist/externalist distinction as a bit of a red herring. Autonomy has both "internal" and "external" conditions, both for its development and its exercise. If one were to insist on the distinction, then my account would be "externalist" by default since it is not purely "internalist."

In some capability accounts, it seems that autonomy is thought of as aiming for or enacting a kind of [capacity for] self-expression; in others, as aiming for or enacting a kind of [capacity for] self-transcendence.[37] These two dimensions need not be mutually exclusive. The notion of autonomy as norm-generation, execution, assessment through reflexive communication would allow for both as dimensions of autonomy. Feinberg's suggestion (Feinberg, 1989, 31) that autonomy consists in self-rule, self-possession, in "being one's own man" might represent the autonomy as authenticity strand or what Buss (2014) refers to as the coherentist approach to personal autonomy.

Another set of issues, already alluded to earlier and in Chapter 1, involves the distinction between "proceduralist" and "substantivist" views of autonomy. Capability accounts could be "procedural" or "substantive," that is, defining autonomy (1) as the possession of certain "procedural" capabilities, such as critical reflection on desires, capacity for reflection and identification with "first-order" desires, and/or a capacity for legislation or the development of a repertory of "autonomy skills" or equal capabilities among persons; or, (2) more substantively, as the aiming for or realization of certain kinds of goals, such as self-fulfillment, self-realization, personal integration.[38]

Recapping the distinction between proceduralist and substantive accounts of autonomy from Chapter 1, according to a proceduralist approach (e.g., Dworkin, Frankfurt, Meyers), personal autonomy consists in the possession or exercise of certain abilities, irrespective of the substantive content of the choices. A substantivist theorist worries that an apparently autonomous choice might merely express inculcated values or beliefs over which one has exercised no control or ones which, even though endorsed, are repressive or stultifying.[39] But, more than just objecting to unreflective internalization of roles, a substantivist approach argues that choices ought to conform to objectively autonomy-conducing standards. Thus, the [strong] substantivist objects to the idea that subordination could be autonomously chosen. In contrast, a proceduralist would worry that *self*-determination has been compromised if standards are imposed on, rather than shaped by, the self.

*Moral* autonomy is thought to involve the adopting, legislating, or endorsing of moral norms or principles. If one were to follow a Kantian line of thinking, one would hold that a self could be autonomous only when a self is moral, because it is only then that a self is truly rational and that normativity is independent of arbitrary and causally determinative conditions (including desires and inclinations). I do not follow the Kantian line here, even though I have suggested that autonomy be understood as self-legislating normatively directed behavior. If autonomy means the capacity for and the exercise of self-governance, then autonomy involves the generation of norms, and not only the ability to pursue desires, interests, and preferences. However, unlike Kant and the substantivist, by norm, I do not necessarily mean something rational or fixed. Rather, autonomy means that the self realizes the capacity to generate guidelines, rules, or policies (norms) by which it directs or governs itself and to assess its norms and own observance of them. Norms can take many different forms and operate at many different levels of comprehensiveness; they need not be universal standards of rationality or consensus (even if there may be some contexts in which universal norms are appropriate) or social standards. Norms must also be seen as produced by selves; and they may be diverse and revisable in specific contexts or for specific purposes. Thus, my account is not purely procedural, since on my view autonomy does involve the development and enactment of norms and norm-governed judgment and action. It is not substantive, in that I do not propose specific standards that a norm must meet in order to count as "really" autonomous.

There are interesting and vexing questions about whether specific instances of behavior, choice, action, and planning should be characterized as autonomous. Given the possible opaqueness of human conduct, to others and sometimes even to oneself, some instances may simply not be clearly identifiable. Even one of the standard proposals for autonomous behavior—endorsing and achieving integration of desires and interests—may not be necessary for or the mark of autonomy. If the self is plurally constituted, then integration of desires and interests may not be *the* goal of autonomy. It may be *a* goal, but there may be other normative goals, such as cultivation of diversification, or the development of different perspectives in the self so as to increase the richness of experience or to enhance the capacity for norm-generation. Diversification, conflict or a problem encountered may be catalyst for or a constituent of norm-generation. A self may experience "internal" conflict or diversification (e.g., in experiencing a sexual orientation which is not recognized in the self's social world) or may experience a biological source of a problem (e.g., in experiencing physical limitations in one's own body) which prompts or contributes in some important way to norm-generation by the self.

## 12. Summing Up

I have proposed that autonomy be understood as self-rule or self-governance that involves three main features:

(1) Defining, evaluating, generating, or endorsing norms, policies, rules, standards by which to guide oneself; this process takes place in what I call norm-generating reflexive communication;
(2) The capacity or power to enact or execute those norms and the enacting of them, the executive aspect;
(3) Assessability, whereby the self can assess (and re-assess) its own compliance with norms that it has generated for itself, as well as assess and re-assess norms themselves.

On my account, autonomy means that a self may generate, execute or assess a new norm, or it may assimilate social norms and make them its own, such that a norm is the product of the self's own reflexive activity. Independence from social conditions consists in being able to partially detach oneself from social roles and conventions. Autonomy does not require abandoning assimilated social norms, but it does require inventive manipulation of them in reflexive communication. Autonomy is not incompatible with being socially located and related. In fact, in some cases, autonomy might be enhanced by or developed as a feature of such relations.

The account also allows for conceptualizing both local and global autonomy. Autonomy can be thought of, not only as attributable to a whole individual, but rather as about the ways in which the individual generates its own norms. A self may be autonomous in some respects, and not in others. As noted earlier, to say that a quadriplegic is not autonomous with respect to [most] physical movement or activity would not entail that she is not autonomous with respect to verbal expression. The notion of norm-generation, execution, and assessment in reflexive communication allows for recognition of behavior as autonomous that has often been dismissed as merely emotional, intuitive, natural, manual, and so on, such as that of the carpenter, the athlete, the caregiver.

I have not addressed political issues regarding the scope of power and that are important in social and political matters of equity and opportunity. I don't mean to downplay the possible effect of power. Nor am I unmindful of conditions of dependency and interdependency. I am arguing for broadening what counts as autonomy. A cared for person (e.g., a quadriplegic) may have some autonomy. A caregiver of a dependent person may be exercising autonomy (self-rule) no less so than the executive who reflexively communicates with herself as she sets company policy or than a rational deliberator or a self-concerned preference maximizer. Any one of these may be constrained in various ways. The self-concerned preference maximizer may have a very limited range of preferences, or may have a narrow context in which preferences can be maximized. The executive may be constrained by a narrow profit-maximization goal, rather than allowed to consider other ways of measuring corporate policy. That the corporate executive may have more power, or be someone whose actions have wider consequences or reap greater financial and social rewards—none of these features entails that the self is any more self-governed than the caregiver. The differences just enumerated concern the values, and distribution of power and rewards in society. A powerful and well-rewarded person may be free from constraints of poverty, have more opportunities and choices. But, that doesn't necessarily mean they are more autonomous (self-governed). Such a person could be impulsive, have poor self-regulation, be unreflective about her or his role and position by having simply internalized social norms about power and money, and so on. What matters for autonomy is the reflexive norm-generating, executing, and assessing relations in which the self engages. The view of autonomy as self-rule is meant to recognize that autonomy can be realized by selves in many different ways and facets of life, rather than associated only with certain kinds of lives. Of course, autonomy does require being able to exercise (self) control. And social conditions, economic opportunities, political position, power relations, all can affect whether a self has control, what its scope is, and whether and to what extent a self develops "autonomy skills" and which ones. The point is only that having power and position is conceptually and practically distinct from autonomy. Autonomy does not require independence from others and social relations, and could be consistent with the maintaining of and even reliance on relationships, community, collaboration, and even care.

Autonomy presupposes a temporally extended self. Self-rule takes time and usually implies the possibility of recurrence, repetition, and re-enactment, as well as reference to the past, to an originating normative stance. That the self is a process, is temporally structured and extended, is what makes it meaningful to say that pre-commitments are commitments *of* the self. The self sets norms for itself. In doing so and complying with them, it may further (e.g., enhance, redirect) its own narrative unity or purposive structure. It might also mean that at a particular time a self could follow its own rule and by doing so be autonomous (self-ruled or self-guided) even if at a time, the self is not actively endorsing the rule, as might be the case in some pre-commitment arrangements.

## Notes

1. Dunnett (1997a, 133).
2. Dunnett (1997a, 512).
3. Bratman (2012, 77).
4. Meyers (1989) analyzes ways in which the social environment can encourage or oppress the development and exercise of "autonomy competency," her focus being the impact of oppressive socialization on women's autonomy.
5. This is the point of Sen's "capability view." A self is not free to realize its personal goals, if its range of social and cultural functioning enables and validates only one particular social role (e.g., mother and housewife). This is a restriction in what Sen calls "agency freedom." See for example, Sen (1985).
6. Christman's own model of the socio-historical self is rooted in narrative and dialogical approaches to the self.
7. E.g., Code (1991, 2000). Abrams (1999) argues that "agency" rather than "autonomy" should be the preferred concept because the latter carries too much metaphysical and Kantian baggage (805).
8. E.g., Friedman (2000), Kittay (1999). Friedman elsewhere advanced an interesting and thoughtful view of autonomy that is compatible with the idea that a self is socially constituted and located (Friedman, 2003). Feminists are not alone in challenging the view of the subject as atomistic and self-transparently free. Communitarians, such as MacIntyre (1984, 1988) and Sandel (1998) have also argued against such views. See also, Hiley (1988), Honneth (1995), Schmitt (1995).
9. It might be complicated to sort out cases in which a self remains autonomous in virtue of a prior commitment from those in which a self is trapped or

coerced by a prior commitment. I'm less interested in that problem than the more general point that conceiving of autonomy as self-rule presupposes that the self is temporally extended, is a process.

10. Arpaly (2003) suggests that "autonomy" is an umbrella term covering a loose set of separate target concepts. It could have skeptical implications for articulating a general concept of autonomy, or, at minimum, could "raise questions about the general usefulness of the concept of autonomy to our theorizing about moral responsibility" (118).

11. Mele goes on, however, to use such terms as "free will" and "free action" as interchangeable with "autonomy" (e.g., 1995, 9), which, I think, elides what is distinctive about autonomy, namely, that it is normative.

12. Plato's *Republic* is famously based on such an analogy. And, Aristotle draws the analogy, for example, in discussing the akratic person in *Nicomachaen Ethics* VII, 10, observing that the incontinent person is like a city which passes good laws, but doesn't follow them.

13. I'm not sure that all of Mele's instances and types of autonomy involve the legislative or normative character that I take to be distinctive of autonomy.

14. See Meyers' (2000, 2005) work on autonomy skills.

15. I am relying on a distinction made by Buchler between modes of human judgment, assertive, active, and exhibitive. Judgment, broadly construed, is discrimination of some aspect(s) of the world and can take place in assertion, action or arrangement (exhibitive judgment). Examples of exhibitive judgments would include a poem, an arrangement of words that exhibits some meaning, rather than asserting a proposition that can be evaluated as true or false; or, a floral arrangement that exhibits structure, color, and other features of flowers. Exhibitive and active judgments are ways of discriminating some aspect(s) of the world, just as much as assertions are. These are functional distinctions, though, and any judgment (utterance, action, product) may take place in more than one mode (Buchler, 1979, 1985).

16. The writer Isabel Allende has the rule to always start a book on the eighth of January. While she says that this is "more from superstition than discipline," it is a self-imposed and executed rule that has organized her life for decades (Allende, 2008, 2).

17. Matsumura (2014) analyzes court treatments of disputes over such disposition in light of theories of personal identity. He rejects the notion that future selves cannot be held to previously made commitments. He invokes a notion of narrative identity, drawing on the work of Schechtman and others, to argue for a strong notion of self-continuity against the idea that there is a succession of different selves as has been suggested by some legal theorists (e.g., Kronman, 1983).

18. Elster (1982). Adaptive preferences are preferences adjusted to the circumstances of what is possible, and therefore, it has been argued, are formed "nonautonomously," that is, they form the basis for choice without themselves having been freely chosen. This process is distinct from preferences that are acquired simply from experience and learning, and is argued to have problematic consequences for theories of justice that are based on welfare understood in terms of preference satisfaction. On my view, it would be possible to be autonomous with respect to an adaptive preference insofar as one engaged in a process of reflexive communication and determined whether or to what extent such a preference ought to function as a norm for oneself (albeit in constrained circumstances). It is also possible that adaptive preferences are autonomy inhibiting, with respect to one or more aspects of autonomy, the legislative, executive, or the assessment aspect.

19. Loretta Lynch, 83rd Attorney General of the United States, reported that "her great-great-grandfather, a free black man in North Carolina, fell in love with her great-great-grandmother, a slave [and that] '[U]nable to purchase her, in order to marry her he had to stay on and re-enter bondage'" (http://nyti.ms/1yiR73H; page visited 11/09/2014). Sneddon imagines a similar case (2013, 69).

20. The subordination cases also seem to be different from someone choosing to submit to the authority of someone because of their knowledge or expertise. In the latter case, there is an endorsement of knowledge-based norms albeit ones that the self may not fully understand. For example, in saying that one will be guided by the science, one is taking as one's norm the consensus of the knowledge community. Such consensus is subject to evaluation and scrutiny (assessment), even if one recognizes oneself as not having the requisite skills or background to conduct such evaluation.

21. Hill (1973) suggests that servility "is a failure to understand and acknowledge one's own moral rights" (93) and thus "manifests a certain absence of self-respect" (97). This is morally objectionable on Kantian grounds because it shows a failure to respect morality (99). However, a deferential housewife (or a slave) could be autonomous if she preserves an attitude of self-respect and recognizes herself as having moral standing. Oshana (1998) rejects purely internalist accounts of autonomy (whereby autonomy is living in accord with one's own preferences) and argues that personal relations and social institutions that allow one to exercise control over one's choices play a role in determining whether someone is autonomous. Thus, a disempowered and subservient housewife or a slave cannot be autonomous (Oshana 86–91). Unlike the slave who cannot choose to exit slavery, a monk who has given himself over to monastic rule is autonomous in so far as he can control the choice to remain under monastic rule (although not in so far as he is subject to it) (Oshana 92). Sneddon (2013) argues that laws limiting the right to sell oneself into slavery limit autonomy of choice but for the sake of the moral value of autonomy of persons, namely, the capacity to frame and pursue a plan for oneself (129).

22. This example uses Buchler's tripartite theory of judgment. See Note 15. I also used this example in Wallace (1993).

23. See McGandy (1997).

24. David Foster Wallace describes well the development of this ability by an athlete to control the body and adjust its movements in the activity itself without necessarily involving self-conscious intervention. He also draws an interesting analogy to being an "experienced driver" (Wallace, 2006).

25. Tronto recognizes reflexive judgment as a component of care (1993, 2001, 189).

26. There is a burgeoning literature on shared agency that is beyond the scope of this discussion. But, for more detailed and extensive analysis of shared agency or a "we-mode" of agency or planning, see for example, Bratman (2014) and Tuomela (2013).

27. An addict might also act intentionally, but perhaps not autonomously. Fulford and Radoilska (2012) distinguish between addiction and compulsion, and delusion. Addiction and compulsion can undermine intentional agency over time, but could also be compatible with voluntary individual actions, and therefore, might mitigate responsibility without fully excusing what the addict does. Delusion, they argue, more likely represents a breakdown in intentional action, rather than being an impediment to it, and therefore, might fully excuse what the delusional person does. Delusion, on their view, would also be a greater internal obstacle to autonomy (51).

28. Lymond is the main protagonist in the *Lymond Chronicles*, a series of historical fiction which takes place in 16ᵗʰ-century Europe. For this episode see Dunnett (1997b), and especially 356–358, where Lymond realizes the addiction.

29. Holton (1999) distinguishes between these two, arguing that the akratic acts against better judgment and the person with weakness of will against a prior resolution. In a related vein, Mele (1995) distinguishes between autonomy and self-control. He argues that the latter is not sufficient for the former, because self-control is compatible with a person being self-oppressed or self-victimized or acting under a compulsion. Autonomy, Mele suggests, requires, in addition to self-control, an authenticity condition, the possession of continuous mental health.

30. See the dialogue from the screenplay by Mike Figgis for the film *Leaving Las Vegas* (www.dailyscript.com/scripts/leavinglasvegas.html).

31. Advanced directives in health care are meant to capture those norms for an individual in anticipation of an individual's possible incapacitation. In that sense they are a kind of Ulysses arrangement. A Ulysses arrangement is one whereby the self makes a pre-commitment to acting (or not acting) in some way in the future, at a time when one anticipates being unable to exercise self-directed agency. The term refers to Ulysses, who directs his sailors to lash him to the mast before sailing past the Sirens so that he can hear their song without being lured to his death. See Elster (1979).

32. Pettit and Smith (1993).

33. This is the crux of the disagreement between substantivist and proceduralist accounts of autonomy; see Section 11.

34. See for example, Berlin (1969) and John Stuart Mill's *On Liberty*. R. Dworkin's (1994) conception of autonomy as "moral independence," that is, being entitled to respect for one's chosen way of life, seems closer to this "negative" way of defining autonomy than it does to a capability account of autonomy. Brison's (1998) distinguishing of six different philosophical accounts of autonomy in the free speech literature has been helpful to me in sorting out some of the various approaches to autonomy. See also Buss's (2014) distinction between four basic approaches to personal autonomy which she calls coherentist, reasons-responsiveness, reasoning-responsiveness, and incompatibilist.

35. Such as (1) critical reflection on desires, capacity for reflection and identification with "first-order" desires, and/or a capacity for legislation or (2) the development of a repertory of "autonomy skills" or equal capabilities among persons. For (1) see, e.g., Frankfurt (1971), Rawls (1971), Scanlon (1972, 1979), G. Dworkin (1988), Haworth (1986). For (2) see, e.g., Meyers (1989), Christman (1991), Sen (1982, 1985, 1992, 1995).

36. Such as self-fulfillment, self-realization, personal integration. In Meyers' (1989) account of autonomy or competency skills the aim is personal integration and presumably some degree of such integration would have to be achieved if the competency skills are the skills they purport to be. According to Brison (1998), Redish (1984) and Baker (1978) posit a self-realization condition for autonomy.

37. The distinction comes from Yaffe (2000) for whom "self-expression" involves expression of certain crucial psychological states and "self-transcendence" involves responsiveness to evaluative facts.

38. For proceduralist accounts see, e.g., G. Dworkin (1988), Frankfurt (1988), Haworth (1986), Meyers (1989), Rawls (1971), Scanlon (1972, 1979). For more substantive accounts see, e.g., Christman (1991), Sen (1982, 1985, 1992, 1995). On personal integration, see, for example, Meyers (1989). On self-realization see, for example, Redish (1984) and Baker (1978).

39. Stoljar (2000) and Benson (2000, 2005) both argue for substantivist accounts of autonomy, Stoljar for a strong and Benson for a weak substantivist account. See also Benson (1994) and MacKenzie and Stoljar (2000b, 19–21) for discussion of the substantive versus proceduralist accounts. Double (1992) calls the substantivist approach an "objective, content-specific" account of autonomy, in contrast to his own recommended account, an "open-ended, individual management style" account.

# 7 Responsibility and the Network Self

[O]ur responsibility for what we do and for its outcome is inseparable from our status as persons.

(Tony Honoré)[1]

When they are naturally characterized as responsibility judgments, "responsibility" always bears the sense of "proper identifiability."

(Joel Feinberg)[2]

The value of autonomy . . . lies in the scheme of responsibility it creates: autonomy makes each of us responsible for shaping his own life according to some coherent and distinctive sense of character, conviction, and interest. It allows us to lead our own lives rather than be led along them, so that each of us can be, to the extent such a scheme of rights can make this possible, what he has made himself.

(Ronald Dworkin)[3]

The story is about carrying your past with you on your back at all times and trying to make a life nonetheless, even daring to use the very unwanted gifts that that past has left you with to help others and as a way of survival and redemption.[4]

Be the change you want to see in the world.[5]

## 1. Introduction

In this chapter I consider another "practical" dimension of selves, namely, the sense in which selves are the appropriate target for responsibility ascription.

I am interested in three different aspects to this issue: (1) responsibility as an identity-presupposing concept; (2) the temporal scope of responsibility, that is, responsibility as both backward and forward-looking; and (3) responsibility in collective contexts. The bulk of this chapter will address the first issue. I will make some suggestions for what the cumulative network model of the self (CNM) might contribute to the second and third issues. But, each of the latter is a large topic in its own right, and some of the issues in connection with those, particularly in

connection with responsibility in collective contexts, I will have to leave
for another project.

I should note what I am *not* addressing. Many discussions of responsibility are tied up with considerations of whether selves are really free,
whether actions are truly voluntary, or under the control of the agent,
and intentional. I am not addressing such issues. I am also not concerned
with descriptive issues concerning psychological or moral capacity or
with the conditions, social, legal, moral, under which someone ought to
be held responsible in whatever sense of responsibility is under consideration, causal, outcome, role, legal, moral, and so on. In different contexts,
responsibility practices may have somewhat different, specific criteria for
resolving these empirical issues. I make no attempt to sort any of this out.
Here's what I do address:

(1) Responsibility as an identity-presupposing concept: when we think
    about responsibility, we often think of agent responsibility in a
    backward looking sense, namely, who is the person who did, and
    therefore, is responsible for an action.[6] Thus, when thinking about
    causal and moral responsibility and criminal liability, the issue is,
    who in the present is the agent of and therefore responsible for a
    previous action, as in "is P in the courtroom the same P as the per-
    son who committed the crime?" This way of putting it suggests the
    possibility that there are two different persons, "P in the courtroom"
    and "P who committed the crime," and the problem is to figure out
    how they are related. If the P in the courtroom is *not* the P who
    committed the crime, then there would be two persons identified
    in the question and the correct answer to the question is, "No." P
    in the courtroom is one person and P who committed the crime is
    another. But, if P in the courtroom *is* the P who committed the crime,
    then there is one person, P, who satisfies or is picked out by both
    descriptions.

Standard four-dimensionalist philosophical theories of personal identity suggest that the self is a series of person-stages, distinct parts or counterpart selves that are causally and otherwise related in the right ways to
form a single whole person or person-career (as discussed in Chapter 3).
This invokes the two Ps idea, Ps who are different "person-stages" related
in appropriate ways to one another. As the underlying basis for identification of the singular agent, I find that unsatisfying. I'm interested in
exploring how CNM is a better approach for conceptualizing the target
for ascription of agential responsibility as a singular agent.

I will also contrast the normal case of responsibility ascription with
weird cases where there is not a single self, that is, fission and fusion
cases, such as the malfunctioning teleporter and brain transplant cases.
In Chapter 4 I argued that fission and fusion disrupt the network such

that the emergent selves or self cannot be identified as *the* original self continuing in a new body. However, even if agential responsibility could not be ascribed to the emergents, are there other ways in which responsibility practices might deal with such cases and distribute responsibility across emergents?

(2) The temporal scope of responsibility: our responsibility practices also include notions such as remedial, precautionary, and compensatory responsibility, as well as the notion that a self may assume responsibilities and obligations for the future. Responsibility is both a backward looking and a forward-looking concept. A self is "determinate" with respect to its past, but it also is incomplete and, qua active and autonomous, contributes to the shape of its future. On CNM, the processual nature of the self makes sense of the idea of ascribing a forward-looking sense of responsibility to the self, the idea of "taking responsibility." I mean this in two senses. First, in something like what Fischer and Ravizza (1998) suggest—that a person recognizes the conditions which helped to create who she is and takes on responsibility for being that person or agent.[7] In this regard, a self takes up her or his past incorporating it into who and what the self is. Second, the self takes responsibility for how it moves forward, for how it projects itself into the future with its cumulative past.

(3) The scope of responsibility in collective contexts: our responsibility practices also include considerations of when and to what extent selves are responsible in collective contexts. I explore how CNM would understand the basis for an individual having responsibility in a collective or systemic context or sharing in responsibility for the cumulative action or outcome of the behavior of a group, collection or social system. I do not consider what specific responsibilities an individual might have, but rather how CNM might offer a perspective for conceptualizing the self as an agent or as a target for responsibility ascription (of some kind) in a collective context.

A network self is not just causally influenced by, but is constituted as a network by its social relations (and many other psycho-biological-physical relations). The self has "identities" in virtue of its social locations and of the norms and practices in which it participates or which it embodies, enacts, and represents. Since every relation entails mutual relevance, the self is also relevant to, constitutive of its social locations. The self may have individual responsibilities within those social locations and may share responsibility for the character of the communities by which it is constituted and for the behaviors and ways in which those communities live. Communities do not have to have been chosen by the self in order for it to share responsibility. They may just be where the self finds itself. One does not choose the culture and society into which one is born, and one may not choose the behavioral patterns and norms that define a particular location that one does choose. But, that does not entail that one has no responsibilities in virtue of those locations and the norms and behaviors that they structure. The topic of responsibility in collective contexts is large and much has already been written on it. I will not address most of it here, but confine myself to suggesting only what CNM might have to contribute to the issue of conceptualizing the self as a target for responsibility ascription in collective contexts.

## 2. Re-identification and Agential Responsibility

A primary concern in matters of ascription of responsibility is that the right agential target be identified. In backward looking responsibility contexts, we want to know that the self at time $t_2$ *is* the self that performed an action at $t_1$, such that it is one and the same self that performed an action and that is held accountable or responsible. In moral and legal, especially criminal justice contexts, the concern is that identification correctly target the agent so that innocent persons are not unjustly punished. In forward-looking responsibility contexts, we want to know that an obligation or "a responsibility" is attached to the right self.

Re-identification, as discussed in Chapter 3, is not about sameness or qualitative identity, nor about continuity alone, but whether it is that one "thing" present at each time. ("Thingness" should not be construed in any substantivizing way. The "thing" under discussion here is a process, a cumulative network that is changeable and evolving.)

I have been bothered by the implications of standard four-dimensionalist accounts of persons because they posit that the self that is present at any time is a different self (a different temporal part or a distinct person, "person-stage") from the self at any other time. The current self is *another* self, not *the one* that performed some deed at another, previous time. This approach would account for responsibility as a self now being responsible for the deed of that other, distinct self, in virtue of a temporal part or counterpart relation. While this is one way of explaining it, it seems to me to weaken the basis for responsibility ascription.[8] This explanation could allow for disavowal, for non-ownership of actions *on the grounds* that they were done by different selves; the present self (temporal part or counterpart) is literally a different self from the self that performed an action.

In contrast, the CNM approach proposes that the self is a cumulative network, a process that is a changeable totality, present at each time, rather than a succession of different, static spatio-temporal slices or objects. Of course, disavowal is possible as a psychological or intentional state. A self can change considerably over time and in that sense seek to disavow a former action or aspect of itself. A self may come to regret previous actions and normative stances, or be so transformed that previous actions seem incomprehensible to oneself and others as that self's own. But, according to CNM such disavowal or change is not grounded in there being literally different selves. On the contrary, such experiences only make sense as relations one has to oneself, not relations between different selves.

To the question, "Is this person in the courtroom *the one*, the person, who did some act?" CNM gives the following account. If the answer is affirmative, it is because the person in the courtroom is the self up to this time. The self who is present in the courtroom today is the cumulative network of traits, the summed up self that retains, as one of its traits, its past as the self who did the earlier action. Therefore, it *is* the self who did the act and can be the proper target for agential responsibility. CNM by itself, doesn't tell us what evidence to collect or how we should go about collecting it. All it says is that identifying a self as responsible for a past act (or omission) is intelligible and justifiable, even though the self may have evolved and have many different traits in the present from those it had at the time of the action.

For example, suppose in one's college years, political activism was a strongly relevant constituent of oneself, and that in the course of that activism one engaged in activity that led to violence. Suppose the relevance of political activism to one's life subsequently becomes attenuated. Perhaps one regrets past actions as a political activist, and maybe even renounces previously held political views. However, in at least some respects, the self would not be who one is in the present were it not for that past. Even though political activism may not be a current social trait, it is a constituent of the history, the past which is a trait, of the self. The self *is* the self who as political activist participated in violence, even if in later years one regrets what one may have participated in and the harm that violence may have caused.

How the self is now with the past that it has is explained by causal and counterfactual dependency relations, psychological, biological, and social relations, and how these are configured and unified to constitute the particular self. If the self as it is now is counterfactually dependent on its own history, it must acknowledge a relation to its own past deeds.[9] The character or integrity of the cumulative whole network of traits is changeable, but at any time it includes its own past and therefore, at any time the self is the one cumulative whole.

Recapping from Chapter 3, CNM interprets the re-identification question as being about numerical unity rather than identity. By unity I just mean the "one thing-ness" of the self. The question can't be asking for identity qua indiscernibility. The process self at the time of committing the crime is discernible from the process self as present in the courtroom. As phases of the process self they are not exactly similar for a self could have many different traits in the present, could have altered considerably from a previous time, including the time of the crime. But, phases have overlapping traits and each includes as one of its traits its history. The person present in the courtroom is the changeable totality, the cumulative network of traits up to this time, that is the agential "owner" of the crime.[10] The assigning of responsibility and many other experiences depend on some notion of numerical (personal) unity. In Chapter 3, Section 4, I noted Beatty's (1970) comment that "in seeking forgiveness of the other, the offender is asserting both that he is and is not the man who committed the offense" (251); and Griswold's observation (2007) that the experience of forgiveness depends on a recognizable continuity of the self.

The re-identification question is about identifying the agential target of or location for responsibility ascription. It doesn't address other issues about responsibility, such as whether the self has been reformed or transformed, or whether it is able to take on responsibility in the sense of admitting guilt or avowing that it is indeed the person responsible. That this person is the one may not require conscious awareness or memory of the deed. Such psychological continuity is a normal constituent of the cumulative nature of a self, and may be necessary for *mens rea* and fitness to stand trial, but the latter are different matters from re-identification and numerical unity. Nor does the re-identification question address what kind of responsibility the person has, causal or outcome responsibility, role responsibility, or moral responsibility and guilt. It does not address whether the self is due praise or blame. Nor does it consider whether the person has the appropriate capacities for being held responsible and should be punished, or is someone who has "remedial responsibility"[11] from whom a specific response, such as an apology or some remedial or compensatory action, is called. These are separate issues resolution of which would rest on further determination of the capabilities and specific roles of the self in question and on other responsibility practices. Re-identification is about a prior consideration—Who is the self to whom that action belongs? And for that, it seems to me, we want a theory that conceptualizes the self as *the one*, the self to whom the action belongs.

## 3. Agential Ownership

Normally, the self who is constituted as agential owner of the action would have control in some sense over and be causally connected to an action (or omission) in some way, would recognize liability, accountability, and possible obligation going forward, and would have a singular agential perspective. This suggests that there are two temporal axes, forward and backward, that are relevant to agential responsibility ascription.

(1) Singularity of agential perspective (backward and forward). By this I mean not just that the self has particular abilities to avow responsibility and to engage in voluntary, intentional action. Rather, the

action (which could also be a contribution to a collective or cumulative action) belongs to the doer of it (the utterer of the words, the shooter of the gun, the donor of the gift, the writer of the essay). Usually, by "doer" we mean "author," although sometimes there is a split between authorship and doing, as when someone authorizes an act, but someone else executes it. In such cases, each may be contributing to a cumulative action by doing different actions. For example, the "authorizer" utters words or signs a memo authorizing the "executor" to market and negotiate sale of a house. Each participates in a cumulative action, selling the house.[12] What each self does, belongs to that self. In this case, the self may "own" a particular action and may be a shared owner of the cumulative action. The self carries forward that ownership even when the self's awareness or agency becomes compromised, say by illness or disability. That might alter what responsibility practices apply, but the singular ownership is not undermined by alteration in the content or direction of the agential perspective. The summed up self includes that past as one of its present traits and moves forward with that history. A self could move forward regretting its own previous perspective and action, enthusiastically embracing and affirming them, recognizing liability, or even forgetting them.

(2) Causal (and/or other appropriate legal, contractual, etc.) connection (backward). Having some such connection(s) is usually thought, at least for standard understandings of responsibility, to be necessary for an agent to be morally responsible. This condition is articulated by Martinsen and Seibt (2013), in the context of discussing the notion of shared ecological responsibility, as an agent being *agentively liable*.[13] An agent may also have compensatory or remedial responsibilities (forward-looking responsibility) in virtue of its backward looking connections to an event or outcome, although an agent can also have forward-looking responsibilities independently of backward connections, as for example, when one may have responsibility to remediate even though one may not have been the cause of harm.

There could be cases in which the self lacks the normal intentional perspectives associated with being the agential owner. Intentional and dispositional features of the agential perspective, while typically features of the agential target of responsibility, may subsequently not obtain, or may only obtain in an attenuated sense. For example, in cases of mental illness, dementia, amnesia or other compromised intentional states, blame and punishment, praise and approbation, or other practices associated with responsibility ascription may not be appropriate.[14] But, incapacities do not undermine the constitutive relationship of the self's past. The self may still be the agential owner of the action, and thus the appropriate target of agential responsibility ascription even when the practices associated with such ascription cannot be fully enacted.

It seems important to maintain the distinction between re-identification and capacity for participating in responsibility practices. A self changes and can survive considerable, even drastic change. Discussions of whether someone is still a self or a person, still that particular self or person, often focus on things like cognitive disability or loss of cognitive and memory functions, as in dementia or amnesia. However, re-identification may not require that the person have conscious awareness or memory of the deed. Schechtman makes a similar point when she argues that a "person life" is the correct target of forensic considerations, is the object about which responsibility judgments could be made (Schechtman, 2014, 102; 107–108).

Many terrible things that can happen to selves may compromise their capacity to participate in responsibility practices. On CNM, comprehensive amnesia and Alzheimer's disease happen to, are constituents of a self. They are damage to the bodily/psychological (sub-)network of the self. That damage may have profound effects on other, e.g., social, intentional, communicative, (sub-)networks of the now compromised or damaged self. With cognitive damage, there may be shedding, so to speak, of many constituting social roles, as for instance in the case of Clive Wearing, the severe amnesiac discussed in Chapter 3, or as in an Alzheimer's patient, but other social roles may still persist. Participation in communicative, social, and meaning relations, may still be possible and ongoing, however rudimentarily, as with selves cognitively disabled from birth. However, cognitive disability does not necessarily undermine being that self, that cumulative network, however limiting it may be. What we find valuable about various abilities may not set the threshold for being a self at all, or for being identifiable as that particular self, now diminished, disabled, or dying. Or for being the proper target or locus for responsibility. The Alzheimer's patient who has no memory of her prior deeds is still the proper target of identification for responsibility, even if, due to diminished capacities, responsibility practices are not realizable.

## 4. Responsibility Ascription and Distribution in Fusion and Fission Thought Experiments

I now want to explore the thought experimental cases from Chapter 4, the fusion or fission cases expressed in body/brain transplants, teleporter, and the Swampman scenario. The thought experiments originated as devices to test intuitions about whether the "same" self continues (or not) in the products of fusion and fission.[15] In Chapter 4 I argued that according to CNM fusion and fission disrupt the network that is the self, such that the "same" self does not survive such operations. In the hypothetical cases (1) of a brain from one self being combined with the body of another self (fusion) or (2) of duplication in spontaneous biological fission, teleporter duplication or Swampman duplication (fission), none of the fused or fissioned selves can be identified as the prior self, *the one* that did an action. Therefore, it would seem that fusion and fission, two-to-one and one-to-two transformations, by disrupting the network, also disrupt the assignment of responsibility. The normal conditions for identification and re-identification do not obtain.

According to CNM what matters is whether *the network* continues and functions as the proper target of identification. In the *single* antecedent/successor thought experimental case, the self can plausibly be said to continue and therefore be the target for responsibility ascription as the agent, even with a wholesale bodily replacement. But, in fusion or fission cases the self does not continue. When the original self does not continue and singular agential responsibility cannot be ascribed to the resulting selves, perhaps there are other bases on which to ascribe some responsibility. That is not such a strange idea since our responsibility practices already include a variety of bases for ascribing responsibility, even when not agential responsibility. Selves can be responsible for actions done by others, such as parents being (legally) responsible for actions done by their minor children, or an employer for actions done by an employee.[16] There are role, contractual, legal, or potentially other causal relations, often involving practices established for the distribution and management of risk, that support responsibility assigning practices to persons other than the agent.

While identification and re-identification of the agent is central to ascription of agent responsibility, responsibility and the demand for responsibility ascription is much broader. As just noted, our responsibility practices extend well beyond singular agential responsibility and attach responsibility to targets other than the particular agent as is the case with criminal, and in some sense, moral responsibility. Perhaps, then, there are other ways to think about distributing responsibility in fission and fusion cases where the original self does not survive. The emergents in the fission and fusion thought experimental cases would appear to meet at least some conditions for responsibility ascription. If that is the case, then responsibility practices would probably evolve to address situations where there is some appropriate target for responsibility ascription, even if not the agent itself.

In what follows, I will explore (1) how in the thought experimental cases of singular replication the singular emergent can be justifiably identified as the appropriate target for agential responsibility ascription, and (2) whether in the thought experimental cases of fission or fusion our current system of responsibility practices could allow or suggest ways to distribute responsibility. Even if the emergents may not be appropriate targets of agential responsibility, they might still be appropriate targets of some responsibility.

## 4.1. Singular Replication

In singular replication—teleporter, Swampman—the network, the self, has not been disrupted. That would suggest that responsibility ascription could go through just as it would in the normal case.

In the single result of the teleporter, the network continues because there is a one to one mapping of the self that entered the teleporter onto the self that emerges from the teleporter. Thus, the single teleporter emergent would be identified as the appropriate target of agential responsibility. (1) It is the unique, singular possessor of the agential perspective. It takes up the past of the original self as its, and is therefore re-identifiable as the summed up self that had acted in the past and continues forward with the agential perspective of that self. (2) It has causal (and intentional) connection, mediated by artificial, technological means, to the action. The single, emergent self is counterfactually dependent on the prior history of the self. Just as the original self has to acknowledge its relation to and ownership of its past deeds, so, too, with the single teleporter emergent self. If the *network* maps onto the body that emerges, then it inherits, so to speak, responsibility, just as the self in the normal case does.

A possible objection might be that since the new material body couldn't *literally* have been the cause of the previous action, the absence of biological, causal relations weakens responsibility ascription. But, it is the network, not just the body, that is the self and the target of responsibility ascription. The network, I have argued, is not disrupted by the "normal" functioning of the teleporter that results in a single emergent. In addition, the objection might be circumvented in the teleporter case on the grounds that there are *some*, just not the usual, causal relations that tie the existence of the replicant body to the original network in some appropriate way. Swampman, however, is an accident whose existence has no causal or intentional ties to Davidson. Swampman body has only formal qualitative similarity. Would responsibility ascription go through in such a case?

In Chapter 4, I said that Swampman singular would take up and continue the network self, Davidson. While Swampman body lacks the right causal chain, neither we nor Swampman would know that according to the conditions of the thought experiment. The thought experiment is assuming that the world operates differently than it actually does, and that a fully constituted, mature, functioning organic body can simply come into being *de novo*. In a world with such different causal mechanisms, perhaps responsibility practices would have evolved differently than they have. But, if we are assuming the possibility of such replication of a fully formed human being, as in the teleporter case, and if we are transferring our responsibility practices roughly as they are to this new scenario, then Swampman, like the teleporter emergent, would have the singular agential perspective of Davidson. Still, given our usual assumptions about causation, it might seem odd or just plain wrong to consider Swampman agentially responsible in just the way Davidson is.

But, why not, if we're willing to assign responsibility to the singular teleporter emergent? In each case, there is production of a fully formed human being with all the capacities of a human being and of that *particular* human being without the replicant body having gone through normal biological, developmental processes. If we accept that such a body is the self that entered the teleporter, then why not accept that Swampman is Davidson? How causation in the Swampman experiment operates is not much more mysterious than how it operates in the teleporter experiment. The teleporter experiment seems more plausible perhaps because tele-porting is a familiar staple of science fiction and thought experiments, even though we really have no idea how such a replicant would be nearly instantaneously produced. In either case, the production of each is mys-terious at least as far as known causal processes and laws of nature are currently understood. If the Davidson network maps on to Swampman body, then Swampman inherits all the traits and responsibilities of David-son. On the other hand, a difference might be that in the teleporter case the agent (allegedly) exerts some control over if or when the otherwise mysterious production of the replicant occurs, whereas with Swampman, there is no such control. The existence of Swampman body has no coun-terfactual dependency relations to Davidson.

According to CNM, Swampman qua Davidson embodies Davidson's history and agential perspective (just as the singular teleporter emergent does). Maybe one way to think about this is that the *network* has (some of) the right counterfactual dependency relations, even if Swampman body does not. If it is the network that matters, then Swampman is for all prac-tical purposes Davidson, and will move forward living the Davidson life. Responsibility practices consider both backward and forward-looking considerations. If the Davidson life ought to include responsibility for who Davidson has been and what Davidson has done, and if Swamp-man lives the Davidson life, then Swampman is no less a proper target of agential responsibility than the teleporter emergent.[17]

According to CNM, what matters is the cumulative network. Nor-mally, that coincides with a particular continuant body. Both the tele-porter and Swampman experiments ask whether the self continues with a new body. Psychological theories of the self say yes, because the mental states continue; but this would be true when there are duplicate selves as well. Animal theories of the self would say no, because the body itself has been destroyed and a new one put in its place. CNM says that the network may continue with a new body in the singular replicant case in so far as the network of traits maps on to or coincides with the new body.

## 4.2. Fission

What about responsibility ascription and fusion and fission (duplication) cases? In fission cases, CNM says that either there is some clear basis for distinguishing between the two, or the network self is disrupted and there are two new selves, albeit with causal and psychological connections to the original self, and the singular agential perspective has been disrupted.

Even so, setting aside doubts about how causation operates in the teleporter case, one might argue that even though the two emergents are not the original self, the successor selves have causal connections that, while not supporting continuation of the one self (the agent of the action), might support some responsibility ascription.

In fission, neither duplicate uniquely embodies the singular agential perspective of the original self. Neither is that original self, and there is not a singular agential perspective or self that can live the life of the original self (unless arbitrarily selected to do so, or unless there is some distinguishing feature). How then can the emergents be responsible? Consider an analogy with social organizations. Suppose one organization, say a department in a university, splits into two departments. The original department has ceased to exist. "Stuff" in the form of members may still exist even though the *department* does not still exist. However, there are almost certainly ongoing responsibilities and tasks from the original department that are transferred to the two new departments. For example, suppose there are students who were majors in the original no longer existing department, who are distributed between the two new departments. The new departments take on obligations and fulfill commitments to those students made by the original no longer existing department. Similarly, suppose the original department had made a purchase payment for which is outstanding at the time of the split. Presumably the two new departments are the proper targets of responsibility for discharging the debt, even though neither one of them actually made the purchase since neither one of them existed at the time. Perhaps responsibility for the debt is assigned to one of them, or perhaps it is apportioned on some basis between them.

One potential limitation of the social organization analogy is that there is some intentionality in the creation of the two departments. They did not spontaneously divide or come about as a result of malfunction. But, suppose the splitting of the department was not chosen or endorsed by the department, but imposed by administrative fiat or was the result of administrative error that for some reason would be difficult to reverse. Presumably, the same kind of distribution of responsibility would still occur and make sense. This suggests that both practical considerations as well as causal connections and other social (and legal) mechanisms are in play in identifying appropriate targets and in distributing responsibility. Such considerations could also play a role in responsibility practices vis à vis individuals.

Another limitation of the analogy is that the departments are different from one another, and those differences are the bases for distributing responsibilities between them. In fission or replication of a self the two new selves, are, by hypothesis, exactly similar to one another in the instant immediately following replication. Therefore, it might not be clear if and how responsibilities should be distributed if there is nothing to distinguish them. Still, if some assignment of responsibility to subsequent existents makes sense, as suggested by the organizational analogy, then at least some case could be made for doing so in the case of fissioned or duplicate selves, and some method could be devised for determining how to do so appropriately even though neither can be identified as the singular agent.[18]

If the responsibility involved is not what I have been calling agential responsibility, then moral or criminal guilt might not apply and punishment might be mitigated. However, this could present a difficulty in the duplicating teleporter case. Suppose that, instead of being the result of malfunction, duplication were an option one could choose. If duplication meant no transfer of moral or criminal guilt, then would teleportation become a way for a self to evade criminal liability, on the grounds that since the previous self no longer exists, no one bears agential responsibility for actions or commitments of that self? That doesn't seem to be a very palatable result. Some sort of responsibility practice might evolve to deal with such a possibility, for instance, by extending criminal liability beyond the doer of the act. Some of our responsibility practices already do this. For example, someone who authorizes a criminal act may be criminally liable even though the authorizer is not the agent who did the act, e.g., shot the victim. In such a case, the authorizer and the actor are both criminally liable, although exactly what each is liable for (and the penalties) may differ.

Or, responsibility practices might evolve such that if duplication were a genuine possibility, guilt would transfer. An argument for that might go like this: The original teletransportation scheme rested on the presumption that the person who emerged is, for all practical purposes, the person who entered. Either one alone would have been held accountable; if both survive, both should be. The deal made in the teletransportation scheme would be that the entering self understands that teletransportation entails risks of malfunction and duplication and accepts that *whoever* emerges takes on responsibility for the deeds of the original (in this instance, two emergents). I don't know exactly what that would mean if neither one can be said to be *the* self, *the* agent, who did the prior self's deeds, but perhaps a responsibility practice could evolve to deal with such a case.

One might object and argue that a previously existing but now nonexistent self cannot obligate (or pass on responsibility to) a presently existing self. But, if responsibility doesn't transfer to an emergent self on the grounds that it is a different self, then the whole scheme of the thought experiment collapses. But, if one accepts the scheme of the thought experiment, then duplication (either by choice or by malfunction) would not necessarily undermine some responsibility ascription, *even though* duplication disrupts the singularity of the agential perspective and neither can be said to be *the* self. This would be consistent with the organization analogy that shows that some of our current responsibility practices allow for responsibility ascription and distribution in some cases even when the agent cannot be re-identified or no longer exists.

But, what about Swampman? In contrast to biological fission and teleporter duplication, Swampman duplicated has neither the *singular* agential perspective of Davidson (as he does in the singular case) nor the causal connections that the other fission cases would allegedly have to their originals. Swampman qua duplicate Davidson body is a new, unexpected (and causally unexplained) being on the scene, one who, because Davidson still exists, cannot take up the self of Davidson. There are several possibilities. If Davidson and Swampman could be distinctly and reliably identified, then (1) perhaps Davidson would be the proper target of responsibility ascription and the proper approach to duplicate Swampman would be to give him a lot of therapy and help him forge a distinct self and life for himself. Or, (2) perhaps the dispositional similarity to Davidson would entail some different responsibility practice vis-à-vis Swampman. Or, (3) if Davidson and Swampman cannot be distinctly identified, then perhaps the case is like the duplicate teleporter case or the spontaneous biological fission case, and both would be responsible in some sense.

In the first option, where both Davidson and Swampman can be reliably identified, what would justify treating Davidson as responsible and Swampman as a target for therapy and development of a new life? In *singular* replication, I suggested that the absence of the "right" causal connections may not, by itself, rule out Swampman being for all practical purposes Davidson. Singular Swampman is the new body of the Davidson network, similar to the teleporter emergent being the new body of the self that entered the teleporter. But, in duplication, the network is disrupted; there is now both Davidson and Swampman. If it is plausible for one to be responsible, there has to be a condition or distinguishing feature that justifies treating them differently. The only difference is that Davidson is constituted by the "right" backward causal connections and Swampman is not. If they can be reliably identified as Davidson and as Swampman, then (and as I argued in Chapter 4) there is an argument to be made that Davidson, but not Swampman, continues Davidson and is responsible.[19]

Of course, Davidson has causal relations whether known or not. However, if Davidson and Swampman are *not* identifiable as distinct, this difference would, presumably, be inaccessible to both Davidson and Swampman and to anyone else, and therefore, could not be a basis for distributing responsibility differently between them. For all practical purposes, when they can't be identified as "original" and "duplicate," each appears to be equally a candidate for some responsibility ascription, like the teleporter duplicate, and even if not agential responsibility.[20]

The duplication case presents a different problem from the singular case. In the singular case, the question is whether Swampman embodies sufficient conditions to be Davidson. I have argued that he does, or that it is at least plausible to argue that he does. In duplication, the question is whether there is a basis, a sufficient reason, for distinguishing between the two. In the Davidson/Swampman context, I am suggesting that being constituted by the right causal connections and being identifiable as such might be a decisive factor for making such a distinction, even though having those connections is not necessary for responsibility ascription in the singular replicant case. As I argued earlier and in Chapters 1 and 2, the self is constituted by a cluster of conditions. While some subset of conditions must be present for the self to continue as that self, it may be that there is no necessary condition that must be present in all contexts. In different contexts, different factors may be relevant.

Admittedly, the reasoning here is a bit unstable, and I'm not really sure how responsibility practices would or should evolve to deal with such cases. If CNM is right, reasoning is unstable because in fission, the network is disrupted. When we can't identify *the* agent—and that is the basic problem with duplication, there is no single agent to identify—it is unclear how (and whether) responsibilities of a prior single self distribute over duplicates. I have suggested though that responsibility practices might evolve such that some responsibility ascription would be possible. However, one might want to push back against any assignment of responsibility because duplication is just an accident. In each, the malfunctioning teleporter and Swampman, it is a matter of sheer accident or luck that each duplicate exists. Good luck for the duplicate in so far as existence itself is good; bad luck with respect to the problems and uncertainties it creates. But, in the malfunctioning teleporter case, the emergent that is the duplicate was the intended outcome and absent the survival of the original would have been responsible. The accident of malfunction seems to change the kind and distribution of responsibility but not necessarily remove it altogether. Swampman—singular or duplicate—though, is just an accident. In the singular case, I argued in Chapter 4 that his accidental and causally mysterious origins do not rule out his continuing the network, Davidson, in which case responsibility could plausibly be ascribed to him. In the duplicate case, whether it should be or not may depend on additional factors, such as whether Davidson original can be reliably identified, and if he can, determining whether the distinguishing factor of causal origin may be decisive. If they can't be distinguished, then the situation might be partly like the biological fission case or the teleporter case, and responsibility could be distributed between the two or ascribed to both.[21]

## 4.3. Fusion

In a fusion case, such as the brain of one self being combined with the body of another self, CNM says that the resulting self is neither of the

original selves, but is a new self. The new self has its own agential perspective, but, as I argued in Chapter 4, that perspective is not the singular
agential perspective of either of the original selves. There are causal relations to both prior selves, intentional and some dispositional relations
to at least one, and some dispositional relations to the other in so far as
dispositions (and capabilities) are dependent on prior regimens and practices, and bodily systems as well as on the brain. But, in contrast to the
fission cases where obligations and responsibilities going forward might
be distributed, in the fusion case it seems that they would compound.

Consider the reverse of the previous analogy to splitting departments
in a social organization. Suppose, instead of a department splitting into
two departments, two departments merge into one. The two previous
departments cease to exist even though individual members may still
exist. Or, to make it more analogous to the brain transplant cases, suppose the leadership team of one department were combined with the
non-leadership members of another department to form a new department, and both previous departments as such cease to exist. In either
case, there is a new institutional, functional unit with a new authoritative
structure and scope of activity. Duties, debts, activities of the previous
departments may or may not transfer to the new department. It would
probably depend on the type of duty, debt, and activity, as well as on the
context and functionality of the new department.

Is this scenario analogous to the brain transplant cases? One difference is that a "leadership team" is not as defining of the character of a
department or organization as a brain and the psychological traits that
go along with it are for a self. In the organizational analogy, a leadership
team might be subordinate to the purposes of the department or unit in
ways that the brain is not often thought to be subordinate to the body
or the rest of the self. We might even say that the department remains
the "same" department with new leadership. In contrast, psychological
theories of the self treat brain transplants (better described as body transplants) as cases where the emergent self *is* the self of the brain, on the
presumption that the self, the person, goes with the brain. According to
psychological theories, the responsibilities of the new, fused self would
just be those of one of the prior selves, namely, the one of the brain. But, if
the organizational analogy has some plausibility, then just as a leadership
team might have to assume responsibilities of a group's prior leadership
team and not simply replace those with its own prior responsibilities, so
too, might a new fused self have to assume new responsibilities and not
simply carry over those from the self of the brain.

In Chapter 4, I argued that the new self is a fusion of parts of two
selves, and is a new self, not either one of the previous selves. Similarly,
even granting limits to the organizational analogy, it does suggest that
a combining of "parts" of selves involves those parts adapting to and
coordinating with one another in ways that will be distinctive of a new

compositional product. For the network self, this might mean that some, but not all, duties and responsibilities carry over from the brain-self, and some duties and responsibilities carry over from the other body self. The new, fused self may not have many of the capabilities that the self from which the brain came had. It also has different familial, biological, and social relations and traits, and may have some biological and emotional dispositions that come from the body, not the brain of the new fused self. There could be a variety of bases on which we might ascribe responsibility to this new self for things done or planned for by either or both of the previous selves from which its parts come. But, since it is not either one of those previous selves, whatever responsibility is ascribed to it, it cannot be the agential responsibility of either one of them. If brain (or body) transplantation and fusion were a genuine possibility, then responsibility practices might have to evolve to also deal with the possibility that someone might choose transplantation in order to avoid full responsibility or criminal liability. As noted earlier with fission, criminal liability might be dissociated from criminal guilt. Or, responsibility practices might evolve such that guilt would transfer, or evolve in yet some other way.

To recap: the thought experiments originated as devices to test intuitions about whether the "same" self continues (or not) in the products of fusion and fission. Even when the original self does not continue and its agential responsibility cannot be ascribed to the resulting selves, there could be other bases on which to ascribe some responsibility. If any of the thought experimental cases, or something similar to them, were to become real possibilities, then responsibility practices would evolve to address them. I'm not sure exactly what such practices would look like. All I have done here, importing conclusions from Chapters 3 and 4, is argued:

(1) that in the thought experimental cases of singular replication the singular emergent can be justifiably identified as the appropriate target for agential responsibility ascription. In the singular case, the cumulative network continues;

(2) that in the thought experimental cases of fission or fusion, while the emergents may not be appropriate targets of agential responsibility, our current system of responsibility practices could allow for a variety of ways to distribute and ascribe responsibility to such emergents.

## 5. Forward-looking Responsibility and the Incomplete Self

Just as a self is constituted by its relations to its past, it is also constituted by its relations to its future and to its possibilities. It is one cumulative network, a changeable totality that retains its past and projects itself into the future.

A process self is always in a state of "natural debt" and, until death, is incomplete. By "natural debt" I just mean that the self is not all self-made. There are aspects of the self, e.g., genetic code, family of origin, dispositions, some social and cultural habits and normative perspectives, that the self inherits or that it just finds itself constituted as. At the same time, "debt" implies something to discharge going forward. Inherited features of the self are both determining and may set boundaries or conditions on what is possible, while at the same time contributing in a positive way to what is possible. The self is not necessarily passive in its taking up of such inherited features. Rather, the self can affirm, disavow, "own up" to features as truly one's own and so on. This is both acknowledging who one is and in moving forward, taking responsibility for that even as the self may aim to reshape and extend (or diminish) what it is given.

This may be something like what Watson, quoting Dewey, refers to as responsibility as self-disclosure, the "attributability face" in contrast to the "accountability face" of responsibility.

> [W]hen any result has been foreseen and adopted as foreseen [by the agent], such result is the outcome not of any external circumstances, not of mere desires and impulses, but of the agent's conception of his own end. Now because the result thus flows from the agent's own conception of an end, he feels responsible for it. . . . The result is simply an expression of himself; a manifestation of what he would have himself to be. Responsibility is thus one aspect of the identity of character and conduct. *We are responsible for our conduct because that conduct is ourselves objectified in action.*[22]

Feinberg (1970b) refers to "representational attributability" (251), not an agential or causal notion of responsibility or liability, but responsibility in the sense of responding to or answering for oneself.[23] Fischer and Ravizza (1998) propose a similar notion—that a person recognizes and takes on responsibility for being that person or agent.[24] If the self is incomplete and if it has the requisite agential capacities—e.g., semantic, symbolic, physical, cognitive, the capacities of adaptive intelligence in a Deweyan and Buchlerian sense—then a self is not a passive recipient or byproduct of its relational locations. Even though some of those locations may be "given," the self is not necessarily passive with respect to them. Rather, the self responds to and contributes to how those relations shape it.[25] In so doing, the self both has and is responsible for the character of its singular agential perspective.

The self may also add features to itself, for example, by deliberate choice of career, citizenship, intimate partner, parenthood, and so on. By singular, I don't mean that the self qua responsible agent has to achieve perfect harmonization of its many perspectival constituents. Perhaps the I-as-professor-of-philosophy is not very well "harmonized" with I-as-neighbor-of-a-non-intellectual; perhaps that perspective (I-as-philosopher) is largely suppressed in the context of choices, interactions, and actions in relation to that neighbor relation. Or, perhaps the I-as-feminist experiences conflict with the I-as-daughter or the I-as-spouse. In taking responsibility as *an* agent, the self does not lose its plurality, it does not lose the fact that the self is a community of selves. Because the self is a community and therefore, "internally" diversified, it has the capacity to detach from any one of its perspectives and shape the role that perspective will play in the self's overall process of action choice, interaction in the world. As discussed in the previous chapter, this is crucial to autonomy and to the idea that a self takes responsibility for itself, for being and becoming, who it is.

## 6. The Network Self and Responsibility in Collective Contexts

Our responsibility practices have also begun to evolve to address when and to what extent selves are responsible in collective or systemic contexts. The topic of responsibility in collective contexts is large and much has been written on it.[26] I will not address most of it here, but confine myself to suggesting what CNM might have to contribute.

First, a principled point about relatedness. Every relation entails mutual relevance (albeit not necessarily in the same way), that is, every relation is reciprocal, even if not symmetrical (or transitive).

According to CNM, a self is not just causally influenced by, but is constituted as a network by its relations, psychological and bodily, familial, social. The self has "identities"—e.g., mother, philosopher, feminist, consumer, citizen, carbon emitter—in virtue of its social locations and of the norms and practices in which it participates or which it endorses, embodies, enacts, and represents. Applying the principle of mutual relatedness, then, the self would also be relevant to, constitutive of its social locations in some sense.

Some of a self's relations or locations seem to have miniscule relevance to who a self is. A self's relations in large scale social or ecological contexts, where one has "identities" such as resident of developed world, consumer, carbon emitter and so on, may seem trivial as constitutive of the self. Conversely, an individual may seem only trivially relevant to the larger scale social context. It is certainly true that sometimes, maybe even often, the relations are trivial in one or both respects. But, not always, and even if they are in one respect, they might not be in another. Reviving an example from Chapter 2, as a resident of New York City, one of several million people, one may merely extend the scope of New York City and have no impact on its integrity.[27] Its scope, its comprehensiveness is a trait of (strongly relevant to) the integrity of New York City, but a self, qua individual resident, is not strongly relevant to what New York City is.

However, that doesn't mean an individual couldn't be strongly relevant. On the contrary, some individual resident *could*, in virtue of political office, community activism, economic or cultural influence, also be strongly relevant to, contribute to, the integrity of New York City. Moreover, an individual could be strongly relevant to a sub-complex constituent of New York City, e.g., to the character of a particular neighborhood. The individual's contribution might thereby be strongly relevant to New York City in some respect, depending on the contribution. Or, the neighborhood might be strongly relevant to the overall integrity of New York City in virtue of the individual's contribution.

In addition, an individual resident may participate in a cumulative activity that is characteristic of the pattern of living in New York. For example, an individual moves her car and thereby contributes to the cumulative collective activity of clearing the street for alternate side of the street street-cleaning.[28] The self's intention and explicit conceptualization of her action may be "I am moving my car," without thinking about it as a contribution to the collective action of clearing the streets for street-cleaning. But, even without explicit formulation of her action in collective terms, she is so contributing, and enacting and perpetuating practices and cultural norms that define that particular activity.

Even if the individual resident is in general merely a constituent of the scope of New York City, there could be a context in which the individual functions as a representative of New York City in some sense. Suppose in some context the individual is the sole person present who is from New York City and communicates information about New York City to others present, or functions as a "representative" New Yorker (in patterns of behavior or speech, for instance). As such the individual could spread the reach of New York cultural norms.

There is a variety of ways in which an individual might be relevant to, or constitutive of, some aspect of a collective structure, practice, action or activity. If there is mutual relevance and the self is, in some sense, constitutive of its social locations, then the self may have individual responsibilities within those social locations; it may share responsibility for the character of the communities by which it is constituted and for the behaviors and ways in which those communities live.

Intentionality is often taken to be central to determining whether and to what extent an individual may be responsible or share in responsibility for some action. But, it is not always and whether it is or not may also depend on the kind of responsibility that is ascribed to an individual. I want to suggest that mutual relevance is the underlying basic condition for responsibility ascription in collective contexts. Communities do not have to have been chosen by the self in order for it to share responsibility. They may just be where the self finds itself. One does not choose the culture and society into which one is born, and one may not choose the behavioral patterns and norms that define a particular location that one does choose. For example, in choosing to become a mother, the self does not necessarily choose all the norms and expectations of motherhood, and may, indeed, rebel against some of them.

By having responsibility in a collective context I don't mean only having responsibilities in virtue of occupying a particular role (such as mother, parent, teacher, lawyer, building inspector) in virtue of which there may be specific responsibilities assigned to that role, in some cases governed by formal and informal rules of professional conduct. Rather, how an individual behaves in the role and fulfills role-defined duties may have wider impact. For example, the tactics of a personal injury attorney may reenact the norms of that profession and thereby contribute to perpetuating them and reinforcing the stereotype of the "ambulance chasing" lawyer. Or, an individual may conduct herself differently and contribute to a possible shift in the norms of the profession, or in the local context of practice. Thus, an individual may have some responsibility for how the profession conducts itself, the perpetuation of its norms, and for its reputational standing.

The individual does not just internalize or take on individual responsibilities. One also participates in the particular social location with the structures and norms, formal and informal, that define it. In doing so, one acquires and by one's own activity shapes one's "identity," for example, qua personal injury attorney, while also contributing to the scope or character of that profession, even if the contribution is miniscule. An individual may also have responsibility in a collective context by sharing responsibility or being "co-responsible" for a collective outcome or for contributing to a cumulative action in a system or practice with direct or emergent outcomes.[29] For example, where individual actions (clearing the street for street-cleaning, driving, other fossil-fuel dependent forms of consumption) may contribute to a collective outcome (a cleared street, accumulation of greenhouse gases in the atmosphere), an individual may have co-responsibility for an outcome even though the individual's contribution alone is miniscule and would not be sufficient to produce the outcome and even though the individual may not intend the collectively produced outcome.

Recognition of the self as having social "identities" and as thereby contributing in some way to the collective or systemic context of such "identities" helps to conceptualize the self as having responsibility in collective or systemic contexts. Whether in any specific context a self has or shares in responsibility, and if so, how and to what extent, would require much additional action-theoretic analysis, as well as analysis of causal, moral, legal, and cultural responsibility practices. All CNM suggests is that at the ground level, so to speak, the social constitution of the self and the reciprocal nature of relation constitute a basis for ascribing to the individual some responsibility in collective contexts.

One worry might be that CNM doesn't recognize boundaries and sets the extensional limits of the self too broadly. It is true that CNM casts a wide net. Moreover, the identities of the self may not all be of the self's choosing or within the self's control. However, this is not necessarily a defect of the theory. Rather, it could be viewed as a healthy corrective to theories that define the self too narrowly or to tendencies that selves might have to allow one's preferences to artificially restrict what is relevant to the self. To take a simplistic example, suppose a self lives in a multifamily dwelling where noise is transmitted easily through shared walls. A self who thinks of itself as "free to do what it wants within its own home" and who plays loud music at 3 a.m. has failed to recognize itself as also being an apartment-dweller, a neighbor-with-shared-walls. CNM says that being a neighbor-with-shared-walls is an identity of a self that may have accompanying responsibilities. There are many different ways in which the self is socially constituted, some having pervasive, and some having more restricted, impact on the self and others. Viewing the self (and the self viewing itself) through the lens of CNM would allow for better recognition of the identities, and responsibilities, one may have in virtue of multiple social relations and locations, even if, at the same time, it engenders the need to work out criteria for specifying the exact nature and scope of responsibility in collective contexts.

## 7. Some Objections

It might be objected that while the neighbor-with-shared-walls makes sense because there is a direct action that affects other persons in a recognizable interpersonal context, in wider system contexts, such as the global economic system or global carbon emissions, any individual's action(s) and contribution to or participation in the system are so mediated by multiple interactions and causal relations that responsibility is too dispersed or fragmented to meaningfully attach to an individual.

Moreover, in a contemporary context where one may be not only a member of a tribe or clan or village, but may also be a participant in a global economic system, is a carbon emitter, a member of national and international social organizations, the range of possible responsibilities would be so great that they would dissolve the force of the concept. If the social system(s) of which the self is a constituent, however small, has broadened, then so, too, have the identities of the self. Even if local (and familial) identities tend to be the most immediately felt, social structures and relations have evolved such that social identities have expanded to include wide, system identities. But, no one can respond to, can take on responsibility for, all the possible constituent locations of the self. For responsibility to be meaningful, it has to be circumscribed and allow for actionable response. Therefore, there need to be boundaries to what we consider possible bases for responsibility.

It may be psychologically difficult to think of one's identities and responsibilities in wide, system terms, but the objection is not about the psychological difficulty, but challenges a possible implication of CNM that responsibility could potentially have indefinitely wide scope for an individual. Since on CNM a self has many identities, this way of thinking would lead to overburdening individuals. A self has only so much time in the day and has to limit and set priorities among its activities and responsibilities. One might say, "Look, I can't be responsible for how the profession I participate in is defined. I can only 'do my job.' This other stuff is not in my sphere of control." Or, the parent who is driving her children to school thinks of herself as just that, a parent fulfilling a parental responsibility to educate her children, rather than as a consumer of fossil fuel, a carbon emitter, and a contributor to global warming. One might argue that the individual's participation or contribution as a carbon emitter or as a professional practitioner is so miniscule that it can't be the basis for an identity let alone for having responsibilities. Or, even if one admitted that one might have some responsibility, it would always be trumped by other more salient priorities, such as the responsibilities of being a good parent or of fulfilling one's professional duties.

One line of reply is to grant that, as in the New York City example, an individual may only be a constituent of the scope of a large scale system, in these instances, global carbon emissions or the character of a large, social profession. However, with respect to some systems and where much is at stake, e.g., global carbon emissions, every addition makes some difference—it is one more additional carbon molecule—even if no single addition is the producer of the concerning outcome (global warming and climate change). Seeing oneself as a contributor to an outcome, even when one alone does not make a significant difference, may still be a legitimate basis for thinking about the scope of one's responsibilities, in this case, as being co-responsible for an emergent outcome of social and economic patterns of behavior in which one participates. To have such co-responsibility that would imply that one should alter one's behavior is perhaps analogous to conceptualizing oneself as having a responsibility to "do one's bit" for the war effort, when one's country is engaged in defense of itself against an aggressor.[30]

Another line of reply is to consider what is meant by contribution or participation. Even if one's contribution to a specific outcome is miniscule, one's participation in a system may contribute to perpetuating the system and may represent the values and norms embodied in that system (of consumption, of mobility, of professional practice) as positive or as harmless or morally unproblematic.[31] By enacting the practices of a system, one expresses a normative stance or normative identity, and thereby could have some responsibility for the values and norms by which one lives. Consider being a member of a slaveholding and slave endorsing society. Even if one did not oneself own or trade slaves, one might still contribute to perpetuating the system and representing slavery as having an alleged "positive" value. One's participation in the system could take many different forms, for example, one might benefit economically (e.g., by being able to purchase cheaper goods) and socially (e.g., in virtue of there being less competition for benefits that society offers and that slaves would not be permitted to access). Or, suppose one is a member of and endorses the values of an organization that advocates racial superiority. Even if the individual does not herself engage in lynchings or other overt acts of racially motivated harm and therefore is not responsible for such deeds herself, she may still be responsible for perpetuating beliefs and norms that create a climate that encourages or validates such deeds (Striblen, 2013).

Similarly, as a resident of the United States, one's mode of living is constituted by indefinitely many features of that social arrangement, most of which one did not choose or initiate. One participates in those arrangements—whether by using petroleum and petroleum-based products, paying taxes that support various governmental policies (including ones that the self professes to oppose), or more deliberatively by voting in elections. One therefore may causally contribute, even if in indiscernible and often unconscious ways, to the nature of those arrangements. Moreover, as constituted by those arrangements, the self inhabits and is inhabited by attitudes that reflect evaluative and cognitive positions. One is also, therefore, responsible in some sense for those attitudes, as well as for the actions that flow from them; the attitudes in so far as they fall within the scope of one's capacity for evaluative and normative judgments, and the actions in so far as one has the possibility and capacity to behave differently. Even if the self expresses them unreflectively and has not explicitly or voluntarily chosen them, one could properly be asked to defend or justify both the attitudes and the actions of the community or social arrangement in which the self participates.[32] Or, one might have responsibility to remediate or contribute to remediation. One may not be *morally* responsible in the sense of deserving blame, praise, punishment or reward for many of the ways in which one participates, but there may be a variety of ways in which it is meaningful to ascribe responsibility to the individual in such collective contexts.

Does this mean that in cases of morally problematic norms and practices, such as slavery, an individual has a *duty* to actively seek to change it, to oppose it, for instance, to boycott businesses which use slaves, or to engage in abolitionist political activity? Does it mean that an individual has a duty to join forces with others in collective action to remediate, or as a member of an otherwise unrelated collection of individuals to come up with some collective decision procedure for what, if any, action to take?[33] There is a large literature addressing such issues, and I'm not going to try to address that here. The point I want to reiterate is that CNM offers an account of why it is appropriate to ask that question of an individual. The individual's social locations (informal as well as formal and intentional) are constitutive of the individual, that is, they contribute to the overall integrity of the individual. Because relation is reciprocal (albeit not necessarily symmetrical) the individual in turn may affect or have the capacity to affect its social locations. The answers to practical and moral questions about what an individual's specific responsibilities might be will depend on many other considerations. The point is only that the individual can be conceptualized as a legitimate target for responsibility ascription.

Of course, the extent to which one merely inherits as opposed to choosing, affirming or actively advancing the norms, attitudes, and behaviors of a group or collective may affect the nature and scope of one's responsibility or co-responsibility in a collective context. Some collective contexts are consciously chosen communities in which there is a fair amount of reflection and commitment. Others are communities in the sense of participating with others in parallel communicative and judicative directions.[34] But, what CNM says is that all are constituents, "identities," of the self qua a cumulative network. It is therefore at least possible that one bears some responsibility for behaviors and attitudes that are made in virtue of or that express those collective locations. Even when, in virtue of one of its identities (e.g., qua user of petroleum products) the self is merely living a "way of life" that contributes to the consequences of that way of life as lived by the community or set of persons who continue to so act, one may share in the responsibility for those consequences.

But, it might be argued, one may not be aware of the consequences, or even if one is, may not believe that one is responsible, and may disavow responsibility on the grounds that one's contributions are too insignificant to make a difference. But, to the first point (lack of awareness), just as ignorance of the law does not necessarily relieve one of responsibility for obeying it, ignorance of consequences by itself may not relieve one of responsibility. A self might not know or believe at the time of acting that its action is wrong. But, by itself that would not relieve the self of causal responsibility, and might not relieve it of moral responsibility either (if, for instance, it is a case where one ought to know, or where information is readily available). To the second point (insignificance of individual contribution), as a member of a community (the set of persons with experiential parallelism), each person makes some difference, however immediately indiscernible, and therefore, there is at least some case to be made for ascribing responsibility to each for the consequences of the community's cumulative and collective behavior.

What I am suggesting is that the responsibility of a community may be shared by the members of that community—even in the absence of self-conscious and intentional joint commitments and even if they are not themselves conscious of the consequences—because they are constituted by, participate in and produce as a set the behaviors and consequences of those behaviors that are the responsibility of the community. Whether that responsibility is causal, moral, vicarious, remedial, or whether it entails liability in some legal or compensatory sense and so on are additional questions to be considered. If the very constitution, the integrity of a self, is at least partially social, then that is a basis for considering the self as bearing some responsibility for not only its contribution (which may be miniscule), but as sharing in the community's responsibility for the actions of the set in which the self participates.

## 8. Conclusion

In this chapter I've suggested that CNM avoids some unsettling implications of standard four-dimensionalist accounts of persons. On the stage theory account, the person who performed an action cannot be the person who is responsible for the action. The two are counterparts of one another. They belong to one person-career, but each is a distinct three-dimensional object (space-time region) related such as to be counterparts. Similarly, a temporal parts theory says that an action would be done by a person part, while a different person part (with appropriate unity relations) would have responsibility ascribed to it. According to CNM, on the other hand, the person at any time is the cumulative upshot of what it has been and the leading edge of the process. As such the self is who it is in virtue of who it has been; its past is a trait (not *a* part). Thus, there is numerically one thing (cumulative network) that bears responsibility for its action.

It might be argued that this is just a semantic difference, and that stage theory (or temporal parts theory) can account, just as well as CNM can, for how to identify the appropriate target of responsibility ascription. Stage theory can give an account of re-identification (persons are counterparts with appropriate unity—causal, similarity, and contiguity—relations). But, I am suggesting that CNM is preferable because conceptualizing the self as a cumulative network, as a diachronically and synchronically unified process provides a more coherent basis for conceptualizing distinctive self features such as agency and responsibility. There is practical need for an account of a self as a single, unified "thing" that is the target of forensic concerns, and CNM provides such an account. One might be concerned that identifying the self as a process weakens the sense in which a self is an agent. But, as I have argued, conceptualizing the self as a cumulative network doesn't mean that a self doesn't have many of the functional features associated with selves, such as first-personal experience, agency and autonomy, and now responsibility. It just means that one has to reconceptualize those and I have proposed ways of doing so.

According to CMN, the processual nature of the self also gives a better foothold for thinking about the ways in which a self can be responsible in both backward and forward-looking senses. And, finally, by recognizing that selves are also socially constituted, that is, by recognizing that the cumulative network is inclusive of social and cultural traits, CNM can offer an account of why it makes sense to attribute responsibility to a self in a collective context (e.g., as having individual responsibility for some contribution, or as co-responsible, or as sharing in collective responsibility). There is much valuable work already done in the area of collective responsibility. All CNM does is suggest that recognizing social features as constitutive "identities" and hence possible loci of responsibility advances the understanding of individuals having responsibility in collective contexts.

## Notes

1. Honoré (1999, 10).
2. Feinberg (1970a, 138, n. 17).
3. Dworkin (1986, 6).
4. As found on io9.com. Comment by Nene Ormes and Karin Waller with the Science Fiction Bokhandeln in Malmö, Sweden, about the book *Zoo City* by Lauren Beukes (http://io9.com/10-great-novels-that-arent-about-what-you-heard-they-we-1679984927).
5. Attributed to Mahatma Gandhi. "Falser Words Were Never Spoken," by Brian Morton, *The New York Times* www.nytimes.com/2011/08/30/opinion/falser-words-were-never-spoken.html?_r=0 (visited 14 January 2015).
6. Our responsibility practices sometimes involve ascribing responsibility to someone other than the agent, e.g., in some cases of strict liability, or cases where a parent is responsible for a child, or for the actions of a minor. We might think of these as different forms of vicarious (but legitimate and real senses of) responsibility, where liability is transferred to someone other than the person(s) who did the action (and where guilt, moral or otherwise, may be dissociated from liability).
7. "Partly as a result of moral education, the child typically acquires the view of himself as an agent, in at least a minimal sense. That is, he sees that upshots in the world depend on his choices and bodily movements. Further, the child comes to believe that he is a fair target of certain responses—the 'reactive attitudes' and certain practices, such as punishment—as a result of the way in which he exercises his agency. We claim that it is in virtue of acquiring these views of himself (as a result of his moral education) that the child takes responsibility. More specifically, it is in virtue of acquiring these views that the child takes responsibility for certain kinds of mechanisms: practical reasoning, non-reflective habits, and so forth" Fischer and Ravizza (1998).
8. Recall Baker's (2009) criticism of four-dimensionalism as having an "anemic" conception of persons, cited in Chapter 1.
9. At the same time, causation and counterfactual dependency include many things that are not strictly speaking constituents of the self. If the traffic light had not changed just when it did, the driver would not have hit the car. The driver may be responsible for hitting the car but not for the changing of the traffic light even though the driver hitting the car is (partially) counterfactually dependent on the changing of the traffic light. The changing of the traffic light is not a trait of the driver, even though it is a trait, a constituent of an event of which the driver is also a constituent.
10. The cumulative whole self at a time may also include the possibilities of the self with respect to subsequent stages, qua possibilities, not qua actualities. Modality is another topic altogether. I mention possibility only to indicate

that notions such as dispositions and capability, as well as the notion that a living process self is incomplete, have to entail some notion of possibility.

11. Miller (2001, 2004) on remedial responsibility.

12. Each may also have co-responsibility for the cumulative action, even though neither is *the* single agent of it.

13. "[I]n order for the agent/agents of an individual or collective action A to be *agentively liable* for an event E, A should be connectable to E by relations that are either (R1) conventional, or (R2) causal and linear or unidirectional, or (R3) if part of a multiply connected causal network, not due to emergent consequences within complex systems" (Martinsen and Seibt, 2013, 171).

14. See Chapter 6, Note 27, citing Fulford and Radoilska (2012) on the possible impact of addiction, compulsion, and delusion on capacity for responsibility, which I am arguing is different from the question of ownership.

15. As I said in Chapter 4, and following Gendler (1999, 2002, 2007), I do not think that fission and fusion thought experimental cases in the personal identity literature are useful for identifying necessary and sufficient conditions for the identity or continuation of persons. The features of personhood or selfhood, of selves as they generally are, are contingently related and when they are taken apart and isolated, as they are in thought experiments, there is instability in our responses. Nonetheless, thought experiments may be helpful in shifting perspective, reframing an issue or seeing what is salient in a morally valenced situation.

16. The parent might also be personally responsible for faulty child-rearing practices, negligence, or for that matter, life-enhancing child-rearing practice; or the employer might be personally responsible for poor employee training and supervision. But, these are distinct from the specific responsibility issue under discussion.

17. The Swampman case is different from imposter cases, where a self attempts to take over the roles and live the life of another cumulatively constituted self. The imposter already has a history and cumulatively formed self, as does (or did) the other self. In so far as an imposter case involves taking on *another* pre-existing self's identity, it would be more like fusion cases. On the other hand, an imposter case could involve creating or being given a whole new identity, an invented, not a stolen identity, for example, a person placed in witness or other forms of "identity" protection programs. Swampman is neither of these, but, like the teleporter emergent, a *de novo* wholesale bodily replacement of Davidson.

18. In contrast, Oderberg (1996) argues that because the original self has ceased to exist, the only self that could be held responsible no longer exists, and the fissioned selves are not proper objects of responsibility ascription.

19. This would be a difference with the duplicating teleporter case in which, even in the case of malfunction, both emergents have some causal and intentional connections. Thus, even if an "original" and a "duplicate" could be identified in the teleporter case, an argument could be made that both should have some responsibility, rather than one being sent off for therapy.

20. This might suggest yet another, different argument about Swampman, even when Davidson is identifiable. If responsibility is in some respects constitutive of who one is and if Swampman is qualitatively identical to Davidson, then one might argue that they should be treated similarly. For Swampman, however accidental his existence, is still constituted as he is, namely, as Davidson, and therefore, is dispositionally identical. What would it be like to feel, think, remember, desire, intend, and so on, just as Davidson, and yet not *be* Davidson or be responsible for what one would feel that one owned? One might wonder just how effective therapy could be in transforming Swampman and

helping him forge a distinct and new direction. I don't know how to assess such an argument, but I can see some plausibility to it.

21. Exactly how luck affects responsibility ascription has been a matter of some philosophical discussion. There is an extensive philosophical literature on luck; Nelkin (2013) provides an excellent overview (and bibliography) starting with the well-known discussion between Nagel and Williams. Nagel points out that it may be paradoxical to ascribe responsibility to persons once we start to recognize the extent to which what a person does is under the influence of many things that are not under the person's control (1979, 36). (Nagel distinguishes four types of luck, resultant, causal, circumstantial, and constitutive.) Still we are, he says, "unable to view ourselves simply as portions of the world" (1979, 37). He says he has no solution for the tension between what he calls the external view of agency, whereby actions are events that happen in the world, and the internal view of agency, whereby we see ourselves and others as bearing some responsibility for what we do (1979, 38).

Honoré (1999) argues that responsibility ascription is rooted in what he calls outcome responsibility, and does not require either fault or desert. (In Nagel's classification of different kinds of luck this would be "resultant luck.") Fault and desert "increase the credit or discredit for the outcome of our behavior that we incur in any event" (31). Outcome responsibility has this grounding role because it is, Honoré argues, "crucial to our identity as persons" (29). We become persons in virtue of authorship for actions and decisions, ascription of which gives us identity, character, and a history. In virtue of authorship, we have "outcome responsibility" (whether there is fault or blame involved or not). Honoré argues (controversially it seems to me) that the "*system* of responsibility" is fair and requires us to "bear the risk of bad luck both in the way we are constituted and in the external circumstances in which we find ourselves" (9). In Honoré's approach, our identities are not solely under our control, and therefore, luck may play a role not only in outcomes, but in the very constitution of who we are (Nagel's "constitutive luck").

While Williams (1981) would disagree, Nagel's and Honoré's arguments suggest some plausibility to the idea that luck does not necessarily remove responsibility ascription. An argument could also be given that the luck of a bad outcome not resulting doesn't remove *moral* responsibility for acting negligently or malevolently, even if one wouldn't be held legally responsible for an outcome that didn't happen. Negligent behavior itself (e.g., driving under the influence, child neglect) or malevolent behavior (e.g., attempted murder) may have legal consequences even when it doesn't have a bad outcome.

There may also be cases where responsibilities are imposed on one through the accident of one's birth, or ordinary situations in which one simply finds oneself by accident or luck (good or bad)—Nagel's "circumstantial luck," where one has no causal part in producing the situation and yet may have some kind of responsibility. For example, one might happen upon a situation where one may have a (remedial) responsibility to act either individually or in concert with others. Held (1970) describes several examples involving collections of persons who under some circumstances could be reasonably said to be morally responsible for acting even though they played no role in bringing about the situation that calls for remedial action.

22. Dewey (1969), as quoted by Watson (2004, 260), emphasis by Watson. (from Dewey's 1891 *Outlines of a Critical Theory of Ethics, Part I, Chapter III,* 160–161.)

23. Feinberg suggests an analogy between an individual being responsible for herself in this sense and a group such as a nation being responsible, both

collectively and distributively, for traits in its group structure that can be ascribed to no given individual as their cause (Feinberg, 1970b, 250).

24. See Fischer and Ravizza (1998) as quoted in Note 7, this chapter.

25. At the same time, its responses contribute to those social and communal locations, even if in small and undetectable ways. (See also Parfit, 1986, Chapter 3, on moral mathematics.)

26. Work on responsibility in collective contexts has focused on a range of issues: whether and how *collectives* can be responsible, on the structure of intentionality, on individual responsibility in collective contexts. As just a sample from the literature in this area, May (1992) offers a "social-existentialist" account of an individual sharing responsibility for harm produced by a group. For an account of "joint commitment" as the underlying intentional structure of a group of individuals having collective responsibility see Gilbert (1989). Tuomela (2013) develops an ontology of groups based on the notion of a we-mode of intentionality (versus an I-mode). For an account of moral responsibility at an individual and collective level in contexts of collective action, see Isaacs (2011). Young (2006) develops a social connection model of responsibility, an account of responsibility for addressing social injustice in collective contexts. Martinsen and Seibt (2013) apply Young's concept to ecological responsibility. For an account of random collection of individuals having responsibility, see Held (1970).

27. Whether being a resident of New York City is strongly or weakly relevant to the individual resident may depend on contingent factors, but that is not important for the point I'm making here.

28. The bane of the existence of a New York City car owner who chooses to regularly park on the street rather than in a parking garage. Such parking is however free and permit-free, and the inconvenience "cost" for the individual may be small compared to the financial burden of garaging a car in New York City.

29. See Martinsen and Seibt (2013) for a discussion of the concept of shared ecological responsibility, and the notions of cumulative action and emergent consequences. In "Five Mistakes in Moral Mathematics," (Parfit, 1986, Chapter 3), one of the main points I take Parfit to be making (apart from the criticism of some standard interpretations of utilitarianism) is that we tend to underestimate the difference (beneficial or harmful) of our actions because we tend to look at them singularly, rather than recognizing them as constituents of sets of actions. What I am suggesting is that if it makes sense to say that the self bears some responsibility for its contribution to a set of actions (even when it doesn't participate self-consciously or intentionally or by making a "joint commitment" in Gilbert's sense, Gilbert, 1989), it is because the self *is* partially constituted by its location in that set and contributes to the cumulative effect that the set of actions has.

30. Leaving aside the complicated issue of what constitutes a legitimate war and war effort.

31. See Striblen (2013) for an interesting discussion of how an individual may contribute to sustaining group norms. See also Smith (2005) on responsibility for attitudes.

32. See Smith (2005, 2008) on what she calls the rational relations view of responsibility, a view that, in recent analytic literature on moral responsibility, is classified as a non-volitionist account of responsibility (in contrast to a volitionist account in which deliberate, explicit choices are necessary conditions for someone being responsible for something).

33. In developing her social connection model of justice, Young suggests that in response to global economic injustices one may have a duty to participate in

collective corrective or remedial action (Young, 2006). Held considers the question whether a random collection of individuals can be responsible for failing to act, or for failing to come up with decision procedure by which to settle on a collective action (Held, 1970). In the context of global warming and climate change, there have been efforts made to develop ways of distributing responsibility for remediation or compensation; see, for example, discussion of The Greenhouse Development Rights (GDR) Framework in Martinsen and Seibt (2013). For the GDR see Baer et al. (2008).

34. Recall experiential parallelism and community in Chapter 5, borrowed from Buchler's definition of community (1979, 44).

# References

Abrams, Kathryn. (1999). From Autonomy to Agency: Feminist Perspectives on Self-Direction. *William and Mary Law Review*, 805–846.

Ainslie, George. (1986). Beyond Microeconomics. In Jon Elster (ed.), *The Multiple Self* (pp. 133–175). Cambridge: Cambridge University Press.

Ainslie, George. (1992). *Picoeconomics: The Strategic Interaction of Successive Motivational States Within the Person*. Cambridge: Cambridge University Press.

Alcoff, Linda Martín. (1988). Cultural Feminism Versus Post-Structuralism: The Identity Crisis in Feminist Theory. *Signs*, 1 (3), 405–436.

Alcoff, Linda Martín. (2006). *Visible Identities: Race, Gender and the Self*. New York: Oxford University Press.

Alford, C. Fred. (1991). *The Self in Social Theory: A Psychoanalytic Account of Its Construction in Plato, Hobbes, Locke, Rawls, and Rousseau*. New Haven: Yale University Press.

Allen, Amy. (2008). *The Politics of Our Selves: Power, Autonomy, and Gender in Contemporary Critical Theory*. New York: Columbia University Press.

Allende, Isabel. (2008). *The Sum of Our Days*. Translated by Margaret Sayers Peden. New York: Harper Collins.

Andersen, Susan and Serena Chen. (2002). The Relational Self: An Interpersonal Social-cognitive Theory. *Psychological Review*, 109 (4), 619–645.

Anscombe, G.E.M. (1975). The First Person. In Samuel Guttenplan (ed.), *Mind and Language* (pp. 45–65). Oxford: Oxford University Press.

Anscombe, G.E.M. (1984). Were You a Zygote? *Royal Institute of Philosophy Lecture Series*, 18, 111–115. (Reprinted in A. Phillips Griffiths, ed. *Philosophy and Practice*. Cambridge: Cambridge University Press, 1985).

Anzaldua, Gloria. (2001). *La Conciencia de la Mestiza*: Towards a New Consciousness. In Kum-Kum Bhavnani (ed.), *Feminism and Race* (pp. 93–107). Oxford: Oxford University Press.

Armstrong, David M. (1980). Identity Through Time. In Peter van Inwagen (ed.), *Time and Cause: Essays Presented to Richard Taylor* (pp. 67–78). Dordrecht: Reidel.

Arpaly, Nomi. (2003). *Unprincipled Virtue: An Inquiry into Moral Agency*. New York: Oxford University Press.

Baer, Paul, Tom Athanasiou, Sivan Kartha and Eric Kemp-Benedict. (2008). *The Greenhouse Development Rights Framework: The Right to Develop in a Climate Constrained World* (Second edition). Heinrich Boell Foundation, Christian

Aid, EcoEquity, and the Stockholm Environment Institute. Retrieved from http://gdrights.org/2009/02/16/second-edition-of-the-greenhouse-development-rights.

Baeten, Elizabeth. (1999). Rethinking the Socially Constituted Self as the Subject of Ethical Communication. *The Journal of Speculative Philosophy*, 13 (1), 1–18.

Baier, Annette. (1985). *Postures of the Mind: Essays on Mind and Morals*. Minneapolis: University of Minnesota Press.

Baker, C. Edwin. (1978). Scope of the First Amendment Freedom of Speech. *UCLA Law Review*, 25, 964–990.

Baker, Lynne Rudder. (2000). *Persons and Bodies: A Constitution View*. Cambridge: Cambridge University Press.

Baker, Lynne Rudder. (2007). *The Metaphysics of Everyday Life: An Essay in Practical Realism*. Cambridge: Cambridge University Press.

Baker, Lynne Rudder. (2009). Identity Across Time: A Defense of Three-dimensionalism. In Benedikt Schick, E. Runggaldier and L. Honnefelder (eds.), *Unity and Time in Metaphysics* (pp. 1–13). Berlin: Walter de Gruyter.

Baker, Lynne Rudder. (2013). *Naturalism and the First Person Perspective*. Oxford: Oxford University Press.

Bapteste, Eric and John Dupré. (2013). Towards a Processual Microbial Ontology. *Biology and Philosophy*, 28, 379–404.

Barabási, Albert László. (2002). *Linked: The New Science of Networks*. Cambridge, MA: Perseus Publishing.

Barclay, Linda. (2000). Autonomy and the Social Self. In Catriona Mackenzie and Natalie Stoljar (eds.), *Relational Autonomy: Feminist Perspectives on Autonomy, Agency, and the Social Self* (pp. 52–71). New York: Oxford University Press.

Baxter, Donald. (1989). Identity Through Time and the Discernibility of Identicals. *Analysis*, 49, 125–131.

Baxter, Donald. (1999). The Discernibility of Identicals. *Journal of Philosophical Research*, XXIV, 37–55.

Baxter, Donald. (2001). Loose Identity and Becoming Something Else. *Noûs*, 35 (4), 592–601.

Beatty, Joseph. (1970). Forgiveness. *American Philosophical Quarterly*, 7, 246–252.

Benson, Paul. (1994). Free Agency and Self-Worth. *Journal of Philosophy*, 91, 650–668.

Benson, Paul. (2000). Feeling Crazy: Self-Worth and the Social Character of Responsibility. In Catriona Mackenzie and Natalie Stoljar (eds.), *Relational Autonomy: Feminist Perspectives on Autonomy, Agency, and the Social Self* (pp. 73–94). New York: Oxford University Press.

Benson, Paul. (2005). Feminist Intuitions and the Normative Substance of Autonomy. In James Stacey Taylor (ed.), *Personal Autonomy: New Essays on Personal Autonomy and Its Role in Contemporary Moral Philosophy* (pp. 124–142). Cambridge: Cambridge University Press.

Berlin, Isaiah. (1969). Two Concepts of Liberty. In Isaiah Berlin (ed.), *Four Essays on Liberty*. Oxford: Oxford University Press.

Berman, Saul J. (2011). *Not for Free: Revenue Strategies for a New World*. Boston: Harvard Business Review Press.

Bird, Alexander and Emma Tobin. (2012). Natural Kinds. In Edward N. Zalta (ed.), *The Stanford Encyclopedia of Philosophy* (Winter 2012 edition). Retrieved from http://plato.stanford.edu/archives/win2012/entries/natural-kinds/.

Black, Max. (1952). The Identity of Indiscernibles. *Mind*, 61, 153–164.

Blackburn, Simon. (1997). Has Kant Refuted Parfit? In Jonathan Dancy (ed.), *Reading Parfit* (pp. 180–201). Oxford: Blackwell.

Bloom, Paul. (2008, November). First Person Plural. *The Atlantic*. Retrieved from www.theatlantic.com/magazine/archive/2008/11/first-person-plural/307055/.

Bloom, Paul. (2010). *How Pleasure Works: The New Science of Why We Like What We Like*. New York: W.W. Norton and Company.

Bostrom, Nick. (2003). Human Genetic Enhancements: A Transhumanist Perspective. *Journal of Value Inquiry*, 37 (4), 493–506.

Bourdieu, Pierre. (1990). *The Logic of Practice*. Translated by Richard Nice. Palo Alto: Stanford University Press.

Bovey, Simon. (2010). *The Un-Gone* [Vimeo and YouTube]. Retrieved from http://vimeo.com/6312563 and from www.simonbovey.co.uk/.

Boyd, Richard. (1991). Realism, Anti-foundationalism and Enthusiasm for Natural Kinds. *Philosophical Studies*, 61, 127–148.

Boyd, Richard. (1999). Homeostasis, Species and Higher Taxa. In R. Wilson (ed.), *Species: New Interdisciplinary Essays* (pp. 141–186). Cambridge, MA: MIT Press.

Braddon-Mitchell, David and Caroline West. (2001). Temporal Phase Pluralism. *Philosophy and Phenomenological Research*, 62 (1), 59–83.

Bratman, Michael. (2005). Planning Agency, Autonomous Agency. In James Stacey Taylor (ed.), *Personal Autonomy: New Essays on Personal Autonomy and Its Role in Contemporary Moral Philosophy* (pp. 33–57). Cambridge: Cambridge University Press.

Bratman, Michael. (2007). *Structures of Agency: Essays*. Oxford: Oxford University Press.

Bratman, Michael. (2012). Time, Rationality, and Self-Governance. *Philosophical Issues (Action Theory), A Supplement to Noûs*, 22, 73–88.

Bratman, Michael. (2014). *Shared Agency: A Planning Theory of Acting Together*. Oxford: Oxford University Press.

Brison, Susan J. (1993). Surviving Sexual Violence: A Philosophical Perspective. *Journal of Social Philosophy*, 24 (1), 5–22.

Brison, Susan J. (1997). Outliving Oneself: Trauma, Memory and Personal Identity. In Diana Tietjens Meyers (ed.), *Feminists Rethink the Self* (pp. 12–39). Boulder: Westview Press.

Brison, Susan J. (1998). The Autonomy Defense of Free Speech. *Ethics*, 108, 312–339.

Buchler, Justus. (1979). *Toward a General Theory of Human Judgment* (Second, revised edition). New York: Dover Publications.

Buchler, Justus. (1985). *Nature and Judgment*. (Reprint.) Lanham: University Press of America.

Buchler, Justus. (1990). *Metaphysics of Natural Complexes* (Second, expanded edition). Kathleen Wallace and Armen Marsoobian, with Robert Corrington (eds.). Albany: SUNY Press.

Buss, Sarah. (2014). Personal Autonomy. In Edward N. Zalta (ed.), *The Stanford Encyclopedia of Philosophy* (Spring 2014 edition). Retrieved from http://plato.stanford.edu/archives/spr2014/entries/personal-autonomy/.

Butler, Joseph. (1736/1852). *The Analogy of Religion, Natural and Revealed*. London: Henry G. Bohn.

Cameron, James. (Director). (2009). *Avatar*. United States: Twentieth Century Fox Film Corporation.

Cameron, Ross P. (2008). Turtles All the Way Down: Regress, Priority and Fundamentality. *Philosophical Quarterly*, 58 (230), 1–14.

Campbell, Scott. (2005). Is Causation Necessary for What Matters in Survival? *Philosophical Studies: An International Journal for Philosophy in the Analytic Tradition*, 126 (3), 375–396.

Canavero, Sergio. (2013). Heaven: The Head Anasomatosis Venture Project Outline for the First Human Head Transplantation With Spinal Linkage (GEMINI). *SNI: Neurosurgical Developments on the Horizon*, 4 (2), 335–342. Retrieved from www.surgicalneurologyint.com/downloadpdf.asp?issn=2152-7806;year=2013;volume=4;issue=2;spage=335;epage=342;aulast=Canavero;type=2.

Castañeda, Hector-Neri. (1977). On the Philosophical Foundations of the Theory of Communication: Reference. *Midwest Studies in Philosophy*, II, 165–186.

Christensen, Wayne D. and Mark Bickhard. (2002). The Process Dynamics of Normative Function. *The Monist*, 85 (1), 3–28.

Christman, John. (1989). *The Inner Citadel: Essays on Individual Autonomy*. New York: Oxford University Press.

Christman, John. (1991). Autonomy and Personal History. *Canadian Journal of Philosophy*, 21, 1–24.

Christman, John. (2004). Relational Autonomy, Liberal Individualism and the Social Constitution of Selves. *Philosophical Studies*, 117, 143–164.

Christman, John. (2009). *The Politics of Persons: Individual Autonomy and Socio-historical Selves*. Cambridge: Cambridge University Press.

Clark, Andy and David Chalmers. (1998). The Extended Mind. *Analysis*, 58, 7–19.

Code, Lorraine. (1991). *What Can She Know? Feminist Theory and the Construction of Knowledge*. Ithaca: Cornell University Press.

Code, Lorraine. (2000). The Perversion of Autonomy and the Subjection of Women: Discourses of Social Advocacy at Century's End. In Catriona Mackenzie and Natalie Stoljar (eds.), *Relational Autonomy: Feminist Perspectives on Autonomy, Agency, and the Social Self* (pp. 181–209). New York: Oxford University Press.

Collins, Patricia Hill. (1990). *Black Feminist Thought*. Boston: Unwin Hyman.

Condon, Richard. (1959). *The Manchurian Candidate*. New York: McGraw-Hill Book Company.

Crenshaw, Kimberlé. (1991). Mapping the Margins: Intersectionality, Identity Politics, and Violence Against Women of Color. *Stanford Law Review*, 43 (6), 1241–1299.

Crenshaw, Kimberlé. (1993). Beyond Racism and Misogyny: Black Feminism and 2 Live Crew. In Mari J. Matsuda et al. (eds.), *Words That Wound* (pp. 111–132). Boulder: Westview Press.

Dauben, Joseph W. (1977, May). C.S. Peirce's Philosophy of Infinite Sets. *Mathematics Magazine*, 50 (3), 123–135.

Davidson, Donald. (1982). Paradoxes of Irrationality. In R. Wollheim and J. Hopkins (eds.), *Philosophical Essays on Freud* (pp. 289–305). Cambridge: Cambridge University Press.

Davidson, Donald. (1985). Deception and Division. In Ernest LePore and Brian McLaughlin (eds.), *Actions and Events: Perspectives on the Philosophy of Donald Davidson* (pp. 138–148). London: Basil Blackwell.

Davidson, Donald. (1987). Knowing One's Own Mind. *Proceedings and Addresses of the American Philosophical Association*, 61, 441–458. (Reprinted in Donald Davidson. *Subjective, Intersubjective*. Oxford: Clarendon Press, 2001).

Dennett, Daniel. (1991). *Consciousness Explained*. Boston: Little, Brown and Co.

Dennett, Daniel. (1992). The Self as a Center of Narrative Gravity. In F.S. Kessel, P.M. Cole and D.L. Johnson (eds.), *Self and Consciousness: Multiple Perspectives* (pp. 103–115). Hillsdale: Lawrence Erlbaum Associates.

Dennett, Daniel. (2001). Where Am I? In D.R. Hofstadter and D.C. Dennett (eds.), *The Mind's I: Fantasies and Reflections on Self and Soul* (pp. 217–229). New York: Basic Books.

Descartes, René. (1964). *Philosophical Essays (Discourse on Method, Meditations, Rules for the Direction of the Mind)*. Translated by Laurence J. Lafleur. Macmillan, Library of Liberal Arts.

Descartes, René. (1988). *Descartes Selected Philosophical Writings*. Translated by John Cottingham, Robert Stoothoff and Dugald Murdoch. Cambridge: Cambridge University Press.

Dewey, John. (1969). *The Early Works of John Dewey, 1882–1898, Vol. 3, 1889–1894, Early Essays and Outlines of a Critical Theory of Ethics*. Edited by Jo Ann Boydston. Carbondale and Edwardsville: Southern Illinois University Press.

Dewey, John. (2008a). *The Later Works of John Dewey, 1925–1953, Volume 1: 1925, Experience and Nature*. Edited by Jo Ann Boydston. Carbondale: Southern Illinois University Press.

Dewey, John. (2008b). *The Later Works of John Dewey, 1925–1953, Volume 10: 1934, Art as Experience*. Edited by Jo Ann Boydston. Carbondale: Southern Illinois University Press.

Double, Richard. (1992, March). Two Types of Autonomy Accounts. *Canadian Journal of Philosophy*, 22 (1), 65–80.

Dunnett, Dorothy. (1997a). *Checkmate*. New York: Vintage Books, Random House (first published 1975).

Dunnett, Dorothy. (1997b). *Pawn in Frankincense*. New York: Vintage Books, Random House (first published 1969).

Dworkin, Gerald. (1988). *The Theory and Practice of Autonomy*. Cambridge: Cambridge University Press.

Dworkin, Gerald. (1989). The Concept of Autonomy. In John Christman (ed.), *The Inner Citadel: Essays on Individual Autonomy* (pp. 54–62). New York: Oxford University Press.

Dworkin, Ronald. (1986). Autonomy and the Demented Self. *Milbank Quarterly*, 64 (Supp. 2), 4–16.

Dworkin, Ronald. (1994). *Life's Dominion*. New York: Random House.

Ekstrom, Laura Waddell. (1993). A Coherence Theory of Autonomy. *Philosophy and Phenomenological Research*, 53, 599–616.

Ekstrom, Laura Waddell. (2005). Autonomy and Personal Integration. In James Stacey Taylor (ed.), *Personal Autonomy: New Essays on Personal Autonomy and Its Role in Contemporary Moral Philosophy* (pp. 143–161). Cambridge: Cambridge University Press.

Elster, Jon. (1979). *Ulysses and the Sirens*. Cambridge: Cambridge University Press.

Elster, Jon. (1982). Sour Grapes—Utilitarianism and the Genesis of Wants. In Amartya Sen and Bernard Williams (eds.), *Utilitarianism and Beyond* (pp. 219–238). Cambridge: Cambridge University Press (Reprinted in John Christman, ed. *The Inner Citadel: Essays on Individual Autonomy* (pp. 170–188). Oxford: Oxford University Press, 1989).

Ereshefsky, Marc and Maximillian Pedroso. (2013). Biological Individuality: Case of Biofilms. *Biology and Philosophy*, 28, 331–349.

Feinberg, Joel. (1970a). Action and Responsibility. In Joel Feinberg, *Doing and Deserving: Essays in the Theory of Responsibility* (pp. 19–51). Princeton: Princeton University Press.

Feinberg, Joel. (1970b). Collective Responsibility. In Joel Feinberg, *Doing and Deserving: Essays in the Theory of Responsibility* (pp. 222–251). Princeton: Princeton University Press.

Feinberg, Joel. (1989). Autonomy. In John Christman (ed.), *The Inner Citadel: Essays on Individual Autonomy* (pp. 27–53). Oxford: Oxford University Press.

Fischer, John and M. Ravizza. (1998). *Morally Responsible People Without Freedom*. Retrieved from www.ucl.ac.uk/~uctytho/dfwCompatFischerRavizza.htm (visited 19 June 2007) (from final chapter of *Responsibility and Control: A Theory of Moral Responsibility*. Cambridge: Cambridge University Press, 1998).

Fodor, Gerald. (1998, 15 January). The Trouble with Psychological Darwinism. *London Review of Books*, 20 (2).

Forrest, Peter. (2006). The Identity of Indiscernibles. In Edward N. Zalta (ed.), *The Stanford Encyclopedia of Philosophy* (Fall 2006 edition). Retrieved from http://plato.stanford.edu/archives/fall2006/entries/identity-indiscernible/.

Frankenheimer, John. (Director). (1962). *The Manchurian Candidate*. United States: M.C. Productions.

Frankfurt, Harry. (1971). Freedom of the Will and the Concept of a Person. *Journal of Philosophy*, 68 (1), 5–20 (Reprinted in his *The Importance of What We Care About*. Cambridge: Cambridge University Press, 1988).

Frankfurt, Harry. (1988). *The Importance of What We Care About*. Cambridge: Cambridge University Press.

Frankfurt, Harry. (1999). *Necessity, Volition and Love*. Cambridge: Cambridge University Press.

Freeman, Lauren. (2011). Reconsidering Relational Autonomy: A Feminist Approach to Selfhood and the Other in the Thinking of Martin Heidegger. *Inquiry*, 54 (4), 361–383.

Friedman, Marilyn. (2000). Autonomy, Social Disruption and Women. In Catriona Mackenzie and Natalie Stoljar (eds.), *Relational Autonomy: Feminist Perspectives on Autonomy, Agency, and the Social Self* (pp. 35–51). New York: Oxford University Press.

Friedman, Marilyn. (2003). *Autonomy, Gender, Politics*. Oxford: Oxford University Press.

Fulford, K.W.M. (Bill) and Lubomira Radoilska. (2012). Three Challenges from Delusion for Theories of Autonomy. In Lubomira Radoilska (ed.), *Autonomy and Mental Disorder* (pp. 44–74). Oxford: Oxford University Press.

Gallagher, Shaun. (2000). Philosophical Conceptions of the Self: Implications for Cognitive Science. *Trends in Cognitive Science*, 4 (1), 14–21.

Gallagher, Shaun. (2013). A Pattern Theory of Self. *Frontiers in Human Neuroscience*, 7 (443), 1–7.

Gallagher, Shaun. (2014). Pragmatic Interventions into Enactive and Extended Conceptions of Cognition. *Philosophical Issues (Extended Knowledge). A Supplement to Noûs*, 24, 110–126 (*Extended Knowledge* 2014).

Gallagher, Shaun and Anthony J. Marcel. (1999). The Self in Contextualized Action. In Shaun Gallagher and Jonathan Shear (eds.), *Models of the Self* (pp. 273–299). Thorverton: Imprint Academic.

Gendler, Tamar Szabó. (1999). Exceptional Persons: On the Limits of Imaginary Cases. In S. Gallagher and J. Shear (eds.), *Models of the Self* (pp. 447–465). Thorverton: Imprint Academic.

Gendler, Tamar Szabó. (2002). Personal Identity and Thought Experiments. *The Philosophical Quarterly*, 52 (206), 34–54.

Gendler, Tamar Szabó. (2007). Philosophical Thought Experiments, Intuitions, and Cognitive Equilibrium. *Midwest Studies in Philosophy*, XXXI, 68–86.

Gergen, Kenneth J. (2009). *Relational Being: Beyond Self and Community*. Oxford: Oxford University Press.

Gert, Bernard. (1971). Personal Identity and the Body. *Dialogue*, 10, 458–478.

Gibbard, Alan. (1990). *Wise Choices, Apt Feelings: A Theory of Normative Judgment*. Cambridge, MA: Harvard University Press.

Gilbert, Margaret. (1989). *On Social Facts*. London: Routledge.

Griswold, Charles. (2007). *Forgiveness: A Philosophical Exploration*. Cambridge: Cambridge University Press.

Habermas, Jurgen. (1992). *Postmetaphysical Thinking*. Cambridge, MA: MIT Press.

Haraway, Donna. (1991). *Simians, Cyborgs and Women: The Reinvention of Nature*. New York: Routledge.

Hare, R.M. (1963). *Freedom and Reason*. Oxford: Clarendon Press.

Harré, Rom. (1995). The Necessity of Personhood as Embodied Being. *Theory and Psychology*, 5 (3), 369–373.

Haslanger, Sally. (2012). *Resisting Reality: Social Construction and Social Critique*. Oxford: Oxford University Press.

Hawking, Stephen. (2000, January 23). Unified Theory Is Getting Closer, Hawking Predicts, Interview. *San Jose Mercury News*.

Haworth, Lawrence. (1986). *Autonomy: An Essay in Philosophical Psychology and Ethics*. New Haven: Yale University Press.

Held, Virginia. (1970). Can a Random Collection of Individuals Be Morally Responsible? *Journal of Philosophy*, 67 (14), 471–481.

Hermans, Hubert J.M. (1996a). Opposites in a Dialogical Self: Constructs as Characters. *Journal of Constructive Psychology*, 9, 1–26.

Hermans, Hubert J.M. (1996b). Voicing the Self: From Information Processing to Dialogical Interchange. *Psychological Bulletin*, 119, 31–50.

Hermans, Hubert J.M., T.I. Rijks and J.J.G. Kempen. (1993). Imaginal Dialogues in the Self: Theory and Method. *Journal of Personality*, 61, 207–236.

Hiley, David R. (1988). *Philosophy in Question: Essays on a Pyrrhonian Theme*. Chicago: University of Chicago Press.

Hill, Thomas E. (1973) Servility and Self-Respect. *The Monist*, 57 (1), 87–104.

Holton, Richard. (1999). Intention and Weakness of Will. *The Journal of Philosophy*, 96 (5), 241–262.

Honneth, Axel. (1995). *The Fragmented World of the Social: Essays in Social and Political Philosophy*. Edited by Charles W. Wright. Albany: SUNY Press.

Honoré, Tony. (1999). *Responsibility and Fault*. Oxford: Hart Publishing.

Hull, David. (1976). Are Species Individuals? *Systematic Zoology*, 25, 174–191.

Hull, David. (1978). A Matter of Individuality. *Philosophy of Science*, 45, 335–360.

Hull, David. (1980). Individuality and Selection. *Annual Review of Ecology, Evolution and Systematics*, 11, 311–332.

Hume, David. (1978). *Treatise on Human Nature*. Edited by L.A.Selby-Bigge, second edition with text revised and variant readings by P.H. Nidditch. Oxford: Clarendon Press.

Isaacs, Tracy. (2011). *Moral Responsibility in Collective Contexts*. New York: Oxford University Press.

Ismael, J.T. (2007). *The Situated Self*. Oxford: Oxford University Press.

James, William. (1950). *Principles of Psychology*. Vol. 1. New York: Dover Publications, Inc. (first published 1890, New York: Henry Holt and Co.).

James, William. (1971). *Essays in Radical Empiricism and a Pluralistic Universe* (with an Introduction by Richard Bernstein). New York: E.P. Dutton and Co.

Johnson, Mark. (2005). Cognitive Science. In John Shook and Joseph Margolis (eds.), *A Companion to Pragmatism* (pp. 369–377). New York: John Wiley & Sons.

Johnston, Mark. (1987, February). Human Beings. *The Journal of Philosophy*, 84 (2), 59–83.

Kitcher, Philip. (2007, Autumn). Does 'Race' Have a Future. *Philosophy and Public Affairs*, 35 (4), 293–317. (Reprinted in Kitcher. *Preludes to Pragmatism* (pp. 145–165)).

Kitcher, Philip. (2012). *Preludes to Pragmatism: Toward a Reconstruction of Philosophy*. Oxford: Oxford University Press.

Kittay, Eva Feder. (1999). *Love's Labor: Essays on Women, Equality and Dependency*. New York: Routledge.

Kolak, Daniel and Raymond Martin. (1987). Personal Identity and Causality: Becoming Unglued. *American Philosophical Quarterly*, 24, 39–47.

Korsgaard, Christine M. (2003). Personal Identity and the Unity of Agency. In Raymond Martin and John Baressi (eds.), *Personal Identity* (pp. 168–183). Oxford: Blackwell.

Kripke, Saul. (1972). *Naming and Necessity*. Cambridge, MA: Harvard University Press.

Kronman, Anthony. (1983). Paternalism and the Law of Contracts. *Yale Law Journal*, 92, 763–798.

Kurtz, Roxanne Marie. (2006). Introduction. In Sally Haslanger and Roxanne Marie Kurtz (eds.), *Persistence: Contemporary Readings* (pp. 1–26). Cambridge, MA: MIT Press.

Kymlicka, Will. (1989). *Liberalism, Community and Culture*. Oxford: Clarendon Press.

Latour, Bruno. (1988). *The Pasteurization of France*. Translated by Alan Sheridan and John Law. Cambridge, MA: Harvard University Press.

Latour, Bruno. (2005). *Reassembling the Social: An Introduction to Actor-Network Theory*. Oxford: Oxford University Press.

Lewis, David. (1983a). Survival and Identity. In David Lewis (ed.), *Philosophical Papers*. Vol. 1 (pp. 55–77). Oxford: Oxford University Press (Originally published in Amelie Rorty. *The Identities of Persons* (pp. 17–40). Berkeley: University of California Press, 1976).

Lewis, David. (1983b). *Philosophical Papers*. Vol. 1. Oxford: Oxford University Press.

Lewis, David. (1986). *On the Plurality of Worlds*. Oxford: Blackwell Publishers.

Locke, John. (1975). *An Essay Concerning Human Understanding.* Edited by P.H. Nidditch. Oxford: Clarendon Press.

Lugones, María. (1992). On Borderlands/la Frontera: An Interpretive Essay. *Hypatia*, 7, 31–37.

Lugones, Maria and Elizabeth V. Spelman. (1999). Have We Got a Theory for You! Feminist Theory, Cultural Imperialism, and the Demand for 'The Woman's Voice'. In Marilyn Pearsall (ed.), *Women and Values* (pp. 14–24). Belmont: Wadsworth.

Lyotard, Jean-Francois. (1988). *The Differend.* Translated by George Van Den Abbeele. Minneapolis: University of Minnesota Press.

Lysaker, Paul and John Lysaker. (2008). *Schizophrenia and the Fate of the Self.* Oxford: Oxford University Press.

MacIntyre, Alasdair. (1984). *After Virtue* (Second edition). Notre Dame: University of Notre Dame Press.

MacIntyre, Alasdair. (1988). *Whose Justice? Which Rationality?* Notre Dame: University of Notre Dame Press.

Mackenzie, Catriona and Natalie Stoljar (eds.). (2000a). *Relational Autonomy: Feminist Perspectives on Autonomy, Agency, and the Social Self.* Oxford: Oxford University Press.

Mackenzie, Catriona and Natalie Stoljar. (2000b). Introduction: Autonomy Refigured. In Catriona Mackenzie and Natalie Stoljar (eds.), *Relational Autonomy: Feminist Perspectives on Autonomy, Agency, and the Social Self* (pp. 3–31). New York: Oxford University Press.

Mackie, David. (1999). Animalism *Versus* Lockeanism: No Contest. *The Philosophical Quarterly*, 49, 369–376.

Mackie, John. (1980). The Transcendental 'I'. In Zak van Straaten (ed.), *Philosophical Subjects: Essays Presented to P.F. Strawson* (pp. 48–61). Oxford: Clarendon Press.

Mahowald, Mary. (1972). *An Idealistic Pragmatism: The Development of the Pragmatic Element in the Philosophy of Josiah Royce.* The Hague: Martinus Nijhoff.

Mann, Thomas. (1941). *The Transposed Heads, a Legend of India.* Translated by H.T. Lowe-Porter. New York: A.A. Knopf.

Marsoobian, Armen, Kathleen Wallace and Robert S. Corrington (eds.). (1991). *Nature's Perspectives: Prospects for Ordinal Metaphysics.* Albany: SUNY Press.

Martinsen, Franziska and Johanna Seibt. (2013). Climate Change and the Concept of Shared Ecological Responsibility. *Environmental Ethics*, 35 (2), 163–187.

Matsumura, Kaiponanea. (2014). Binding Future Selves. *Louisiana Law Review*, 75, 71–125.

May, Larry. (1992). *Sharing Responsibility.* Chicago and London: University of Chicago Press.

McDowell, John. (1997). Reductionism and the First Person. In Jonathan Dancy (ed.), *Reading Parfit* (pp. 230–250). Oxford: Blackwell (Reprinted in John McDowell. *Mind, Value, and Reality* (pp. 359–382). Cambridge: Harvard University Press, 1998).

McGandy, Michael J. (1997). Buchler's Notion of Query. *Journal of Speculative Philosophy*, XI (2), 203–224.

McKenna, Erin. (2002). The Need for a Pragmatist Feminist Self. In Charlene Haddock Seigfried (ed.), *Feminist Interpretations of John Dewey* (pp. 133–159). University Park: Penn State University Press.

Mead, George Herbert. (1934). *Mind, Self and Society.* Edited by Charles W. Morris. Chicago: University of Chicago Press.

Mele, Alfred. (1995). *Autonomous Agents.* Oxford and New York: Oxford University Press.

Merleau-Ponty, Maurice. (1962). *Phenomenology of Perception.* Translated by C. Smith. New York: Routledge & Kegan Paul.

Meyers, Diana T. (1989). *Self, Society and Personal Choice.* New York: Columbia University Press.

Meyers, Diana T. (2000a). Feminism and Women's Autonomy: The Challenge of Female Genital Cutting. *Metaphilosophy*, 31, 469–491.

Meyers, Diana T. (2000b). Intersectional Identity and the Authentic Self: Opposites Attract! In Catriona Mackenzie and Natalie Stoljar (eds.), *Relational Autonomy: Feminist Perspectives on Autonomy, Agency, and the Social Self* (pp. 151–180). New York: Oxford University Press.

Meyers, Diana T. (2005). Decentralizing Autonomy: Five Faces of Selfhood. In John Christman and Joel Anderson (eds.), *Autonomy and the Challenges of Liberalism: New Essays* (pp. 27–55). Cambridge: Cambridge University Press.

Miller, David. (2001). Distributing Responsibilities. *Journal of Political Philosophy*, 9 (4), 435–471.

Miller, David. (2004). Holding Nations Responsible. *Ethics*, 114 (2), 240–268.

Millikan, Ruth G. (1999). Historical Kinds and the Special Sciences. *Philosophical Studies*, 95, 45–65.

Minsky, Marvin. (1988). *Society of Mind.* New York: Simon and Schuster.

Moravec, Hans. (1998). *Mind Children: The Future of Robot and Human Intelligence.* Cambridge, MA: Harvard University Press.

Moravec, Hans. (1999). *Robot: Mere Machine to Transcendent Mind.* Oxford: Oxford University Press.

Morton, Brian. (2011). Falser Words Were Never Spoken. *The New York Times.* Retrieved from www.nytimes.com/2011/08/30/opinion/falser-words-were-never-spoken.html?_r=0 (visited 14 January 2015).

Mouffe, Chantal. (1992). Feminism, Citizenship, and Radical Politics. In Judith Butler and Joan W. Scott (eds.), *Feminists Theorize the Political* (pp. 369–384). New York: Routledge.

Nagel, Thomas. (1971). Brain Bisection and the Unity of Consciousness. *Synthese*, 22, 396–413.

Nagel, Thomas. (1979). *Mortal Questions.* Cambridge: Cambridge University Press.

Nagel, Thomas. (1986). *The View from Nowhere.* New York: Oxford University Press.

Nelkin, Dana. (2013). Moral Luck. In Edward N. Zalta (ed.), *The Stanford Encyclopedia of Philosophy* (Winter 2013 edition). Retrieved from https://plato.stanford.edu/archives/win2013/entries/moral-luck.

Nelson, James Lindemann. (1995). Critical Interests and Sources of Familial Decision-Making for Incapacitated Patients. *Journal of Law, Medicine and Ethics*, 23, 143–148.

Newen, A., A. Welpinghaus and G. Juckel. (2015). Emotion Recognition as Pattern Recognition: the Relevance of Perception. *Mind and Language*, 30 (2), 187–208.

Noonan, Harold W. (1998). Animalism *Versus* Lockeanism: A Current Controversy. *The Philosophical Quarterly*, 48, 302–318.

Noonan, Harold W. (2001). Animalism *Versus* Lockeanism: Reply to Mackie. *The Philosophical Quarterly*, 51, 83–90.

Nozick, Robert. (1981). *Philosophical Explanations*. Cambridge, MA: Belknap Press of Harvard University Press.

O'Brien, John. (1995). *Leaving Las Vegas*. New York: Grove Press (originally published, 1990, Watermark Press).

Oderberg, David S. (1996). Coincidence Under a Sortal. *Philosophical Review*, 105 (2), 145–171.

Olson, Eric. (1997). *The Human Animal: Personal Identity Without Psychology*. New York: Oxford University Press.

Olson, Eric. (2007). *What Are We? A Study in Personal Ontology*. Oxford: Oxford University Press.

Ormes, Nene and Karin Waller. Retrieved from http://io9.com/10-great-novels-that-arent-about-what-you-heard-they-we-1679984927.

Ortega y Gasset, José. (2000). *Meditations on Quixote*. Translated by E. Rugg and D. Marin. Urbana and Chicago: University of Illinois Press (Reprint of 1961 publication by W.W. Norton & Company).

Oshana, Marina A.L. (1998). Personal Autonomy and Society. *Journal of Social Philosophy*, 29 (1), 81–102.

Parfit, Derek. (1986). *Reasons and Persons*. Oxford: Clarendon Press of Oxford University Press.

Pears, David. (1984). *Motivated Irrationality*. Oxford: Oxford University Press.

Pears, David. (1985a). Motivated Irrationality. In Ernest LePore and Brian McLaughlin (eds.), *Actions and Events: Perspectives on the Philosophy of Donald Davidson* (pp. 264–288). Oxford: Basil Blackwell.

Pears, David. (1985b). The Goals and Strategies of Self-Deception. In Jon Elster (ed.), *The Multiple Self* (pp. 59–77). Cambridge: Cambridge University Press.

Peirce, C.S. (1976). *The New Elements of Mathematics by Charles S. Peirce*. Edited by C. Eisele. Vol. 3 (pp. 87–89). The Hague: Mouton.

Perry, John. (1975). *Personal Identity*. Berkeley: University of California Press.

Perry, John. (1976). The Importance of Being Identical. In Amelie Rorty (ed.), *The Identities of Persons* (pp. 67–90). Berkeley: University of California Press (Reprinted in John Perry. *Identity, Personal Identity and the Self*. Indianapolis: Hackett Publishing, 2002).

Pettit, Philip and Michael Smith. (1993). Practical Unreason. *Mind*, 102 (405), 53–79.

Priest, Graham. (2009). The Structure of Emptiness. *Philosophy East and West*, 59 (4), 467–480.

Quill, Timothy. (2015). Terri Schiavo—A Tragedy Compounded. *New England Journal of Medicine* (April 21, 2005), 352, 1630–1633.

Quinton, Anthony. (1962). The Soul. *The Journal of Philosophy*, 59 (15), 393–409.

Railton, Peter. (2006). Normative Guidance. In Russ Shafer-Landau (ed.), *Oxford Studies in Metaethics*. Vol. 1 (pp. 3–33). Oxford: Oxford University Press.

Ramis, Harold. (Director). (1996). *Multiplicity*. United States: Columbia Pictures Corporation.

Rawls, John. (1971). *A Theory of Justice*. Cambridge, MA: Harvard University Press.

Redish, Martin H. (1984). *Freedom of Expression: A Critical Analysis*. Charlottesville: Michi Company.

Reid, Thomas. (1895). *Essays on the Intellectual Powers of Man* (1785). In W. Hamilton (ed.), *Philosophical Works of Thomas Reid*. Vol 1. Hildesheim: George Olms (Reprinted).

Rorty, Amelie. (1976). *The Identities of Persons*. Berkeley: University of California Press.

Rovane, Carol. (1998). *The Bounds of Agency: An Essay in Revisionary Metaphysics*. Princeton: Princeton University Press.

Royce, Josiah. (1968). *The Problem of Christianity*. With Introduction by John E. Smith. Chicago: University of Chicago Press.

Royce, Josiah. (1969a). Mind. In John J. McDermott (ed.), *The Basic Writings of Josiah Royce*. Vol. 2 (pp. 735–761). Chicago: University of Chicago Press.

Royce, Josiah. (1969b). The Philosophy of Loyalty. In John J. McDermott (ed.), *The Basic Writings of Josiah Royce*. Vol. 2 (pp. 855–1013). Chicago: The University of Chicago Press.

Sacks, Oliver. (2007, September 24). A Neurologist's Notebook: The Abyss: Music and Amnesia. *The New Yorker*, 100–111. Retrieved from www.newyorker.com/reporting/2007/09/24/070924fa_fact_sacks.

Sandel, Michael. (1998). *Liberalism and the Limits of Justice* (Second edition). Cambridge: Cambridge University Press.

Sartre, Jean-Paul. (1956). *Being and Nothingness*. Translated by H.E. Barnes. New York: Washington Square Press.

Scanlon, Thomas. (1972). A Theory of Freedom of Expression. *Philosophy and Public Affairs*, 1, 204–226.

Scanlon, Thomas. (1979). Freedom of Expression and Categories of Expression. *University of Pittsburgh Law Review*, 40, 519–550.

Schechtman, Marya. (1996). *The Constitution of Selves*. Ithaca: Cornell University Press.

Schechtman, Marya. (2008). Personal Continuation and a Life Worth Having. In Catriona Mackenzie and Kim Atkins (eds.), *Practical Identity and Narrative Agency* (pp. 31–55). New York: Routledge.

Schechtman, Marya. (2014). *Staying Alive: Personal Identity, Practical Concerns and the Unity of a Life*. Oxford: Oxford University Press.

Schmitt, Richard. (1995). *Beyond Separateness: The Social Nature of Human Beings—Their Autonomy, Knowledge and Power*. Boulder: Westview Press.

Seibt, Johanna. (2009). Forms of Emergent Interaction in General Process Theory. *Synthese*, 166, 479–512.

Seibt, Johanna. (2015). Non-transitive Parthood, Leveled Mereology, and the Representation of Emergent Parts of Processes. *Grazer Philosophische Studien*, 91 (1), 165–190.

Seigfried, Charlene Haddock. (1991a). The Missing Perspective: Feminist Pragmatism. *Transactions of the Charles S. Peirce Society*, 27 (4), 405–416.

Seigfried, Charlene Haddock. (1991b). Where Are All the Pragmatist Feminists? *Hypatia*, 6 (2), 1–20.

Seigfried, Charlene Haddock. (1996). *Pragmatism and Feminism: Reweaving the Social Fabric*. Chicago: The University of Chicago Press.

Seigfried, Charlene Haddock (ed.). (2002). *Feminist Interpretations of John Dewey*. University Park: Penn State University Press.

Sen, Amartya. (1982). Rights and Agency. *Philosophy and Public Affairs*, 11, 187–223.

Sen, Amartya. (1985). Well-Being, Agency and Freedom: The Dewey Lectures 1984. *The Journal of Philosophy*, 82 (4), 169–221.

Sen, Amartya. (1992). *Inequality Reexamined*. Cambridge, MA: Harvard University Press.

Sen, Amartya. (1995). Gender Inequality and Theories of Justice. In Martha Nussbaum and Jonathan Glover (eds.), *Women, Culture, and Development*. Oxford: Oxford University Press.

Shoemaker, David. (2007). Personal Identity and Practical Concerns. *Mind*, 116 (462), 317–357.

Shoemaker, Sydney. (1963). *Self-knowledge and Self-identity*. Ithaca: Cornell University Press.

Shoemaker, Sydney. (1970). Persons and Their Pasts. *American Philosophical Quarterly*, VII (4), 269–285.

Shoemaker, Sydney. (1976). Embodiment and Behavior. In Amelie Rorty (ed.), *The Identities of Persons* (pp. 109–137). Berkeley: University of California Press.

Shoemaker, Sydney. (1979). Identity, Properties and Causality. In P. French, T. Uehling and H. Wettstein (eds.), *Midwestern Studies in Philosophy VI* (pp. 321–342). Minneapolis: University of Minnesota Press.

Shoemaker, Sydney. (1984a). *Identity, Cause and Mind*. Cambridge: Cambridge University Press.

Shoemaker, Sydney. (1984b). Personal Identity: A Materialist Account. In Sydney Shoemaker and Richard Swinburne (eds.), *Personal Identity* (pp. 67–132). Oxford: Blackwell.

Shoemaker, Sydney. (1984c). Sydney Shoemaker's Reply. In Sydney Shoemaker and Richard Swinburne (eds.), *Personal Identity* (pp. 133–152). Oxford: Blackwell.

Shoemaker, Sydney. (1999). Eric Olson, *The Human Animal*. Noûs, 33, 496–504.

Shoemaker, Sydney. (2008). Persons, Animals, and Identity. *Synthese: An International Journal for Epistemology*, 162 (3), 313–324.

Shoemaker, Sydney and Richard Swinburne. (1984). *Personal Identity*. Oxford: Blackwell.

Sider, Theodore. (2001). *Four-Dimensionalism: An Ontology of Persistence and Time*. Oxford: Oxford University Press.

Slater, Matthew. (2015). Natural Kindness. *British Journal of Philosophy of Science*, 66, 375–411.

Smith, Angela. (2005). Responsibility for Attitudes: Activity and Passivity in Mental Life. *Ethics*, 115 (2), 236–271.

Smith, Angela. (2008). Control, Responsibility, Assessment. *Philosophical Studies*, 138 (3), 367–392.

Sneddon, Andrew. (2013). *Autonomy*. London and New York: Bloomsbury Academic.

Sripada, Chandra S. (2014). How Is Willpower Possible? The Puzzle of Synchronic Self Control and the Divided Mind. *Noûs*, 48 (1), 41–74.

St. Augustine. (1961). *Confessions*. Translated with an introduction by R.S. Pine-Coffin. Penguin Books.

Steinhart, Eric. (2001a). Persons vs. Brains: Biological Intelligence in the Human Organism. *Biology and Philosophy*, 16 (1), 3–27.

Steinhart, Eric. (2001b). *The Logic of Metaphor: Analogous Parts of Possible Worlds*. Synthese Library Vol. Dordrecht: Kluwer Academic.

Steinhart, Eric. (2002). Indiscernible Persons. *Metaphilosophy*, 33 (2), 300–320.

Steinhart, Eric. (2008). The Revision Theory of Resurrection. *Religious Studies*, 44 (1), 1–19.

Steinhart, Eric. (2014). *Your Digital Afterlives: Computational Theories of Life After Death*. New York: Palgrave Macmillan.

Stoljar, Natalie. (2000). Autonomy and the Feminist Intuition. In Catriona MacKenzie and Natalie Stoljar (eds.), *Relational Autonomy: Feminist Perspectives on Autonomy, Agency and the Social Self* (pp. 94–111). Oxford: Oxford University Press.

Strawson, P.F. (1959). *Individuals*. London: Methuen.

Strawson, P.F. (1987). Kant's Paralogisms: Self-consciousness and the Outside Observer. In K. Cramer, F. Fulda, R.-P. Horstmann and U. Pothast (eds.), *Theorie der Subjektivität* (pp. 203–219). Frankfurt: Suhrkamp.

Striblen, Cassie. (2013). Collective Responsibility and the Narrative Self. *Social Theory and Practice*, 39 (1), 147–165.

Sullivan, Shannon. (2001). *Living Across and Through Skins: Transactional Bodies, Pragmatism and Feminism*. Bloomington: Indiana University Press.

Tan, Amy. (2001). *The Bonesetter's Daughter*. New York: G.P. Putnam & Sons.

Taylor, Charles. (1989). *Sources of the Self: The Making of the Modern Identity*. Cambridge: Cambridge University Press.

Taylor, Charles. (1992). *The Ethics of Authenticity*. Cambridge, MA: Harvard University Press.

Thomasson, Amie. (2015). What Can Philosophy Really Do? *The Philosopher's Magazine*, 71 (4th Quarter), 17–23.

Tronto, Joan C. (1993). *Moral Boundaries: A Political Argument for an Ethic of Care*. New York: Routledge.

Tronto, Joan C. (2001). Does Managing Professionals Affect Professional Ethics? Competence, Autonomy and Care. In Peggy Desautels and Joanne Waugh (eds.), *Feminists Doing Ethics* (pp. 187–202). Lanham: Rowman and Littlefield Publishers.

Tuomela, Raimo. (2013). *Social Ontology: Collective Intentionality and Group Agents*. New York: Oxford University Press.

Van Inwagen, Peter. (1987). *Material Beings*. Ithaca: Cornell University Press.

Velleman, J. David. (1996). Self to Self. *The Philosophical Review*, 105 (1), 39–76. (Reprinted in Velleman. *Self to Self: Selected Essays* (pp. 170–202). New York: Cambridge University Press, 2006).

Velleman, J. David. (2002). Identification and Identity. In Sarah Buss and Lee Overton (eds.), *Contours of Agency: Essays on Themes from Harry Frankfurt* (pp. 91–123). Cambridge, MA: MIT Press (Reprinted in J. David Velleman. *Self to Self* (pp. 330–360). New York: Cambridge University Press, 2006).

Velleman, J. David. (2006). *Self to Self: Selected Essays*. Cambridge: Cambridge University Press.

Wallace, David Foster. (2006, August 20). Federer as Religious Experience. *The New York Times*. Retrieved from www.nytimes.com/2006/08/20/sports/play magazine/20federer.html?pagewanted=all&_r=0 (visited 1 January 2016).

Wallace, Kathleen. (1993). Reconstructing Judgment: Emotion and Moral Judgment. *Hypatia: A Journal of Feminist Philosophy*, 8 (3), 61–83. (Reprinted in Ngaire Naffine, ed. *Gender and Justice* (pp. 383–406). Ashgate, 2001).

Wallace, Kathleen. (1999). Anonymity. *Ethics and Information Technology*, 1 (1), 23–35.

Wallace, Kathleen. (2000). Agency, Personhood and Identity: Review Article on *The Bounds of Agency: An Essay in Revisionary Metaphysics*, by Carol Rovane. *Metaphilosophy*, 31, 311–322.

Wallace, Kathleen. (2003). Autonomous 'I' of an Intersectional Self. *Journal of Speculative Philosophy*, 17 (3), 176–191.

Wallace, Kathleen. (2007). Educating for Autonomy: Identity and Intersectional Selves. In John Ryder and Gert-Rüdiger Wegmarshaus (eds.), *Education for A Democratic Society* (pp. 165–176). Central European Pragmatist Forum. Vol. 3. New York: Rodopi Press.

Wallace, Kathleen. (2008). On-line Anonymity. In Herman Tavani and Kenneth Himma (eds.), *Handbook on Information and Computer Ethics* (pp. 165–189). Hoboken: John Wiley & Sons.

Wallace, Kathleen. (2009). Personal Identity of an Intersectional Self. In Alexander Kremer and John Ryder (eds.), *Self and Society* (pp. 89–102). Central European Pragmatist Forum. Vol. 4. New Amsterdam: Value Inquiry Book Series, Vol. 207, Rodopi Press.

Walzer, Michael. (1983). *Spheres of Justice: A Defense of Pluralism and Equality*. New York: Basic Books.

Ward, Dave. (2011). Personal Identity, Agency, and the Multiplicity Thesis. *Minds and Machines*, 21, 497–515.

Watson, Gary. (1975). Free Agency. *The Journal of Philosophy*, 72, 205–220.

Watson, Gary. (2004). *Agency and Answerability: Selected Essays*. Oxford: Oxford University Press.

Weatherson, Brian. (2008). Intrinsic vs. Extrinsic Properties. In Edward N. Zalta (ed.), *The Stanford Encyclopedia of Philosophy* (Fall 2008 edition). Retrieved from http://plato.stanford.edu/archives/fall2008/entries/intrinsic-extrinsic/.

West, Caroline. (2008). Personal Identity: Practical or Metaphysical? In Catriona Mackenzie and Kim Atkins (eds.), *Practical Identity and Narrative Agency* (pp. 56–77). New York: Taylor & Francis.

Whitman, Walt. (1891–92). *Leaves of Grass, Song of Myself, verse 51*. Retrieved from https://whitmanarchive.org/published/LG/1891/clusters/27

Wiggins, David. (1980). Personal Identity. In Chapter 6 of *Sameness and Substance*. New York: Oxford University Press.

Wiggins, David. (2001). *Sameness and Substance Renewed*. Cambridge: Cambridge University Press.

Williams, Bernard. (1973). *Problems of the Self: Philosophical Papers 1956–1972*. New York: Cambridge University Press.

Williams, Bernard. (1981). *Moral Luck: Philosophical Papers 1973–1980*. Cambridge: Cambridge University Press.

Witt, Charlotte. (2011). *Metaphysics of Gender*. New York: Oxford University Press.

Wittgenstein, Ludwig. (1972). *The Blue and Brown Books*. New York: Blackwell (first publication, Blackwell, 1958).

Wittgenstein, Ludwig. (2009). *Philosophical Investigations* (Fourth edition). Edited and translated by P.M.S. Hacker and Joachim Schulte. Oxford: Wiley Blackwell.

Yablo, Stephen. (1999). Intrinsicness. *Philosophical Topics*, 26, 479–505.

Yaffe, Gideon. (2000). Free Will and Agency at its Best. In James E. Tomberlin (ed.), *Philosophical Perspectives, 14, Action and Freedom, 2000* (A Supplement to *Nôus*) (pp. 203–229). Cambridge: Blackwell.

Young, Iris Marion. (1986). The Ideal of Community and the Politics of Difference. *Social Theory and Practice*, 12 (1), 1–26.

Young, Iris Marion. (2006). Responsibility and Global Justice: A Social Connection Model. *Social Philosophy and Policy*, 23 (1), 102–130.

Zemeckis, Robert. (Director.) (2000). *Cast Away*. United States: Twentieth Century Fox Film Corporation.

# Index

Note: page numbers in italic indicate a figure and page numbers in bold indicate a table on the corresponding page. Fictional figures appear under first names.